Fundamentals
of
Human–Computer Interaction

Bob Cornick

Computers and People Series

Edited by

B. R. GAINES

The series is concerned with all aspects of man–computer relationships, including interaction, interfacing modelling and artificial intelligence. Books are interdisciplinary, communicating results derived in one area of study to workers in another. Applied, experimental, theoretical and tutorial studies are included.

Fundamentals
of
Human–Computer Interaction

Edited by

ANDREW MONK

Department of Psychology
University of York
York, UK

1985

ACADEMIC PRESS

(Harcourt Brace Jovanovich, Publishers)

London   Orlando   San Diego   New York
Toronto   Montreal   Sydney   Tokyo

Academic Press Rapid Manuscript Reproduction

ACADEMIC PRESS INC. (LONDON) LTD.
24–28 Oval Road
LONDON NW1 7DX

United States Edition published by
ACADEMIC PRESS, INC.
Orlando, Florida 32887

British Library Cataloguing in Publication Data

Fundamentals of human-computer interaction.
    1. Interactive computer systems
    I. Monk, Andrew
001.64   QA76.9.I58

ISBN 0-12-504580-8
ISBN 0-12-504582-4 (pbk.)
LCCCN 84-45602

PRINTED IN THE UNITED STATES OF AMERICA

85 86 87 88   9 8 7 6 5 4 3 2 1

CONTENTS

Chapter 3 *by Neil Thomson*
Human Memory: Different Stores
With Different Characteristics

Chapter 4 *by Neil Thomson*
Thinking and Reasoning:
Why Is Logic So Difficult?

PART TWO
THE USE OF BEHAVIOURAL DATA   65

Chapter 5 *by Andrew Monk*
How and When to Collect Behavioural Data

CONTRIBUTORS

Peter Bailey - Department of Psychology, University of York, Heslington, York, YO1 5DD.

Phil Barnard - MRC Applied Psychology Unit, 15 Chaucer Road, Cambridge, CB2 2EF.

Nick Hammond - Department of Psychology, University of York, Heslington, York, YO1 5DD.

Charles Hulme - Department of Psychology, University of York, Heslington, York, YO1 5DD.

Alison Kidd - R19.2.1, British Telecom Research Labs., Martlesham Heath. Ipswich, IP5 7RE.

G. Reinhard Kofer - K KE ST, Siemens AG, Office Software Prototyping Group, Hofmannstr. 51, 8 Munchen 70, West Germany.

Antony Lo- British Telecom Research Labs., Martlesham Heath, Ipswich, IP5 7RE.

Andrew Monk - Department of Psychology, University of York, Heslington, York, YO1 5DD.

Peter Reid - Software Sciences Ltd., London and Manchester House, Park Street, Macclesfield, Cheshire, SK11 6SR.

Harold Thimbleby - Computer Science Department, University of York, Heslington, York, YO1 5DD.

Peter Thompson - Department of Psychology, University of York, Heslington, York, YO1 5DD.

Neil Thomson - Thomson Computer Services, 71 The Mount, York.

John Waterworth - British Telecom Research Labs., Martlesham Heath, Ipswich, IP5 7RE.

PREFACE

The task of interacting with a 'machine', typically a computer-based system, is no longer restricted to a small group of specialists. With the advent of computer-controlled telecommunications and access to large databases using teletext, most members of the community will, in the relatively near future, have routine daily interactions with computer systems. There is an increasing awareness of the case made by Human-Computer Interaction (HCI) specialists that the design of the user-machine interface in any interactive system is crucial for its efficiency and acceptability, and therefore for its commercial potential.

The assumption that motivates this book is that the time has come for these experts to share some of their specialist knowledge with those at the sharp end of the design process; for example, the system designers and programmers. It is not enough simply to consult an HCI specialist when problems arise. If effective interactive products are to be built and sold, all the personnel involved in the design process must be aware of the basic issues and principles involved.

The aim of this book is to sensitise the systems designer to the problems faced by the user of an interactive system. We hope that it will be read by systems engineers and managers concerned with the design of interactive systems as well as graduate and undergraduate computer science students. The book is also suitable as a tutorial text for certain courses for students of Psychology and Ergonomics.

The book has grown out of a course entitled 'The User Interface: Human Factors for Computer-based Systems' which has been run annually at the University of York since 1981. This course has been attended primarily by systems managers from the computer industry. The enthusiasm and constructive criticism of these people has done much to shape this book. Thanks are also due to all my colleagues at York, in particular to Karin Carter for her work on the references, to Peter and Jenny Bailey for their help 'editing the editor', to my wife, Ruth Monk, and also to Charles Hulme for their considerable help and encouragement and to Marilyn Glicker, Fay McDonald and Annelies Campbell for their help with the production of the book.

ACKNOWLEDGEMENTS

Acknowledgement is made to the Director of Research, British Telecom Research Laboratories, for permission to publish Chapters 7, 13 and 14. Acknowledgement is also due to the following for illustrations for figures:

1.4 - from Pearson, D.E. (1975). Transmission and Display of Pictorial Information, Pentech Press, Figure 6.4 "The CIE Chromaticity Diagram".

1.6 - from Schiff, W. (1980). Perception: An Applied Approach. Boston: Houghton and Mifflin Co. Table 1.4 "Techniques for measuring visual acuity, and optimum resulting values" (p. 28).

1.10 - from Endeavour (1972) 31, 88-94, Digital computers and image processing, Figure 7. (Photographer Harry Andrews.)

1.11 - from Anstis, S.M. (1974). "A chart demonstrating variations in acuity with retinal position." Vision Research, 14, 589-592, Figure 3 (p. 591).

*1.17 - from Lindsay, P.H. and Norman, D.A. Human Information Processing (1st edition). New York: Academic Press. Figure 1-9. (Photographer R.C. James.)

2.1 - from Tinker, M.A. Bases for Effective Reading. Minnesota: University of Minnesota Press.

Table 9.1 - from "The Presentation Graphics Feature and Interactive Chart Utility" (SC 33-011-0), IBM, Winchester, England.

* Originally published in J. Thurston and R.G. Carraher "Optical Illusions and the Visual Arts", c. 1966. Litton Educational Publishing, Inc. and reprinted by permission of Van Nostrand Reinhold Company.

PART ONE

THE USER AS A PROCESSOR OF INFORMATION

The aim of this book is to introduce concepts and examples which allow the designer to think more clearly about the problems faced by the users of interactive systems and their solution. This first section presents over-views of four areas from Cognitive Psychology.

Cognitive Psychology, or 'Human Information Processing' as it is sometimes known, is central to the development of the kind of sensitivity to human factors problems that the book aims to create. It provides the conceptual framework needed to think about the abilities and limitations of the user. If the 'human' part of the human-computer interaction is to be viewed as a part of a complete information processing system then it is necessary to describe him in terms of his information processing capacities. This perspective is not commonly taken outside the behavioural sciences and is developed in detail to ensure a full appreciation of the rest of the material in the book. It is illustrated by describing the strengths and weaknesses of the human information processing system as they relate to the user interface.

The first two chapters are concerned with how we take in information. This kind of human information processing has been studied extensively under the heading of 'Perception'. Chapter 1 discusses such topics as visual acuity, colour vision and our sensitivity to changes in the visual array. The visual system can be usefully characterised as having a limited bandwidth in the temporal and spatial domains and this view is developed to explain the usual recommendations about display parameters such as letter size and refresh rates. Chapter 2 summarises some of the findings from experimental studies of people reading printed and electronically presented text. This chapter also includes a review of work on special problems arising from the use of VDTs.

The third and fourth chapters are concerned with how we store and manipulate information. Human memory is conventionally viewed as a collection of stores of various kinds which have different characteristics. Knowing how these stores function makes it possible to minimise the users' memory problems. Similarly, knowledge of human reasoning processes makes it possible to understand how we manipulate information. Human memory is discussed in Chapter 3 and reasoning in Chapter 4.

CHAPTER 1

Visual Perception: an Intelligent
System with Limited Bandwidth

Peter Thompson

1.1 INTRODUCTION

Vision is our primary sense. Man learns about his
environment largely through his eyes, but the human visual
system has its limitations and its quirks; and an
appreciation of these is an important prerequisite for
making the most efficient use of our visual sense to
communicate information from the world to our higher
cognitive centres.
 The message of this chapter is two-fold. Firstly, the
visual system acts as a low-pass spatio-temporal filter;
this means that there are many things that the eye does not
see and that any visual display need not transmit. Secondly,
vision is an active process, constructing our visual world
from often inadequate information. It is little wonder
therefore that the eye is sometimes deceived.
 An appreciation of both the physical and the cognitive
constraints upon the visual system is important when
designing visual displays.

Light

Visible light is that part of the Electro-magnetic spectrum
to which our eyes are sensitive, the visible range lying
between wavelengths of 400-700 nanometres (nm). At the
short-wavelength end of the visible spectrum is 'blue' light

and at the long-wavelength end is 'red' light. The perceived brightness and colour of light depend largely on the physical intensity and wavelength of the light. However, most of the light we see is reflected light, whose perceived brightness and colour depend upon the properties of the surface from which it is reflected, as well as the properties of the illuminant: generally dark surfaces absorb most light, light surfaces absorb little light; 'red' surfaces absorb most short wavelengths and 'blue' surfaces absorb most long wavelengths, but this is not always the case.

Our Visual Apparatus

For the purposes of this chapter the human visual system comprises the eyes and those areas of the brain responsible for the early stages of visual processing. The human eye focuses an image of the world upsidedown on the retina, a mosaic of light-sensitive receptors covering the back of the eye (see Figure 1.1a). The photoreceptors of the retina are of two different sorts: rods, which are very sensitive to light but saturate at high levels of illumination, and cones, which are less sensitive and hence can operate at high luminance levels. Humans have three different types of cone, each optimally sensitive to a different wavelength, which allow us to have colour vision. Most of each retina's 7 million cones are concentrated in the fovea, the small area of the retina (about 0.3 millimetres in diameter) upon which fixated objects are imaged. The rods, 120 million in each retina, predominate in the periphery. Figure 1.1b shows the distribution of rods and cones on the retina. The point from which the optic nerve leaves the retina is devoid of all photoreceptors, this is called the 'blind-spot', a surprisingly large area of retina totally insensitive to light. The blind spot is located in the temporal retina, that is, in the half of the retina closer to the temple. The other half of the retina is known as the nasal retina, being closer to the nose. The whole of the retina is covered by a network of blood vessels which lie between the visual receptors and the world. However, these are not usually seen because the visual system rapidly ceases to respond to stimuli which remain unchanging on the retina.

(a)

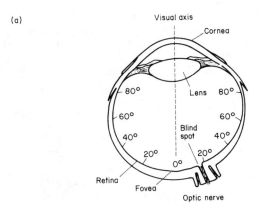

FIG. 1.1a Cross-section through the human eye.   The cornea
and lens of the eye focus light on the sensitive retina.
Objects which we look at directly are imaged on the fovea.

(b)

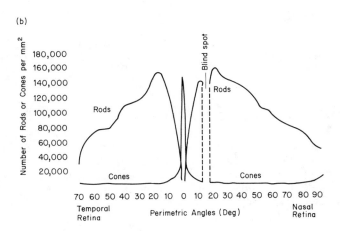

FIG. 1.1b The distribution of rods and cones in the human
retina, left eye.

Visual Angle

The most widely used measure of image size is the degree of
visual angle, see Figure 1.2. An object 1 unit in length
placed at a distance of 57 units from the eye produces an

image of approximately 1 degree of visual angle upon the
retina. Both the sun and the moon subtend angles of about
0.5 degrees (30 minutes). The fovea covers an area of about
1-2 degrees, roughly the size of your thumb-nail at arm's
length, and the blindspot an area of about 5 degrees.

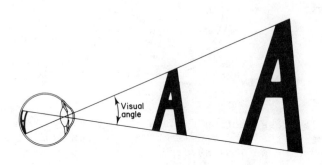

FIG. 1.2 Retinal image size expressed in terms of its visual
angle. Objects with same visual angle have the same size on
the retina.

1.2 LUMINANCE, CONTRAST AND BRIGHTNESS

Luminance generally refers to the light reflected from a
surface, and is an objective measure of radiance. It depends
both upon the illuminance, that is the light falling on the
surface, and upon the reflectance, that is the
light-reflecting properties of the surface. Luminance is
easily measured by a photometer and is defined by the
Commission Internationale de l'Eclairage (C.I.E.), in units
of Candelas per square metre, although the Foot-Lambert is a
commonly used alternative unit (1 cd/m^2 = 0.2919 fL).
    Contrast has been defined by the C.I.E. as follows:

$$\text{Contrast} = \frac{(L_o - L_b)}{L_b}$$

where L_o = object luminance
      L_b = background luminance
This definition allows contrast to take a negative value,
e.g., the printing on this page.
    Contrast is often defined differently by visual
scientists and physicists:

$$\text{Contrast} = \frac{(L_{max} - L_{min})}{(L_{max} + L_{min})}$$

where L_{max} = maximum luminance
      L_{min} = minimum luminance
This contrast, often called the Michelson Contrast can only
take on a value between 0 and 1.

FIG. 1.3a Simultaneous brightness contrast. The two small
grey squares have the same luminance but different brightness.

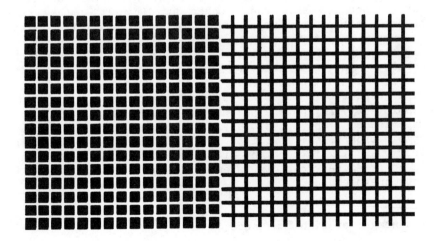

FIG. 1.3b The Hermann Grid. Ghostly dots appear at the
intersections of the lines. Note that no such dot appears at
an intersection if that point is fixated.

Luminance and contrast are physical measures, whereas brightness is a psychological, subjective response to light; its apparent lightness or dimness. Generally the higher the luminance the brighter a light will appear. However this is not always the case. Perceived brightness on one part of a display depends on the brightness of adjoining areas, see Figure 1.3a. Furthermore the juxtaposition of high and low brightnesses can produce disturbing visual effects, Figure 1.3b.

The classic method for measuring brightness involves measuring the difference in luminance which produces a 'just noticeable difference' (j.n.d.), in brightness. The threshold luminance, dL, which can be discriminated from a background luminance, L, obeys Weber's Law:

$$\frac{dL}{L} = k$$

where k, the Weber Fraction, has a value around 0.01-0.02 for the range of luminances encountered in typical displays.

This simple relationship is complicated by the adaptation level of the visual system. Our vision in dim illumination is mediated by rods because of the low sensitivity of cones. Because we have very few rods in the fovea we are relatively insensitive to objects at the point of fixation when using rod vision - our maximum sensitivity is shifted about 20 degrees into the periphery where rods have their greatest density, see Figure 1.1b. Astronomers have long been familiar with the fact that very faint stars in the night sky cannot be seen when looked at directly - they only become visible when imaged away from the insensitive fovea. In normal day-time vision, photopic vision, the rod visual pigment, called rhodopsin, is bleached by the high light levels, and only recovers slowly when we move into low levels of illumination. This process, known as dark-adaptation, can take up to 30 minutes to reach maximum sensitivity. Anyone who has entered a dark cinema will have experienced the temporary blindness caused by the combination of the low light level and bleached rods. Moving from the dark into bright light, known as light adaptation, is achieved very rapidly as cones begin to operate and the rods are bleached.

Advantages of High Luminance

Most normal viewing conditions span photopic (cone) vision, when luminance is above 10 cd/m^2, and mesopic vision (when both cones and rods are operating), between 0.001-10 cd/m^2.

When viewing a VDT the level of light adaptation will be
determined by some weighted average of the room luminance
and the display luminance. The brightest parts of the screen
are unlikely to exceed 1000 cd/m^2 and the total range of
luminance encountered with a VDT will be less than 2 log
units.

There seems to be good evidence that having a high level
of display luminance is advantageous because:

(i) acuity increases with luminance.

(ii) pupil diameter decreases with increased luminance;
this decreases optical distortion and improves depth of
field, c.f. reducing the aperture on a camera when taking
a photograph.

(iii) discomfort from reflected glare may be reduced.
The penalty paid by increased luminance is that flicker
sensitivity increases (see section 1.4). Discomfort from
direct glare may increase with increased display
luminance.

1.3 COLOUR SENSITIVITY

There are three types of cone in the human retina, one is
most sensitive to short wavelengths (the 'blue' cone), one
to the middle range (the 'green' cone), and the other to
long wavelengths (the 'red' cone). Each cone type is broadly
tuned in its sensitivity and responds to a wide range of
wavelengths so that most of the colours we see will have
excited all three mechanisms to some extent. When coloured
lights are mixed together colour addition takes place, which
is quite different from the colour subtraction which results
from mixing paints. Red and green lights mix together to
give yellow; red and green paints mix to give a rather nasty
grey-brown. Yellow surfaces will excite the red and green
cones a great deal but will have little effect on the blue
cones. Because of the distribution of cones in the retina,
colour vision is best in the fovea and less good in the
periphery. Indeed, in the far periphery we have no colour
sensitivity at all.

Colour Naming

No dimension of the visual world illustrates the limitations
of the visual system better than colour. We are able to see

only a small portion of the Electromagnetic spectrum,
between about 400 - 700 nm, even though shorter wavelengths,
in the ultraviolet, can be 'seen' by some insects and longer
wavelengths, in the infrared, by certain reptiles.
Furthermore our ability to discriminate different
wavelengths as different hues is limited. This ability
varies enormously over the visible spectrum. With just three
cone types we are able to discriminate around 128 just
noticeable differences (j.n.d.) of wavelength. We are most
sensitive in the yellow and blue/green portion of the
spectrum where a change in wavelength of only 1 nm can be
discriminated.   At the extremities of the spectrum the
j.n.d. rises to as much as 20 nm.

The discriminations described above are made at equal
luminance and saturation; that is, the discrimination is
made on the basis of wavelength alone. Colour comprises
three aspects of a stimulus, its hue, its brightness and its
saturation, saturation being the amount of white light added
to the saturated hue.   Thus pink is an unsaturated red.
Although we can discriminate around 128 different hues, we
can discriminate many thousands of colours. Indeed, 8000
colour names are listed in the 'Methuen Handbook of Colour',
but it is unlikely that anyone would correctly identify
'Wafted Feather' or 'Angel Wing' without some training.

An important constraint in the use of colour is a
cognitive one - we cannot reliably assign generally accepted
names to many of the colours we can discriminate. Grether
and Baker (1972) have listed ten spectral colours which can
be reliably identified without extended training; these are
listed below:

Wavelength (nm)	Label
642	Red
610	Orange
596	Orange-Yellow
582	Yellow
556	Yellow-Green
515	Green
504	Green-Blue
494	Blue-Green
476	Blue
430	Violet

Of course we could add black, white, and a few
non-spectral colours like brown to this list.

Measuring Colour

Because we have 3 cone mechanisms human colour vision is
trichromatic; that is, any colour can be specified as a
mixture of 3 'Primaries'. The primaries do not have to match
the spectral properties of the cone pigments; indeed, as
long as none of the primaries is simply a mixture of the
other two, any three colours can be used. In C.R.T. colour
displays the primaries (i.e., the phosphors) are commonly
red, green and blue.

The C.I.E. has laid down standard primaries. This allows
us to specify colours in terms of the relative proportions
of each of the standards. If we know the relative
proportions of two of the primaries in a mixture, we can
infer the proportion of the third as proportions must sum to
unity. For example, if the proportion of red primary is
0.04, and the proportion of green primary is 0.29, then the
proportion of blue will be 0.67. This would appear as a
greenish blue.

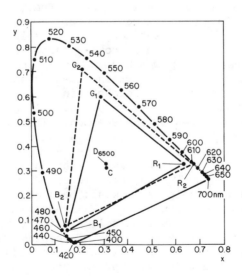

FIG. 1.4 The 1931 CIE chromaticity diagram, showing the
location of the red, green and blue colour televesion
primaries for PAL System (R_1, G_1, B_1) and for the NTSC system
(R_2, G_2, B_2).

The widely used C.I.E. 1931 Chromaticity diagram, Figure 1.4, plots the proportion of the red primary, x, against the proportion of the green primary, y. When the value of both x and y is small then the blue primary predominates. Our example above can be seen to represent a colour close to 490 nm. It can also be seen in this chart that the televison primaries used in Great Britain (PAL System I) and in the U.S.A. (N.T.S.C.) allow representation of no more than half the area of visible colours.

The point marked D6500 in the middle of the figure refers to an average daylight "white light", the 6500 being the colour temperature. The point marked C nearby is an alternative standard white which has a colour temperature of 6740K. A note of caution is called for here: colour specification is a complex topic and the unwary will soon confound chroma,colour, hue, saturation, brightness, colour temperature, value and purity. Excellent chapters on this subject can be found in both Pearson (1975) and Hurvich (1981).

Colour Blindness

One problem with using colour differences to convey information is that a relatively large fraction (about 8%) of the male population has some kind of colour deficiency. This is an inherited defect which affects less than 1% of the female population. The most common defect occurs in the red or green receptors, which results in anomalous colour vision, the confusion of certain hues discriminable by normals, rather than in true colour-blindness. The so-called red/green colour-blind man may simply have large j.n.d.s in the red and green area of the spectrum. This will probably be most apparent at low light levels, which may explain why such people have particular difficulty in discriminating shades of brown, an extra-spectral colour which arises when a surface of low reflectance reflects those wavelengths which with a higher reflectance would be seen as yellow. In many people the existence of a colour anomaly is only manifest when fairly subtle colour discriminations are demanded, therefore a large number of people with some kind of colour blindness are unaware of their deficiency. The first time they are made aware of their problem may be when required to use a colour VDT!

1.4 THE VISUAL SYSTEM AS A SPATIOTEMPORAL FILTER

Flicker Sensitivity

The eye's sensitivity to temporal change is often measured by its Critical Flicker Frequency (C.F.F.). This measure can be regarded as a temporal analogue of an optician's eyechart, which determines the limit of spatial resolution (see section on spatial sensitivity below). Lights flickered very rapidly are perceived as shining steadily; only when the flicker-rate drops below the C.F.F., typically around 50 cycles/second, can the flicker be perceived. Thus we can describe the temporal reponse of the visual system as resembling a temporal low-pass filter, see Figure 1.5.

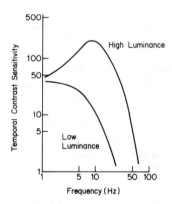

FIG. 1.5 Flicker sensitivity of the eye at two levels of screen luminance.

Flicker sensitivity increases with increasing luminance; therefore a display which appears not to flicker at low luminance levels may well appear to flicker at high luminance levels. Furthermore our sensitivity to flicker is not uniform across the retina and, at high flicker rates,

the periphery can be more sensitive than the fovea; hence
the common observation that a television set appears to
flicker more when viewed out of the corner of the eye. This
means that the larger the display we use, the further into
peripheral vision it will encroach and the more likely it is
that it will appear to flicker at the edges. This can be a
particular problem with VDTs which are viewed from very
small distances compared with those used in viewing T.V.;
the closer an object, the larger its retinal image size.

Spatial Sensitivity

It makes no sense to define visual acuity in terms of the
width of the thinnest line or size of the smallest letter a
person can see unless we also know the distance of that line
or letter from the eye. What we need to know is the size of
the image on the retina, and this is usually measured in
units of visual angle.

There are many measures of visual acuity, some of which
are shown in Figure 1.6. The familiar 20/20 label for normal
vision was developed by Snellen who tested his subjects'
eye-sight 20 feet from his letter chart; the equivalent
score using the metric version of this test is 6/6. Those
who can discriminate letters at 20 feet which most people
can only see at 10 feet are described as having 20/10
vision, which is exceptionally good. Those who can only see
letters from 20 feet which most people can discriminate at,
say, 40 feet, are described as having 20/40 vision. Visual
acuity of 20/200 is the legal definition of blindness in
most of the United States, while to pass a driving test in
the U.K. a candidate must read a licence plate at 75 feet -
requiring an acuity of about 20/47 (6/14).

The measures of visual acuity shown in Figure 1.6 were
obtained using high levels of illumination and a high level
of contrast between the target and the background. In
everyday life conditions are often far from ideal and much
less impressive values of acuity are found. Although high
luminance and contrast improve the visibility of patterns
which reflect their illuminant, transilluminated displays,
such as VDTs, produce irradiation or direct glare at high
luminance levels which reduce acuity.

The Contrast Sensitivity Function

In recent years many visual psychophysicists have measured
visual sensitivity, not with spots or thin lines or with

letters of the alphabet, but with sine-wave gratings. These gratings are characterised by their sinusoidal luminance profile, their orientation, phase, spatial frequency and amplitude. Figure 1.7 contains some pictures of sine wave gratings. Spatial frequency is defined as the number of cycles of grating per degree of visual angle; the amplitude is usually expressed as a measure of Michelson contrast.

TECHNIQUE	EXAMPLES	MINIMUM (ANGULAR) VALUE
1. *Minimum visible* (detecting single line or dot)	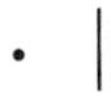 • |	0.5 sec of arc
2. *Minimum separable* (resolution of interspaces between contours)	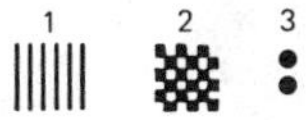  1 ‖‖‖ 2 ▓ 3 ⁞ 4 ⊒⫙ 5 ◗ ◖	30 sec-1 min of arc (20/10 to 20/20)
3. *Recognition* (naming target)	L O B T C L	30 sec-1 min of arc
4. *Vernier acuity* (detecting discontinuity)	 | |	2 sec of arc
5. *Stereoscopic acuity* (detecting depth displacement)	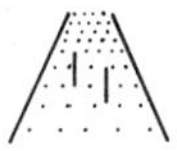 △	1.5 sec of arc
6. *Dynamic acuity* (detecting and locating interspace in moving target)	 ◖ ←	1-2 min of arc up to 60°/sec

Varieties of minimum separable acuity include: (1) Ives grating, (2) checkerboard pattern, (3) dot pairs, (4) Illiterate Snellen, (5) Landolt circles. Note that in several of these, the viewer must not only detect interspaces, but must localize them (Illiterate Snellen and Landolt circle).

FIG. 1.6 Techniques for measuring visual acuity and optimal resulting values.

The sine-wave grating was chosen as an appropriate stimulus with which to measure visual sensitivity by researchers who viewed the visual system as a linear system and therefore brought the techniques of Fourier analysis to vision. A discussion of the role of Fourier analysis in

vision research is not necessary here; suffice it to say
that any two-dimensional function, e.g., the luminance
distribution of a visual pattern, can be decomposed into a
set of sinusoids of appropriate frequencies, amplitudes,
orientations and phases. Furthermore, the response of a
linear system to a sinusoidal input is itself a sinusoid of
the same frequency and orientation; therefore only the
amplitude and phase of the response need to be determined
for each input frequency and orientation to give us the
modulation transfer function, M.T.F., for the system.

FIG. 1.7 Some examples of sine-wave gratings.

To measure the M.T.F. for the human visual system we
measure contrast detection thresholds, the lowest contrast
at which we can detect the presence of a stimulus, for a
range of sine-wave gratings of different spatial
frequencies.

This function, Figure 1.8, is called the spatial contrast
sensitivity function and can be regarded as the spatial
equivalent of the flicker sensitivity function shown in
Figure 1.5, to which it bears a striking resemblance.
    The Contrast Sensitivity Function can be seen as the
spatial filtering characteristic of the visual system. In
recent years neurophysiologists and psychophysicists have
determined that the C.S.F. does not describe a single
filtering mechanism but is the envelope of a number of more
narrowly-tuned spatial filters, or 'channels'. This means
that the neural mechanisms responsible for detecting low
spatial frequencies are quite different from those detecting
medium and high spatial frequencies.

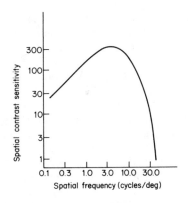

FIG. 1.8 Human spatial contrast sensitivity function.

The Window of Visibility

The medium bandwidth of spatial channels means that the
visual system can only be thought of as carrying out a
Fourier analysis in the crudest sense. However, the
description of visual stimuli in the frequency domain
remains extremely useful. Clearly it is unnecessary to

represent any spatial frequencies higher than about 50 cycles/degree in any image as the visual system simply will not detect their presence. To illustrate this further let us consider the problem of stroboscopic movement - the apparent movement of images presented successively in slightly different spatial positions. That an impression of smooth movement can be gained from a succession of stationary images is exploited both by raster displays like television and by the movies. Moving patterns on such displays are time-sampled versions of real, smooth movement. If an object is spatially displaced by too great a distance in a single frame of stroboscopic movement the smoothness of the motion breaks down. Similarly the illusion of smooth movement is destroyed by too long a temporal delay between successive images. Although the necessary conditions for smooth movement have been investigated by many studies over the years, few generally applicable laws have emerged. More recently, Watson and Ahumada (1983), research scientists at the NASA Ames laboratories, have approached the issue in a new way. Firstly they have described the stimuli not in terms of their size, separation and time between frames, but in terms of their spatial frequency and temporal frequency content. Secondly, they have described what they call the human 'window of visibility'. Because the high-frequency cut-off in spatial vision does not vary much as a function of temporal frequency and because the temporal frequency cut-off does not depend too much on spatial frequency, we can map out a spatiotemporal area in the frequency domain which defines the limits of our visual sensitivity, see Figure 1.9a. Stimulus components lying outside this 'window of visiblity' cannot be seen and can be ignored.

FIG. 1.9(a) The window of visibility. Frequency components of a stimulus which lie outside the window cannot be seen.
(b) On the right of the figure is the contrast distribution for a thin vertical line moving smoothly. On the left is the frequency spectrum for the same moving bar.
(c) The contrast distribution (right) and frequency spectrum (left) for a thin vertical line in stroboscopic motion. Because the frequency spectrum in the window of visibility is different from that for smooth movement (1.9b), the line will not appear to be moving smoothly.
(d) As 1.9c but with a higher sampling frequency. The spectral replicas are now more widely spaced and fall outside the window of visibility. This moving line will appear to be identical to the real smoothly moving time in 1.9b.

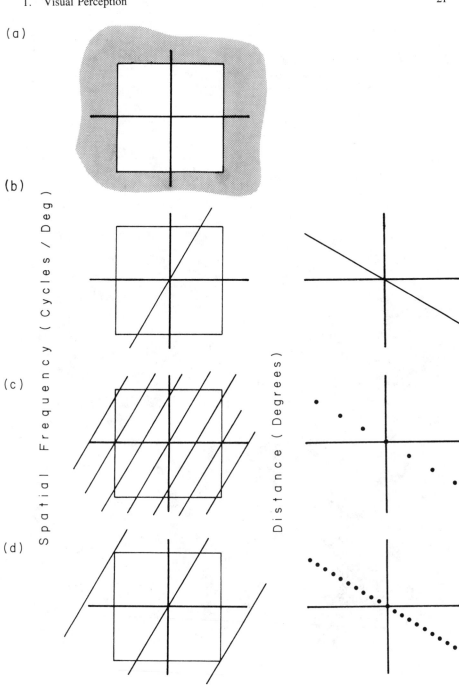

(a)

(b)

(c)

(d)

Spatial Frequency (Cycles / Deg)

Distance (Degrees)

Temporal Frequency
(Cycles / Second)

Time (Seconds)

Therefore for two stimuli to appear to be identical only those frequency components lying within the window need to be identical. Watson and Ahumada showed that the frequency spectrum for stroboscopic motion is the same as that for real motion except for the addition of replicas of the spectrum, see Figure 1.9b-d. These replicas will be more widely spaced as the time sampling of the motion becomes finer. As long as the replicas do not encroach upon the window of visibility the stroboscopic movement will appear exactly like real movement.

One important consequence of this type of approach to visual processing is the realisation that when constructing or decoding visual patterns we need only to concern

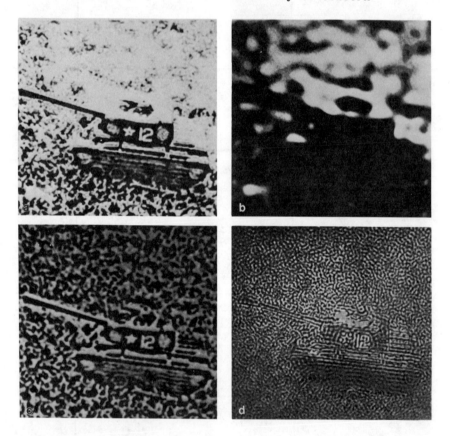

FIG. 1.10(a) Original photographic image.
(b) Same image filtered to pass low spatial frequencies only.
(c) As (b) but with only medium spatial frequencies passed.
(d) As (b) but with only high spatial frequencies passed.
Courtesy of H.C. Andrews

ourselves with a limited amount of information. Firstly, as discussed above, we do not need to consider frequencies which fall outside the 'window of visibility'; secondly, we may find that a very limited range of frequencies contains that information that we require from a scene. Figure 1.10 shows a tank when low-, medium- and high-pass filtered. If our task is simply to read the number on the tank we can throw away all the low and high frequency information in the picture and still read the number with ease.

Retinal Inhomogeneity and Cortical Magnification Factor

Visual sensitivity in peripheral vision is very different from that in the fovea. The highest detectable spatial frequency in central vision is around 40-50 cycles/degree but is around only 9 cycles/degree just 10 degrees into the periphery. Sensitivity declines slightly more rapidly along vertical meridia, less rapidly along the horizontal. Flicker sensitivity is not affected in the same way, indeed sensitivity to high rates of flicker is at least as good in peripheral as in central vision. Recently neuroanatomists and psychophysicists have suggested a simple relationship between visual acuity at different eccentricities and the anatomy of the visual cortex. It is well-known that the visual field is mapped topographically onto the surface of the striate cortex. This map however is distorted, devoting a relatively large area to the fovea and a much smaller area to the peripheral retina. Indeed, it is possible to predict the visual acuity at any eccentricity from the 'cortical magnification factor', M, the extent of striate cortex devoted to 1 degree of visual angle at that eccentricity. Therefore magnifying an image in the peripheral visual field in proportion to 1/M will produce an image equally resolvable at all retinal locations.

Rovamo and Virsu (1979) have presented equations which allow the determination of M at different eccentricities; a few values are given below:

Eccentricity (degrees from fovea)	M (mm/degree)
0	7.99
1.5	5.34
4.0	3.44
7.5	2.28
14.0	1.37
30.0	0.625

A similar conclusion has been reached by Anstis (1974) who found that the height of letters at which they could just be recognised increases linearly with eccentricity up to about 30 degrees into the periphery. Five degrees from the fovea a letter 0.2 degrees high can be recognised while 25 degrees from the fovea the letters must be 1.0 degrees high. Thus the minimum discriminable letter size increases by about 2.5 minutes of arc for each degree of retinal eccentricity. Figure 1.11 shows letters which should be equally readable when fixating the central spot. Note that this array of letters remains equally readable over a wide range of viewing distances. As viewing distance increases the retinal image becomes smaller but closer to central vision.

FIG. 1.11 All letters should be equally readable when centre of this chart is fixated, since each letter is ten times its threshold height.

The lack of high-frequency information should lead to peripheral vision being markedly blurred. Similarly, the insensitivity of central vision at night should lead to a blurring of the visual world. However in both these cases, although our vision is devoid of fine detail, we would not describe it as blurred. It appears that our perceptual processes compensate for the limitations of the visual system and perceive the most probable form of the world, even if this requires that we go beyond the available sense data.

1.5 PERCEPTION AS AN ACTIVE PROCESS

The previous sections have outlined some of the restrictions on visual sensitivity. If we assume that a stimulus can be detected, how sure can we be that it will be perceived accurately? The visual system is not a camera, it does not try to copy the original scene into a picture inside the head; rather it transforms, enhances, distorts and discards information. One side-effect of this processing is that sometimes straight lines appear curved, stationary objects appear to move, white objects appear coloured; sometimes objects can disappear altogether and yet others appear which do not exist. This may sound alarming, but it is a small price to pay for a visual system which works as well as ours.

The Perceptual Constancies

As we walk around the world it has a comforting solid feel about it; buildings stay still, people stay the same size and shape, snow is always white and coal is always black. This is very surprising when we consider the nature of the images on our retinas (sometimes called the proximal stimuli). As we walk along a street the buildings will be bouncing up and down on the retina, people will swell and swell as they approach us, becoming larger, even, than the bouncing buildings. The intensity of the light reflected from the snow will often be a good deal lower than that reflected from coal. These fleeting distorted images are transformed by our perceptual processes into the constant world we know.

Brightness constancy and colour constancy refer to our ability to perceive the correct reflectance and hue of surfaces regardless of their illuminant. Snow looks white in moonlight because, although it reflects little light, it is still reflecting a high proportion of the illuminant. Coal will always look black simply because, no matter how much light it reflects, it has a low reflectance.

Object constancy refers to our ability to perceive the correct size and shape of objects in three dimensional space, despite gross distortions in their proximal stimuli, see Figure 1.12. On occasions these perceptual constancies can be misapplied by the visual system with the result that we suffer from 'visual illusions', see Figure 1.13.

FIG. 1.13 A version of the Ponzo illusion, a case of misapplied size constancy scaling.

FIG. 1.12 Size constancy. The small woman in both figures subtends the same visual angle on the retina, but the operation of size constancy in the upper picture leads her to appear larger than her retinal size should warrant.

In this illusion, the Ponzo illusion, the upper bar is
perceived as being more distant from the observer than the
lower bar. Hence, although of the same retinal size, the
upper bar is perceived as being larger than the lower bar by
virtue of its greater distance. Sometimes we can turn these
illusions to our advantage as has been achieved by the Road
Research Laboratory's successful 'Roundabout' illusion.
Yellow lines spaced closer and closer together across roads
approaching roundabouts deceive drivers into over-estimating
their speed with the result that they slow down.
   One of the most interesting aspects of many of the
illusions to which the visual system is prone is that we are
quite helpless to correct our perceptions even when we know
they are faulty. The Fraser spiral remains a spiral even
after we know it is contructed from concentric circles,
Figure 1.14.

FIG. 1.14 The Fraser Spiral.

Perceptions as Hypotheses

The most probable external world is a relatively stable one, where objects, by and large, are of constant shape, size and colour. Edges are generally sharp, railway tracks are generally parallel and windows are rectilinear. When we come to interpret our visual world our preconceptions and expectations can help to determine our perceptions. Often this helps us to perceive objects as they really are, however on occasions it can distort and twist objects into things that they are not.

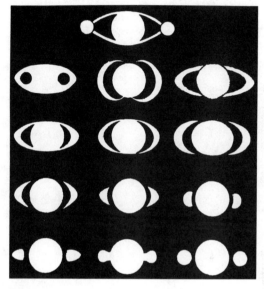

FIG. 1.15 Huygen's early sketches of the planet Saturn.

When Christiaan Huygens first viewed the rings of Saturn through his telescope he did not know the planet had 'rings'. Without the correct perceptual hypothesis he failed to perceive accurately what he saw, Figure 1.15. Sometime after he had drawn these sketches, Huygens realised that the planet was surrounded by flat rings, whereupon his drawings would have changed to reflect his new perceptual hypothesis. Here we have an example of our perception changing dramatically as a result of our changing ideas about the world. Some pictures can be interpreted by two conflicting hypotheses, for example, Boring's "wife/mother-in-law", Figure 1.16. What appears to be a picture of an old crone

one minute will become a young woman the next, although the
picture itself has not changed.   Interestingly it appears
that we cannot entertain both hypotheses about the picture
simultaneously: it is either the wife or the mother-in-law,
never both. When we see this picture for the first time we
immediately "see" one of the two faces although for some
people it will be the wife and for others the mother-in-law,
the appearance of the other figure occurring after some,
often frustrating, period of time.   However, some figures
appear to be a nonsensical jumble at first, only emerging as
a recognisable picture later.   A good example of this is
R.C. James' spotty dog, Figure 1.17. A seemingly irregular
pattern of splodges will on patient inspection transform
themselves into a Dalmation dog.   Once seen it becomes
impossible to look at the splodges again without seeing the
hidden hound.

FIG. 1.16 Boring's wife/mother-in-law.

While it may now be apparent that the visual system does
not passively reflect the world, we should not look on human
perception only as the active interpretation of the visual
world. Before our higher perceptual processes can start to
construct their hypotheses, the raw sense-data has been

dramatically transformed by the passive filters of the more
peripheral visual apparatus. It is only by appreciating all
the stages of processing which are involved in 'seeing' that
we shall understand the real capabilities and limitations of
the visual system.

FIG. 1.17 R.C. James' Spotty dog.

1.6 SUMMARY

Visual stimuli, be they objects in the real world or
patterns on a C.R.T. can be described in terms of their
size, shape, orientation, colour, movement, etc. In many of
these dimensions our visual systems act like a filter,
responding to some parts of the dimension while remaining
oblivious to others. An appreciation of these limitations
is important because it guards us against requiring our
visual system to perform beyond its physical constraints and
because it enables us to achieve an economy of
representation when constructing visual displays - we do not
need to generate those parts of a pattern which will be

invisible to the visual system.

Many of the constraints on vision are established in the early stages of visual processing and can be traced to aspects of the anatomy and physiology of the peripheral visual system. Other constraints appear at a cognitive level. At this higher level, visual processing appears to be an active process which uses past experience and expectations to aid in its construction of a plausible visual world from seemingly ambiguous sense-data.

The rigidity of the physical limitations of the peripheral visual system makes recommendations on the physical dimensions of visual stimuli possible. However, the flexibility of our cognitive apparatus makes many of the decisions of the visual display designer very difficult. Whether the use of colour, highlighted words or flashing symbols will help or hinder the user is often impossible to determine outside the particular task being considered. Fortunately, these decisions can be made after reasonably simple experiments have been carried out.

1.7 FURTHER READING

Gregory's (1966) 'Eye and Brain' remains the most readable introduction to visual perception, but it contains little of the research findings of the past 15 years. Try also Frisby (1979) 'Seeing', a new book which gives an excellent outline of the neurophysiological under-pinning of much psychophysical theorising. The illustrations are particularly good.

Schiff (1980) 'Perception, An Applied Approach' is a good introduction to all the senses. It is not as 'applied' as one might be led to believe from the title, but it does contain useful references to some valuable applied research. Pearson (1975) 'Transmission and Display of Pictorial Information' is an excellent book addressed to communication engineers on the nature of video signals and their efficient transmission.

For a very lucid discussion of the use of sine-wave gratings in neurophysiological and psychophysical research read Campbell and Maffei (1974). Watson and Ahumada (1983) is a most elegant account of the sufficient and necessary conditions for stroboscopic motion which introduces the term 'window of visibility'.

Hurvich (1981) 'Color vision' provides a most readable introduction to colour vision and includes an excellent chapter on colour specification. The proceedings of a symposium including several useful chapters on visual processing as well as a number of chapters on various aspects of image processing are presented in Braddick and Sleigh (1983).

Grandjean and Vigliani (1982) 'Ergonomic Aspects of Visual Display Terminals' is a good collection of papers covering all aspects of VDTs, some of which are concerned with visual function and visual impairments.

CHAPTER 2

Reading: Extracting Information from Printed and Electronically Presented Text

Charles Hulme

2.1 INTRODUCTION

In interacting with computers human operators often receive
and send information in the medium of written language. It
is clearly relevant for those designing and implementing
computer systems to be aware of the sorts of processes
involved in reading. The characteristics and limitations of
the human information processing systems involved in reading
will be relevant for maximising the operating efficiency of
man-machine systems.

In recent years there has been a great deal of research
by cognitive psychologists into the nature of reading
processes. Such research is generally conducted within a
human information processing framework. The processes by
which people read are explicitly fragmented into separate
stages and the processes operating at these stages are
systematically investigated in experimental studies. This
human information processing approach sometimes comes as
something as a surprise to non-psychologists. Basically the
cognitive psychologist views human beings mechanistically
and often explicit analogies are drawn between the
information processing operations carried out by people and
the operations performed by computers. The aim is to try to
elucidate the mechanisms underlying skills such as memory
and reading by trying to establish systematic relationships
between input (stimuli) and output (responses). On this
basis theories are constructed which attempt to specify

FUNDAMENTALS OF
HUMAN–COMPUTER INTERACTION

different stages in the system between input and output.
These stages are specified in terms of the types of code
information is held in and the sorts of transformations it
is subjected to. The next section presents such a view of
the process of reading.

2.2 THE COGNITIVE PSYCHOLOGY OF READING

An Overview of the Reading Process

Reading might be defined as the extraction of information
from text; the process by which we get meaning from a
printed message. There are several sub-processes which are
often distinguished in discussions of this very complex
process.

The reader must first perceive the visual patterns of the
words on a page. On the basis of this visual information he
must decode the meanings of the individual words present.
This process involves going from a visual representation of
a word to some stored representation of that word's meaning.
According to current theories of this process the meanings
of words which the reader knows are stored in a kind of
internal dictionary or "lexicon". The processes by which
the stored information in the lexicon is accessed is the
subject of a great deal of research. It appears that on
some occasions readers may recode visually presented words
into a speech-like representation, while on others access to
the lexicon occurs directly from a visual representation
(see, for example, Coltheart, 1978).

Having identified the meanings of the individual words in
a sentence, the reader must undertake a syntactic analysis.
That is, he must relate the meanings of the individual words
in a sentence according to the rules of the grammar of his
language. The meaning of a sentence will depend not only
upon the individual words but upon the way in which they are
combined. To take a trivial example the following two
sentences have quite different meanings:

> The cat chased the dog
> The dog chased the cat

It appears that in order to perform syntactic analyses of
written messages readers hold the string of words in the
form of internal speech. Using speech is a very good way of
remembering the order of words, which is clearly

crucial in understanding sentences (Kleiman, 1975; Baddeley et al., 1982).

The final stage involved is that the meanings of individual sentences in the passage must be related to each other to reach an understanding of the passage as a whole. In these later stages of reading the reader is clearly performing a kind of problem solving exercise. The ease of understanding a piece of written material will depend not only upon the characteristics of the passage, e.g., how clearly it is printed, its grammatical form, etc., but also upon the reader's past experience and familiarity with the concepts involved.

Eye Movements and the Intake of Visual Information

An average rate of reading for normal adults is somewhere in the region of 250-300 words per minute. A widely held belief, which accords with our subjective experience, is that as we read our eyes sweep smoothly along the printed line. This impression is, in fact, quite false, as first shown by Javal. In fact our eyes move along a line of print in a series of small rapid jerks, which are called saccades. These saccades are punctuated by short periods, called fixations, when the eyes are still. On average, fixations last around 150-300 milliseconds, and the saccades happen much more quickly, taking around 20 milliseconds. The perception of the printed material occurs only during fixations; during the saccades no clear vision is possible. In most situations about 94% of reading time is devoted to fixations.

During the reading of a line of print the eyes sometimes move backwards towards the beginning of the line to re-read some of the material. These backward movements are known as regressions. The number of regressions is related to the difficulty of the material being read. When the material is difficult more regressions occur. When one line of print has been read the eyes make a long return saccade to fixate the beginning of the next line.

This pattern of movements is illustrated in Figure 2.1. It may be possible to observe these eye movements during reading by placing a mirror in front and a little to the right of the reader and then looking at the mirror from behind him. In current research eye movements are normally recorded by using systems which detect the patterns of reflection from small fixed lights placed in front of the eye. (See, for example Rayner, 1978.)

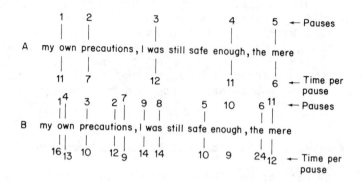

FIG. 2.1 An illustration of the eye movement patterns of a
good and a poor reader. Numbers at the top of the lines show
the sequence of fixations; those at the bottom show the time
taken for each fixation in 50ths of a second.

The Perceptual Span in Reading

The perceptual span refers to the amount of text which can
be processed by the reader in a fixation. Visual acuity is
highest at the fovea of the eye and falls off rapidly
towards the periphery (see Chapter 1, section 1.2). These
physiological factors obviously place constraints on how
much information can be extracted in a fixation. The problem
of how to define the perceptual span in reading proves to be
not as simple as might first appear. This has been most
elegantly demonstrated in a series of experiments by Rayner
(1975). In these studies subjects read short paragraphs
displayed on a CRT display slaved to a computer. The same
computer system also monitors the subjects' eye movements by
means of sensing corneal reflections. Various words in the
text are distorted and changed back to their correct form as
the subject moves his eye past some pre-set boundary. The
dependent measure analysed is how long subjects fixate these
target words, and the assumption is that if a discrepancy is
noticed between the form of the word in peripheral vision
and that when the word is fixated then subjects will fixate

the word longer. These experiments show that if gross
physical cues concerning the letters present in a word and
its overall shape are maintained, for example by changing
"tasted" to "tested", these changes are only noticed at a
distance between one and six character spaces to the right
of fixation. On the other hand, changes in word shape, as
in replacing "tasted" by "tflmed", may be detected seven to
twelve character spaces to the right of fixation. The
implication of such results is that information about the
meaning of the word is only being extracted from a very
narrow window of text but gross cues such as overall word
shape may be being picked up from much further into
peripheral vision. Such a result should not surprise us,
but it means we cannot talk of a single perceptual span in
reading, but rather a number of overlapping spans from which
different types of information are being extracted
simultaneously.

Recognising Individual Words

A great deal of interest has focussed on how a reader
recognises the individual words which comprise a text, i.e.
what sort of perceptual information is utilised in the
process of identifying a word?

It may be useful to organize a discussion of this process
around three very general types of model for word
recognition.

(i) The simplest sort of model we might consider would
be where there was a systematic "scan" of some internal
representation of the word from left to right. This
"scan" would operate sequentially identifying one letter
after another. A listing of the letters present together
with their order of occurrence would provide the
necessary information for the word to be identified.
Models of this sort are referred to as serial letter
identification models. These models would appear to be a
rather slow way of organizing the process of word
recognition.

(ii) A quicker way to organize things would be to have a
process in which all the letters in a word are processed
and recognised at the same time. In other respects the
operation of this model would be the same as in (i).
Models of this type are referred to as parallel letter
identification models.

(iii) According to the last type of model word
identification is not accomplished as a result of a
series of independently carried out letter
identifications. Rather, in addition to information
about letters in the word (or perhaps instead of this)
the reader extracts information about what have been
called supra-letter features. The most common idea is
that the reader uses information about the overall shape
of the word. Processing the shape of the whole word might
be an even quicker process than identifying each letter
separately. The idea of word shape is illustrated in
Figure 2.2.

FIG. 2.2 An illustration of word-shape. The distribution of
ascenders and descenders in a word give it a characteristic
shape outline which is absent when the word is printed in all
capitals.

What evidence is there for these three different views?
Serial letter identification models can be shown to be quite
clearly inadequate to explain our ability to recognise
words. These models predict that it should take longer for
a person to identify a word than a single letter. Many
experimental studies have shown that this is not the case.
Words are often perceived more quickly and more accurately
than single letters. Most research is, therefore, directed
towards the much more difficult problem of deciding whether
parallel letter identification models can explain human
performance, or whether it is necessary to acknowledge a
role for word shape information. There is now a little
evidence that word shape information seems to play a role in
the word recognition process.

One approach to this question has revolved around what
are referred to as Word Superiority Effects; these are
demonstrations that in certain situations people process
words more efficiently than non-words. One task which shows
this effect is a very simple one called simultaneous
matching. Here the person is presented with pairs of words

one above the other.

       e.g.   book
                             book

or on other trials non-words

       e.g.   obok
                             obok

He simply has to respond as quickly as possible; "same" if
the two words or non-words match, "different" if they don't.
    People consistently make "same" judgements faster for
words than for non-words. This effect is greater for words
which are read frequently than for rare words. Could this be
because familiar words are treated as whole patterns rather
than as a string of separate letters?
    One thing that can be done is to distort the shape of a
word by printing it in letters which alternate between upper
and lower case.

       e.g.   bOoK
                             bOoK

When this is done it eliminates the advantage enjoyed by
frequent words compared to non-words in the simultaneous
matching task and the disruptive effect is greater for
frequent than less frequent words (Bruder, 1978). This does
suggest that the overall shape of a word may be important in
the way we perceive it. Word shape is probably more
important in the case of highly familiar (i.e., frequently
read) words than those which we see less often.

2.3 LEGIBILITY

Studies of legibility are concerned with typographical
factors which may influence the ease with which we can read.
The size of type, the style of type, the spacing between
lines, the use of capital and lower case letters, are all
factors which may affect the ease and speed of reading.
    Using conventional printed materials there have been
extensive studies of these sorts of factors. So far these
studies have had relatively little impact on the study of
computer controlled displays, but an awareness of their
methods and findings is certainly relevant to the problem of
conducting such studies. It seems very likely that some of
the factors which have been shown to reduce the legibility
of conventional printed materials will also have similar

effects with other sorts of displays such as those on VDTs.

Measuring legibility

Tinker (1965) and his co-workers carried out an elaborate
research program to investigate the effects of various
physical characteristics on the legibility of text. The
most common method of measuring legibility was the speed of
reading short passages. The subject was given a set
paragraph in which one word spoils the meaning. He was to
cross out that word. An example of one of the paragraphs
used is as follows:

"If father had known I was going swimming he would have
forbidden it. He found out after I returned and made me
promise never to skate again without telling him." (The
word "skate" is to be crossed out.)

Tinker also asked his subjects for ratings of the ease of
reading and the pleasantness of the various printing
arrangements he used. In some cases these agreed closely
with his objective measures of performance but in others
there were discrepancies. Subjective ratings are,
therefore, not a sufficient basis for studies of legibility,
although if performance measures fail to differentiate
displays it would seem reasonable to use what most people
are found to prefer.

All-Capital Printing

Lower case texts are more legible than texts printed all in
capitals. Tinker found that text printed in capitals is
read on average about 14% more slowly than lower case texts,
and in some experiments the slowing was nearly 20%. This is
a large effect which indicates that the use of all capital
presentation should be avoided. Tinker suggests that this
effect may be due to a loss of word-shape information in all
capital printing, but clearly other sorts of explanations
are possible, such as the greater familiarity of lower case
letters or their greater discriminability compared with
upper case letters.

Size of Type

The size of type is measured in points, as in 8-point or 14-point type. A point is roughly 1/72 inch measured vertically. Tinker found that the most commonly used sizes of type (9, 10, 11 and 12-point) were equally legible when set with an appropriate line width and inter-line spacing (leading). It should be remembered, however, that the optimal size for type will obviously depend to some extent on viewing distance.

Line Length and Leading

Line length in printing is measured in picas. A pica is roughly 1/6 inch so that a 30 pica line is about 5 inches long. Leading is the space between lines. The derivation of this term is from the fact that thin strips of lead were used to insert space between successive lines of print. Leading, like type size, is measured in points. Two point leading represents a space between successive lines of roughly 2/72 inch.

Both line width and leading affect legibility. Tinker found optimal leading to be two points, with which lines from 14 to 31 picas (2.3 to 5.2 inches) were equally legible. On the basis of a series of studies using six type sizes set in different line widths and with different leadings Tinker postulated a series of "safety zones" within which these three factors might be varied without any significant effect upon legibility (Tinker, 1965).

2.4 SPECIAL PROBLEMS ASSOCIATED WITH READING FROM CRT DISPLAYS

Potential Health Problems

Now that CRT displays are in such common use there has been concern over their possible effects on health and stress in users. Research is now starting to investigate these matters.

One potential risk which has been discussed is the possible exposure of operators to X-ray and radio-frequency radiation. It has been shown, however, that such emissions by most CRTs in computer terminals are no higher than natural background levels (Terrana et al., 1980). There now seems general agreement that this is not a real risk.

There have been more diffuse worries about the
possibility that VDTs are typically more stressful to work
with than more traditional office equipment. One particular
concern has been with whether or not continual reading of
VDTs causes unusual eye strain. This is quite a complex
question to provide a definite answer to, as it will depend
on the properties of particular displays and the situation
in which they are installed, and must involve studies which
compare the effects of jobs which involve intensive use of
VDTs with other comparable work.

The importance of these design considerations is nicely
illustrated by a comparison of two recent studies.
Gunnarsson and Soderberg (1983) carried out a study
involving employees at the Swedish Telecommunications
Administration who used VDTs in their work. The amount of
time spent working with the VDTs was set at either a
"normal" level or an "intensified" level on different days.
It was found that the higher work load was associated with
an increase in subjective reports of visual strain, and two
physiological measures of this, the near point of
accommodation and convergence, also increased. This
obviously shows that higher work loads increase eye strain
but it would be misleading to conclude that this is
necessarily in any way specific to work with CRT displays.
It is quite conceivable that comparable results would be
found with conventional clerical work.

This sort of conclusion gains support from a study
currently under way at the University of Wisconsin (Sauter
et al., 1983). This involved a comparison of 248 office
workers using VDTs with 85 non-users doing similar work. In
general this study did not find any evidence for higher
stress in the VDT users, and in fact on some indices users
actually fared better than non-users. There was some sign
of greater eyestrain amongst the VDT users, but this in turn
was related to measurements of the adequacy of lighting. So
VDTs may be more taxing to read than conventional printed
materials, but this may at least in part be due to poorly
designed lighting arrangements.

Legibility of CRT Displays

Given the very rapid increase in the use of VDTs in many
different types of work, it is clearly desirable to assess
the legibility of the types of displays most commonly used
with a view to trying to improve them. One sort of question
is whether reading material from a CRT screen is more
difficult than reading conventionally printed material.

Muter, Latremouille, Treurniet and Beam (1982) had subjects read continuous text for two hours, half reading from a CRT display and half from a book. The materials were a set of short stories. Although there were small increases in amounts of dizziness, fatigue and eyestrain reported after reading, there was no difference in this after having read from the CRT display as compared to the book. It was found, however, that although comprehension was equally good in both conditions, subjects read material from the CRT display considerably (28.5%) slower than from the book. This is a very large effect and as the authors point out there are a whole host of differences between their experimental conditions which may contribute to this effect.

One factor is the number of characters per line. Kolers, Duchnicky and Ferguson (1981) found that reading speed on a CRT was 17% slower with 40 larger characters than with 80 characters per line. In the Muter et al. study the CRT displays had 39 characters per line and the book approximately 60 characters per line. The number of words per page also differed considerably, about 400 on a page of the book compared to about 120 on the CRT display. This difference would be further aggravated by the fact that it took nine seconds to fill the CRT screen. Finally, there are more general sorts of differences. Subjects were more familiar with printed text, and they could adjust the angle and height of the book in a way they could not for the CRT display.

So it seems that in line with many people's intuitions, CRT displays may well be slower to read than conventional printed materials. It is far from clear, however, to what extent such differences may be reduced or eliminated by suitable modifications to the displays used. In view of these findings it would seem important to investigate the legibility of conventional CRT displays in the laboratory. This would enable optimal displays to be developed and implemented. A little work of this sort has recently been started.

One factor which is peculiar to CRT displays is the relative merit of positive or negative contrast. Conventional CRT displays consist of bright characters on a dark screen (positive contrast). Theoretically, this might be expected to produce poorer legibility than negative contrast where there is higher overall luminance, because the background is bright and the characters dark. In general higher levels of luminance produce higher adaptation levels which lead to better visual acuity and contrast sensitivity which should improve legibility (see Chapter 1, section 1.2). One problem here is that higher luminance

also makes the visual system more sensitive to flicker
which, with conventional 50 Hz refresh rates, may become
highly noticeable and irritating.

Two studies have reported better performance with
negative contrast displays. Radl (1980) reports higher
rates of transcribing letters from a VDT for 5 minutes with
negative contrast. His subjects also showed a significant
preference for the negative contrast displays. Bauer and
Cavonius (1980) found lower error rates for negative
contrast than positive contast displays in a task where
subjects had to read briefly presented nonsense words and
type them into a terminal, or detect discrepancies between
what was presented and what was printed on a sheet. Once
again users preferred the negative contrast displays. It
would clearly be useful to establish the generality of these
findings over different tasks and longer periods of use, but
the evidence points clearly to a superiority of negative
contrast displays.

More conventional typographical considerations such as
character form, size and spacing are all likely to influence
the legibility of CRT displays as they do printed material.
It is to be hoped that these are soon the subject of
systematic studies.

2.5 SUMMARY

In recent years cognitive psychologists have devoted a
considerable amount of effort to studying the information
processing skills involved in reading. The first part of
the chapter presented a very condensed and no doubt to some
extent partial overview of this research. A major applied
issue in studies of reading is to establish the way in which
typographical factors may improve or hamper reading
efficiency; this is the concern of studies of legibility
which were reviewed briefly in the second part of the
chapter. Reading material presented on computer controlled
VDTs has its own special problems associated with it. It
was argued in the last section that a knowledge of studies
of reading and legibility will have an important bearing on
attempts to solve these problems.

2.6 FURTHER READING

To find out more about the cognitive psychology of reading
you may look at either of two recent books reviewing this
area by Crowder (1982) and by Mitchell (1982).

The best source for more detail on studies of legibility is Tinker's (1965) book. A short book by Gilliland (1972), which is designed for teachers, gives a useful brief summary of some work on legibility.

Work dealing with applied issues in reading from VDTs still tends to be only available in the form of research papers. The volumes by Grandjean and Vigliani (1980) and by Kolers, Wrolstead and Bouma (1980) contain some papers in this area.

CHAPTER 3

Human Memory: Different Stores
with Different Characteristics

Neil Thomson

3.1 INTRODUCTION

Human memory is not a unitary system. Consider the task of
remembering a telephone number you have just looked up in
the directory. You can remember the number if you are not
distracted between looking it up and dialing and if it is
not too long. If however you have to concentrate on
something else while you are trying to remember it you will
forget it. Similarly the task of simultaneously remembering
two telephone numbers that you have never seen before is an
extremely difficult one. Compare that kind of short term
memory with your memory for facts and figures or your
knowledge about the organisation you work in. This long term
memory does not depend on active maintenance neither does it
seem to be limited by the amount you have to remember.
  Human memory is currently believed to be a complex system
of independent storage systems with a central large capacity
store called long-term memory (LTM). Short term memory is
believed to depend on a number of other stores which can
broadly be categorised as input and output buffers. In the
sections that follow the characteristics of these stores
will be briefly described starting with those thought to be
responsible for short term memory.

FUNDAMENTALS OF
HUMAN–COMPUTER INTERACTION

3.2 SHORT TERM MEMORY STORES

Input Buffers

Each type of sensory input, vision, hearing, touch and so on
would appear to have an input buffer associated with it.
Because vision and hearing are our most important senses,
the stores associated with them have been most intensively
studied and are called "iconic" and "echoic" memory
respectively. The general properties and functions of
sensory memories will be discussed with reference to echoic
memory.

Because auditory information is serial by nature, it is
necessary to store information as it arrives until
sufficient is available for processing - no one millisecond
of sound would contain sufficient information to process.
Thus there is a logical necessity for an input buffer. This
is similar to the input buffers used in most computer
operating systems where input characters are stacked up
until there are sufficient to pass to a parser. However, in
the case of the computer, the parser is usually a very
simple routine which processes the characters serially, and
could therefore dispense with the input buffer altogether.
It is retained because it is usually more efficient to parse
a string in a single operation rather than to keep jumping
in and out of the routine. This state of affairs arises
because the speed at which the characters arrive is much
slower than the rate at which the machine can deal with
them.

In the human the situation is far more complex. The
first source of difficulty arises in the lack of delimiting
characters. There is nothing equivalent to "carriage
return", "space" or "/" in the information people have to
deal with. Indeed the segmentation into separate characters
or items which is an essential requirement of a digital
machine is lacking. Although it may sound as though we
leave silent intervals between words when we speak, the
impression is illusory. There are often longer silent
intervals within words than between them and, frequently,
there is no gap at all between words (see Chapter 12 section
12.2). As if this does not impose enough difficulties,
people often have to deal with very poor quality
information, in fact people surpass all machines in
interpreting degraded information - consider the problems of
reading hand-writing for example.

Given the task the human processing system has to perform
on a sensory input, it is not surprising that what we know

of the processes suggests that the parser is far more complex than any found in machines. It would appear not to work in a simple serial manner as this system is not suitable for degraded information or for information lacking segmentation. In any serial process, an error at any stage will cause the rest of the message to be misinterpreted or rejected completely. A more viable system is to extract information in parallel and use information at one point to help disambiguate information extracted at another point. This of course necessitates that the information be stored while this process is performed and this is the function of the sensory store. Unlike computer stores its capacity cannot be measured in units of structure as the material lacks any segmentation and it is more likely that its capacity is limited in units of time.

By definition sensory memory contains information that has not been processed to any degree. It seems to be extremely volatile and may therefore be easily over written, a phenomenon known as backward masking. Thus an auditory stimulus such as the brief sounding of a tone, or a visual stimulus such as very briefly presented letter, will be much harder to identify if it is followed by another similar stimulus rather than no stimulation, i.e. silence or darkness.

Output Buffers

When trying to remember a telephone number or any random string of verbal information, people typically repeat the items over to themselves, a process known as rehearsal. It is believed that what they are doing is recirculating the information through the speech output buffer which can hold about 2 seconds worth of speech. It would not be feasible for them to use sensory memory as any other incoming information would overwrite the items. Using an output store removes this problem so long as they do not try to speak while attempting to retain the string.

The case for output buffers is similar to that for input buffers. It is almost certainly the case that speech is produced in parallel, i.e. a string of motor commands are produced together. Only if this were true could such errors of speech as spoonerisms occur. For "Dear old queen" to be said as "Queer old dean" implies that the "QU" of queen and the "D" of dean were simultaneously present. However, as speech is a serial process, these commands must be stored while they are being executed and this is the role of the output buffer. As with output buffers in computer software,

they allow the fairly rapid process of generating an output
string to proceed unrestrained by the slower speed of the
device which executes the commands.

Although it might be expected that, unlike the input
buffer, output stores would hold segmented information, this
does not appear to be the case. There is evidence that the
capacity of the speech output store is constant in units of
time rather than units of structure (see Baddeley, Thompson
and Buchanon 1975). So, for example, fast speakers can
retain longer strings of random digits than slow speakers
because they can pack more items into 2 seconds.

The evidence for output stores for behaviour other than
speech is rather scarce although some interesting work is
now being done looking at people's ability to remember
sequences of finger movements and it is beginning to look as
if there are output buffer stores for such responses.

3.3 LONG TERM MEMORY

Of all the memory stores, LTM is the least well understood
and no doubt the most complex. While the input and output
buffers bear some resemblance to artificial memories, LTM is
unlike any physical system so far devised.

The most striking characteristic of the store is its
immense capacity. No limit to the capacity of LTM has yet
been found and for all practical purposes it may be
considered infinite. A number of suggestions have been made
concerning the nature of the storage media. Current ideas
include chemical coding in large molecules such as R.N.A.
and neural coding by altering the properties of synapses,
that is, the junctions between neurones in the brain.

At present these are only hypotheses. We don't know where
the information is stored, but we do have considerable
evidence concerning what is stored. The primary code used by
LTM is semantic; i.e., items are stored in terms of their
meaning. While other codes are possible, such as imagery,
motor programs, etc., these are quite probably secondary or
derived from the underlying semantic code.

The semantic code

It is the use of a semantic code that gives LTM many of its
unique properties and, at the same time, makes it so
difficult to study as we have no metric for meaning. Unlike
all physical codes, a semantic code is, by definition,
subjective. Thus, for any particular input, the information

stored will be a function of the nature of the stimulus and
of the interpretation imposed by the person. This arises
because things mean different things to different people. It
raises the awkward question of how the system ever gets
started, for if you know nothing, then nothing will mean
anything and cannot therefore be semantically coded. To use
the jargon of computing, the infant has to "bootstrap"
himself and this problem has led to hundreds of years of
philosophical and psychological argument concerning exactly
what is "known" at birth (or the nature of the bootstrap).
We shall not prolong the argument here!

An important consequence of using a semantic code is that
the information is often quite radically altered during
storage in order for the person to "make sense of it" and so
fit it in with his existing knowledge. Note for example how
information is corrupted when passed from person to person
as in the spreading of gossip or rumour. Each person
imposes his own meaning on the message in order to retain it
and, by so doing, often corrupts it extensively. People used
to thinking about computer storage systems, where the memory
must at all costs preserve the integrity of the information,
might begin to wonder why such a "sloppy" system should have
evolved. Metaphysical questions apart, the use of a
semantic code has considerable advantages over the storage
of more literally coded information.

First, a semantic code is a very high level code. It
bears a similar relationship to low level codes as PASCAL
does to Assembler. Any statement in a high level code does
not necessarily have a unique counterpart in a low level
code. In other words, the mapping of a high level to low
level code is usually one to many and, consequently, if the
high level statement was derived from a set of low level
statements, it is not possible to determine which particular
low level statements were provided. Thus, while we are very
good at remembering the "gist" or meaning of information we
are extremely poor at remembering the material "verbatim".

There are two main advantages of high level codes which
are also present in programming languages. First, a high
level code is nearly always more concise. It employs a
higher level of abstraction than low level codes and,
therefore, requires far fewer statements to express a
particular idea or meaning. Secondly, the higher level of
abstraction employed allows different types of
relationships to become apparent. In other words, the
"vocabulary" of a high level language, in being more
abstract, enables one to produce statements of greater
generality than would be possible in a lower level language.
If we take "meaning" as our high level language, then all

forms of communication can be seen as lower level languages
employed to express that meaning. Thus verbal language,
art, music and gesture are all different types of low level
language used to express a particular idea or meaning. The
lack of any simple correspondence rules between high and low
level languages causes the process of expressing our meaning
to be difficult and frequently "our words beggar our
thoughts".

Representing Meaning

The main problem for anyone attempting to understand LTM has
been the problem of representing meaning. There is no
obvious way of characterising meaning and a great deal of
research is now devoted to trying to devise systems which
can simulate the workings of LTM. Communication between
people involves the exchange of meaning. It is quite
possible to understand all the words someone says without
knowing what he or she is talking about and we only claim to
have communicated when the listener understands our meaning.
However, any one idea can be expressed in a multitude of
ways and attempts to produce systems that understand natural
language before a proper characterisation of meaning has
been devised are, I suspect, doomed to failure.
    It is not difficult to demonstrate that meaning is the
code employed by LTM. If people are asked to remember
passages, lists of words or lists of sentences, they
typically perform very badly if judged on the number of
words they correctly recall. However, if judged in terms
of recall of meaning, they perform extremely well but,
unfortunately, we can only judge how well someone has
recalled the meaning of a passage subjectively. That is, we
have to read the passage ourselves and then read their
recall of it and judge the similarity in meaning between the
two passages.

Retrieval from LTM

The speed at which material can be retrieved from LTM is
impressive. Well-used material can be retrieved extremely
fast for a store with such a large capacity and this must
reflect the fact that the material is highly organized
within LTM. The fact that registration of material is
relatively slow probably also reflects the high degree of
organization employed. Nothing is simply "dumped" into LTM;
its meaning has to be deciphered and the material then has

to be fitted in with our existing knowledge. This involves
processes of reasoning as well as storage processes. The
act of understanding is intimately related to the act of
reasoning and all current models of LTM employ a reasoning
system as part of the total model. This use of reasoning
and the necessity to fit new knowledge into existing
knowledge gives LTM much greater flexibility than a simple
storage device. It enables us to "remember" facts without
having to store them at all. This rather strange statement
might become clearer if you consider this example. Try to
"remember" in which direction (North, South, East or West)
the bathroom window faced in the house you lived in three
houses before your present one (or less if you haven't moved
much). Most people can do this quite successfully although
it takes a fair amount of time. What is very apparent with
this example is that most people have not stored the "fact"
that the bathroom faced East (say). Rather, they are able
to construct this fact from their knowledge of the house,
where the sun set and so on. While it is obvious that
recall involves reasoning in this example, it is quite
likely that most recall is of this type although the
reasoning processes are not so tortuous and are therefore
done very rapidly and perhaps without our being aware of
them. Where possible we do not remember "facts" but rather
remember rules which allow us to reconstruct facts. It
would be rather idiotic to try and estimate the capacity of
LTM by asking people to remember the sequence
2,4,6,8,10,12,14,16 etc. as they would only store the start
and end numbers and the rule underlying the series.

3.4 SUMMARY AND CONCLUSIONS

Human memory can be characterised as a collection of stores
with different characteristics. LTM employs a semantic code
and stores material in a highly organised manner. Retrieval
from LTM is often a process of reconstruction rather than
the output of information held in LTM. This contrasts
strongly with most machine memories which are usually simple
depositories of information where one only gets out what one
puts in. With human memory, on the other hand, one gets out
what the memory system itself puts in.

Memory is a major limitation on human performance and the
designer should always think about the load his system
imposes on the user. To lessen this load it is necessary to
allow for the characteristics of the various stores
involved. Thus, long term memory will only effectively
encode material which is meaningful to the user, and the

designer must ensure that the model the user constructs of
the system is compatible with his own (see Chapter 9). If
relatively   meaningless   material   must   be   remembered
temporarily then a knowledge of the characteristics of our
short term memory is relevant.

3.5 FURTHER READING

This   chapter   has   necessarily   avoided   describing   the
experimental evidence upon which this view of human memory
is based. Baddeley (1983) presents a very readable account
of this work in a much more detailed treatment of the
subject. Standard works on memory which are also to be
recommended are to be found in Norman (1976) and Anderson
(1980). The latter text includes an accessible example of an
attempt to derive a representation for meaning.

    Norman also has a short book (Norman, 1982) which covers
the same ground as this chapter and links the theories he
discusses with an example of user interface design.

CHAPTER 4

Thinking and Reasoning:
Why is Logic So Difficult?

Neil Thomson

4.1 INTRODUCTION

The first two chapters in this section of the book
considered mechanisms for input to the human information
processing system. The chapter preceding this one discussed
human memory. This chapter will consider how the information
is manipulated, specifically the process of inductive and
deductive reasoning.

Of all the human faculties, our ability to reason is the
one which appears to set us apart from the animals. There
is no evidence that any animal, even the higher apes, can
reason. The ability to reason would seem to be intimately
related to our ability to use language and many would
maintain that, in spite of the recent spate of chimps using
sign language, no animal has yet been shown to use language
in a manner similar to people. The study of thought falls
conveniently into two main sections: inductive and deductive
reasoning, and these will be considered under separate
headings.

57

4.2 DEDUCTIVE REASONING

Validity as opposed to truth

Deductive reasoning is the process of arriving at a logically necessary conclusion from initial premises. For example, the conclusion "Elephants are bigger than mice" can be deduced from the two premises "Elephants are bigger than dogs" and "Dogs are bigger than mice". An important point to note is that deduction is concerned with the "validity" of an argument and not with its "truth". Truth, in this context, means congruence with the state of affairs in the world while validity concerns the internal structure of an argument. For example the statement "Mice are bigger then elephants" is completely valid when concluded from the premises "Mice are bigger than dogs" and "Dogs are bigger than elephants". The fact that the premises and conclusion are false (not true) is irrelevant to an evaluation of the validity of the argument. It is worth noting that this independence of truth and validity allows true statements to be derived from invalid arguments and false statements to be derived from valid arguments. For examples listen to any politician speaking!

It is easy to show that people are extremely bad at logical reasoning. Consider the two statements: "Some dogs are greyhounds", "Some greyhounds run fast". Most people consider it legitimate to infer from these premises that "Some dogs run fast". However, this is an invalid conclusion as you were not told that all greyhounds are dogs and it is possible that the greyhounds that run fast were those that are not dogs. If you claim that this is ridiculous because you "know" that all greyhounds are dogs, then you demonstrate well people's inablity to deal with validity independently of truth.

However, any theory which claims that people are stupid is probably itself stupid. People must be able to reason logically or how else would we ever understand each other. The important point demonstrated by some recent research is that people are primarily concerned with truth rather than validity, and consequently, import their existing knowledge into any situation. Consider how stilted communication would become if we had to make explicit every premise. The exchange "Why are you taking an umbrella" - "because of the weather forecast" would become: "The weather forecast predicted rain"; "rain is wet"; "I do not like to be wet"; "Umbrellas prevent one becoming wet in the rain". The resemblance to a computer program is not accidental!

Computers (or more properly compilers) import little if any knowledge to the program and necessitate an extremely verbose explicit form of communication which we would find totally unacceptable in human discourse.

Applying Logic

The study of logic or deductive reasoning is a discipline in its own right and resembles mathematics rather than any natural science (natural sciences being concerned with truth). The operations that most systems of logic use are very simple and Bertrand Russell demonstrated that all could be reduced to the two operations "AND" and "NOT". As most machines can readily perform these operations could we not expect them to be able to perform logic? The answer is a categorical No and the reason is not an inability to perform the operations but, rather, an inability to know which operation to perform. With computers, the programmer performs just this task for the machine. He tells the machine what operations to perform and in what order and it is this ability that machines and animals appear to lack. An example might make this point clearer. If I state that the distance to a vertical pole is 20 feet and that the top of the pole makes an angle of 30 degrees with my position, then it is a trivial calculation to work out the height of the pole. Now most machines can perform the calculation "x= 20(tan 30) " but could not solve the problem because the machine would not know that this was the relevant calculation. What is lacking is the ability to know what operations to perform to get from a starting point (premises) to a desired goal (conclusion). Early attempts to enable machines to do this used "exhaustive" methods where every possible operation was performed on the premise until the desired goal was obtained. It can be easily shown that where there is more than one premise and/or more than one step in the calculation, the number of operations the machine has to perform rapidly becomes ridulously large (known as the exponential explosion).

A better approach has been to examine the ways people solve such tasks and try to incorporate these methods within the machine. The methods are generically termed "heuristic devices". It is important to note that in themselves they are not logical operations but rather are strategies which enable one to determine which logical operations should be performed. A frequently used method and one which is nearly always employed first is that of finding a similar example. People search their memories for problems which are similar

to the one posed and which they have an algorithm for
solving. This may sound a straightforward process but it
involves a faculty which is lacking in most machines, that
of pattern recognition. People are able to see similarities
between different problems which it would be very difficult
to enable a machine to perceive without first giving it our
very sophisticated pattern perception system. A second
method commonly used is to work backwards from the goal.
People often start with the conclusion and derive statements
which necessarily imply that conclusion and then attempt to
map the initial premises onto these derived ones. The whole
process is extremely complex and although some progress has
been made we are a long way from understanding how humans
know what operations should be performed.

4.3 INDUCTIVE REASONING

The term inductive reasoning is almost a self contradiction
as the process of induction is not a logical process.
Induction refers to the production of a general statement
from specific instances. For example the conclusion "All
crows are black" from observing 1,20 or 100000 black crows
is a generalization. It is not a logially necessary
conclusion, indeed it can never be shown to be unequivocally
true. It is not possible to observe all the crows that have
existed, all those that do exist and all those that will
exist and, therefore, one can never know if the statement is
true. However, it would only take the existence of one
white crow to falsify the statement and this leads to the
state of affairs whereby all generalizations can never be
proved to be true but can be proved to be false. This
rather strange situation is expressed in the cliche "The
exception proves the rule" although unfortunately the
meaning of the word "prove" has changed since the statement
was first used and most people now take exactly the opposite
meaning from it. The word "prove" meant "test" in old
English and so the statement should read "The exception
tests the rule" which is exactly in line with the above
statements on induction.

The Exception Tests the Rule

The fact that a general statement can only be falsified
underlies the whole of scientific methodology. Scientists
construct theories and then perform experiments which, if
properly formulated, allow the theory to be falsified. They

do not attempt to prove the theory correct as this is not possible with an inductive statement, and all scientific theories are inductive statements. Thus, ideally, scientists should construct a theory by induction and then attempt to falsify it. If they succeed, they should abandon the theory and try another. However, scientists and non-scientists do not appear to work in this way. To use this approach requires that we be able to use "negative evidence" properly and realise that it is far more important than "positive evidence" to the status of the theory. One white crow is far more important than one black crow given the theory that all crows are black. However, there is substantial evidence that people are unable to use negative evidence and, in fact, will often totally ignore it.

Take for example an experiment by Wason (1966). He showed people four cards. Each card had a letter on one side and a number on the other but because the cards were flat on a table only one side was visible. Each letter could be a vowel or a consonant. Each number could be even or odd. The four cards have "E", "K", "4" and "7", respectively, printed on the side presently visible. Wason went on to explain that he has a hypothetical rule which needs to be tested. The rule is "If a card has a vowel on one side then it has an even number on the other side". Which of the four cards would you turn over to test this hypothetical rule?

If you decided to turn over the cards bearing "E" and/or "4" only, then you have given the same incorrect response as many of the people Wason tested. The mistake was to look only for information confirming the rule. For inductive reasoning only negative evidence is really crucial so one should be looking for counter examples to the rule. Only cards with a vowel on one side and an odd number on the other actually violate the rule so the cards to turn over are the ones with an "E" and a "7" on. Wason found that while people commonly chose the former they much more rarely chose the latter equally crucial one.

One idea that has been advanced to explain this rather odd behaviour is that people will not abandon a theory, no matter how inadequate it may be, until they have an alternative. Note how if you have started thinking about a problem in one way, how difficult it is to see it from a completely new angle. The theory, even if you know it's wrong, blinds you to alternatives because the theory itself will determine in part how you see the evidence (see Wason, 1960 for another demonstration of this kind of behaviour). In other words, people find it difficult to be objective because the processes they use to interpret the world are primarily concerned with meaning which, by definition, is subjective.

This tendency of people to prefer to have a bad theory rather than no theory at all must be understood if one is going to write computer programs to aid human decision making.   An example should make this clearer.   One attempt to help doctors diagnose medical problems used what appears to be a very sensible design.   The doctor recorded all the patient's symptoms and fed them into the program.   The machine then listed all possible ailments that could result from such symptoms.   The problem with such an approach is that, in wishing to be diligent, the programmer had included all possible ailments in his program so that old Mrs Jones could well be diagnosed as having "African doodle bug disease" even though she had never been further than the local shops in the last 50 years.   The programmer might well retort that his program only appeared stupid because it wasn't told that information.   However, if the doctor were to enter all the information he knew about the person, he would be there most of the day and might well feel reluctant to put the fact that Fred Jones is a skiving malingerer on record.   In order to devise a better system it is instructive to see what a doctor does when a patient complains to him.

First, and often before the patient has opened his mouth, the doctor generates a theory about what the patient is suffering from.   He does this using a wide variety of knowledge that he has about the patient's previous medical problems, his life style, "bugs" that are presently doing the rounds, etc.   He then examines the patient using his theory to tell him what to look for so that he does not, by any means, record every possible measurement, but is highly selective.   The advantage of this procedure is speed.   It enables the doctor to come to a conclusion very much more rapidly than if he recorded everything and then deduced what illness the patient had.   The weakness of the system is that the doctor, blinded by his theory, may fail to notice an important symptom which would cause him to change his mind or that, if in a hurry, he may not bother to examine the patient at all but simply send him off with some pills.   Any program that does not recognise that doctors proceed in this way is not likely to be much used. A better approach for our programmer might have been for the doctor to enter his theory into the machine and then be presented with a list of symptoms which the patient ought to have if the doctor's theory were correct.   It might also list illnesses which produce the same or similar symptoms so as to provide the doctor with some alternative theories if his original idea is rejected. The problem of how to build machines with reasoning processes as flexible as human reasoning will be raised again in Chapter 14.

4.4 SUMMARY

In conclusion it should be mentioned that most thought involves both processes of deduction and induction and that the two are often very difficult to separate.   The main points I should like to leave with you are that people are rarely, if ever, illogical but rather, are concerned with truth rather than validity.   Secondly, that people need theories to enable them to interpret the world and will not, as reason demands, abandon a theory because of negative evidence; they need an alternative.

4.5 FURTHER READING

Readers wishing to find out more about the experimental work on thinking are referred to Gilhooly's excellent book (Gilhooly, 1982). This reviews research on problem solving, deductive and inductive reasoning and creative thinking. Two books, one by Mayer (1977) and another by Evans (1982), can also be recommended. An interesting and novel approach to thinking is to relate behaviour to hypothetical mental models. Readers wishing to find out more about this approach should look at Johnson-Laird (1983).

For references to the various attempts to enable machines to solve problems you are referred to section 14.7 in Chapter 14.

PART TWO

THE USE OF BEHAVIOURAL DATA

One possible reason that user interface design has until recently been neglected is the misplaced confidence we tend to have in our ability to examine and evaluate accurately our own behaviour and thought processes. Experimental psychology has demonstrated how inaccurate our introspections about our own behaviour are. Our ability to intuit the behaviour of other people who have different backgrounds, and who may be working in a quite different context, is even more limited.

Experimental Psychology learned very early on in its history not to trust personal hunches and all sound human-factors work is based on empirical data. Learning this system designers might expect the HCI specialists to give them rules, based on empirical data, rather in the way they will be given safety regulations or rules for the ergonomic design of furniture. It is clear, however, that in most cases the HCI specialists cannot do this. They can set out guidelines and examples of the kinds of difficulties faced by the user, but these guidelines do not have the status of rules because the studies which generate them have only limited generality. This point is made with some force in Chapter 9, in Part Three, where the authors found that conclusions drawn in one context, for example 'A fixed argument order enhances performance', are found to be misleading or not to apply in other relatively similar contexts. Thus, while the literature will suggest possible pitfalls and ways of avoiding them, it will often be the case that there are no available studies which can be generalised with confidence to the designer's own specific problem. The conclusion we draw from this is that the designer must be in a position to read and evaluate other people's work and, where necessary, collect his own data.

This second section, then, demonstrates how to collect and evaluate behavioural data as a part of the design process. Taken with the first, it also serves to make the specialist literature more accessible, allowing the designer to read and evaluate papers on specific HCI problems more effectively. There are three chapters in Part Three. Chapter 5 discusses when and how to collect behavioural data, Chapter 6 how to evaluate it. Chapter 7 is by way of a case study in experimental methodology. It is presented as a report on two experiments comparing a range of speech synthesisers.

CHAPTER 5

How and When to Collect
Behavioural Data

Andrew Monk

5.1 THE VALUE OF BEHAVIOURAL DATA

Imagine that you have been asked to lead a team of software
engineers who are going to automate the system for collating
information 'monitored' from private telephone conversations
at a secret defence establishment. You have been provided
with a sketch of the function of the system and you have
some idea of the hardware available. From your initial
deliberations a number of questions arise. One might be
whether to use colour. It is necessary to display complex
graphs representing communication pathways. You could
indicate the nature of a pathway by using different coloured
lines, or alternatively and much more cheaply, by using
different kinds of broken line on a monochrome display. You
remember reading somewhere that colour is an effective way
of identifying the elements of a graph. A search of the
literature reveals that many of the recommendations are
based on little more than anecdote. There are
recommendations based on well-documented experience and
properly controlled experiments but none quite fit the
circumstances of your application. The literature reveals
that colour can often lead to considerably improved user
performance, but that this is not necessarily the case.
  Another question might concern more cognitive
considerations. The initial specification you are working
from gives the critical attributes which are to be used to
classify the conversations. It does not specify how the

attributes are related. Would a hierarchical scheme work and if so how would it be ordered?

The best way to answer the questions whether to use colour and how to organise the classification of conversations is to collect some behavioural data. The first question can be answered in a controlled experiment comparing two otherwise similar set ups. The second can be answered by careful questioning and observation of users of the present paper-based system your system is to replace.

The above scenario illustrates the problems faced by the designer. It is rarely the case that the human factors literature will precisely answer the questions asked of it. It should help to define the problems a user will have and it may suggest some ways that these problems may be minimised but the most appropriate solution will rarely be obvious and the designer will need additional information. Behavioural data should be the major source of additional information used in making a design decision.

5.2 WHEN TO COLLECT BEHAVIOURAL DATA

The scenario developed in the last section will be extended to illustrate the different points in the design process where behavioural data may be usefully collected, starting at the beginning when the old system to be replaced is being studied.

System Analysis

Part of the design team is sent to the defense establishment to find out how the existing paper-based system works. The manager of the department concerned in fact designed the present system. You interview him at length but suspect that what he is telling you is what he expects the users to be doing rather than what they are actually doing. You go on to interview the rest of the department and study the behaviour of two operators in some detail. You find that while the manager views the classification of conversations as essentially hierarchically structured the operators have difficulty using his scheme and have adopted all sorts of tricks to get round the limitations it imposes. Further discussions with operators and the manager together result in a potentially better scheme. At the same time you have identified those parts of the operators' task which are seen to be boring or too demanding so that the new system can avoid these problems if possible.

Specification

The system specification incorporates 'usability specifications' of the kind advocated by Carroll and Rosson (In Press). An example might be

"A skilled operator will be able to enter the classification for a conversation in less than 10 seconds for 50% of conversations classified and less than 20 seconds for 90% of conversations classified."

The figures in the above specification are based on observation of the present system. Notice that the specification includes details of the user population and the margin for error (50% of conversations).

Some of the more important design decisions are made with the aid of small experiments. For example, communication pathway graphs are displayed in monochrome or colour. Tests are performed to see which kind of display results in the best user performance. The tests utilise artificial experimental tasks which are designed to capture the essence of the tasks the operators will perform with these displays in the real system. These experiments show that the colour display results in 30% less errors as well as slightly faster responses than the monochrome one so you decide the additional expense is justified.

Implementation

Having fully specified the system it is emulated at your Human Factors Evaluation Centre and several users with the appropriate background and experience are taught to use it. The centre videotapes the users working with the system and the emulation is instrumented so that a time stamped record of every user-computer transaction is available. In addition the users are interviewed at length. On the basis of this data the Human Factors Evaluation Centre suggests a number of weak points in the design and you make changes to sort them out. Further testing reveals that your changes were effective.

Human Factors Evaluation

Your client has calculated that, in terms of the manpower required and the results obtained, a 10% improvement in

efficiency will pay for the development of the system in
four months. It is thus worth their while to pay for the
development of two systems and then to choose between them
on the basis of efficiency. The client sets up a controlled
experiment in his own human factors laboratory. Of course
your system which was designed with careful attention to the
needs of the user is shown to be 40% more efficient than the
system it replaces and 20% more efficient than the
opposition's system. Your company wins the contract and you
are promoted to the board of directors!

Current design practice may be somewhat distant from the
scenario sketched above, however, as time goes by, more
companies are moving in the direction indicated. The
remainder of this chapter explains how to collect
behavioural data, how to select the users from whom you
collect it and how to design effective experiments. As well
as permiting you to collect your own data this chapter will
make it possible for you to evaluate the data of others and
the conclusions they draw.

5.3 BEHAVIOURAL MEASURES

It is a relatively simple matter to build monitoring
functions into one's prototyping set up. An instrumented
prototype can record errors made (how many, where they were
made) and times (time to complete the task, time to recover
from an error, and so on). The most important measures of
overall efficiency are time to complete the task and some
quantification of correctness.

From this point of view errors detected by the system and
which the user recovers from are important only in so far as
they contribute to the total time taken to complete the
task. This assumes that there is no large systems cost
associated with some errors. Errors which go undetected by
the user are more serious as they indicate the task has not
been completed correctly and must somehow be incorporated
into one's measure of overall efficiency.

Instrumentation of the kind described above provides
objective measures of user performance. More subjective
measures may also be useful. In particular you will need to
observe users at work and debrief them at the end of an
experimental session.

Observation may be very informal and simply involve
sitting in on one or two sessions. At a more formal level
you may decide to videorecord the users as they perform the
task. Another technique is to have the user verbalise his
thoughts as he performs the task. This commentary on the

user's own actions is recorded and transcribed and can then be subjected to what is known as 'protocol analysis'(see Mack, Lewis and Carroll 1983 for a representative study using this technique). Both video recording and protocol analysis are very tedious to score and expensive to do and can probably only to be used to a limited extent. There is also the problem that both these techniques may themselves affect the behaviour of the user. Having the user keep a diary of his experiences with a system is a possible alternative to protocol analysis for long term studies (see Naur 1983 for an example of such a study).

TABLE 5.1 Examples of items from two types of attitude scale.

A. Tick the statements you agree with.

'This system is a real pleasure to use.'
'This system is very tiring to use.'
'Some of the commands are rather obscure.'
'I had no difficulty learning to use the system.'
'This system is an improvement on previous systems I have used.'
'The system does not have a good 'feel' to it.'

B. Give each statement a rating between 1 and 5.
        5 = I strongly agree.
        4 = I agree with reservations.
        3 = I do not agree or disagree.
        2 = I disagree to some extent.
        1 = I strongly disagree.

'I had considerable difficulty learning to use the system.'
'The commands are all straight forward to use.'
'Using the system requires a lot of concentration.'
'The replies given by the system are very 'business like'.'
'The system takes a long time to answer.'
'The system messages are easy to understand.'

Useful insights into the strengths and weaknesses of a system can often be obtained by the careful debriefing of users after they have performed the experiment. Informal questioning may be appropriate as long as care is taken to avoid leading the user into giving you the answers that you want. Being this objective is not as easy as it might seem and if you have some specific questions to ask you might consider constructing some sort of questionnaire. This

could take the form of written questions with open answers
or it might be some sort of attitude scale. The latter is
useful for assessing the user's feelings towards the system.

Table 5.1 gives some examples of items from attitude
scales. Normally one would have more than six items in each
scale, there should be an equal number of statements
expressing positive and negative attitudes to the system and
the items should cover a range of attitudes. Clearly if all
the 'Yes' responses in the questionnaire count towards one
outcome and all the 'No' responses to the other, the final
result could reflect more the user's bias to say 'Yes' than
the question one was originally concerned with. A. is scored
by counting the number of positive items ticked and
subtracting the number of negative items ticked. B. is
scored similarly by adding up the ratings for positive items
and subtracting the ratings for negative items. As well as
computing an overall 'favourability' it may be revealing to
examine the scores for individual items. Repertory grids
may also be used to explore users' attitudes to a system
(see Shaw, 1980).

5.4 SELECTING SUBJECTS

Behavioural scientists refer to the people who take part in
their experiments as subjects. Choosing the users who are
going to be subjects in your experiment is one of the most
important parts of the design of that experiment.

Let us say that in the course of designing some word
processing software we have to decide between two methods of
cursor control, say a touch screen as opposed to special
function keys. A poor way of doing this would be to set up
an instrumented prototype and run several members of the
design team through a series of standard word processing
tasks. The results of such an experiment are very unlikely
to generalize to the secretaries who will be the users of
the final product. First of all the designers will have had
more experience of computer systems in general than the
computer naive secretary. This will lead to quite different
expectancies and thus to quite different patterns of
behaviour. Of course, if the design team has been involved
with this particular project their expectations will be even
more atypical. Secondly, the design team will know less
about the task (formatting documents) than a secretary and
may use a rather different vocabulary to describe it. More
importantly, this will make the way they conceptualise the
task quite different. Thirdly, and not least, the
secretaries will be skilled typists and the way they use the

keyboard may be quite different. For example, using special function keys may allow them to maintain their 'home keys' position so that this method may result in less disruption of typing behaviour.   This would not be the case with less skilled typists.

In general, the principles of sampling subjects for an experiment are the same as those applied in sampling consumers in marketing exercises.   For important experiments, where generalization to a target population is important, for example the comparison of your product with others, you may wish to employ marketing organizations to do the sampling for you. For experiments where generalization is less important it is often sufficient to choose subjects who roughly match the target population in terms of experience under the three categories which arose in the example above: experience with the task, general experience with computer systems and (if you are using keyboard input) typing ability.

While we are considering the topic of user expertise we should consider the problem of practice. The knowledge a user has of a task depends both on prior experience and how practised he or she is at using this particular system. In general, when evaluating a system, one will be interested both in ease of use and ease of learning. Ease of learning is measured in terms of the time required to achieve some asymptotic level of performance. Ease of use is measured in terms of how high that asymptote is. A system which is easy to use may not be the easiest to learn, though experience suggests this is often the case.

5.5 DESIGNING EXPERIMENTS

Some of the behavioural data collected in human factors work is purely observational in the sense that one is simply looking for evidence of problems with the user interface. To collect such data it is necessary carefully to consider the subjects tested and the measures taken as discussed in the previous two sections. When one is designing an experiment - our original example was to compare a coloured display with a monochrome version - there are additional considerations to be taken account of.

Experimental Control

Behavioural science like any other scientific discipline has developed its own methodology for doing experiments. The

aim of this methodology is to control all the different
'variables' which may affect the results of the experiment.
For our discussion of this subject we will take as an
example the experiment considered above which compares two
methods of cursor control.

A useful first step when designing an experiment is to
make a list of all the variables which might affect the
results of the experiment. Table 5.2 contains some headings
you might use in constructing such a list.

TABLE 5.2

Subject	Environment	Procedural
Experience with computers	Noise	Within/Between subjects design
Experience of the task	Other distractions	Training/Practice
Typing ability	Lighting, seating	Scoring
Intelligence/Flexibility		
Anxiety/Motivation		

We have already considered the category Subject Variables
under the heading of 'Selecting Subjects'. This whole
category of variables is 'controlled' by making the subjects
as representative of the target population as possible. The
sample should be representative in range as well as mean
value. Thus, for example, the range of intelligence to be
expected in the target population should be matched in the
range of intelligence of your subjects. Technically this
procedure is described as declaring subjects to be a
'random' variable.

Environmental variables are controlled by fixing them at
levels typical of the environments in which the final
product will be used. For example, the results obtained in
a quiet laboratory may be quite different to those obtained
in the more realistic situation of an open plan office.

Finally we come to the most difficult class of variables,
those that have to do with the way the experiment is
conducted i.e., the experimental procedure adopted. We have
discussed 'scoring' under the heading 'Behavioural
Measures'. We have also briefly discussed the problem of
training and practice in the last section. How the
experiment is structured is discussed in the next section.

TABLE 5.3 Examples of between- and within-subjects designs.
The scores given are solution times in seconds.

A. Between-Subjects

	Group I (System A)		Group II (System B)	
	Subject 1	735	Subject 2	425
	Subject 3	623	Subject 4	367
	Subject 5	791	Subject 6	276
	Subject 7	798	Subject 8	548
	Subject 9	562	Subject 10	418
	Subject 11	752	Subject 12	391

B. Within-Subjects

		System A	System B
Subject 1		651	452
Subject 2		438	321
Subject 3		859	657
Subject 4		672	653
Subject 5		712	752
Subject 6		546	444

Within- and Between-subjects Designs

Typically any experiment will have a 'dependent variable'
and an 'independent variable'.   The dependent variable is
the thing you measure, the independent variable is the thing
you manipulate.   For example, consider an experiment to
compare System A which uses long menus with System B which
uses a larger number of shorter menus.   The question is
whether the subjects can achieve a number of trial goals
faster using System A or System B. The dependent variable
here is time in seconds to complete the test.   The
independent variable is menu length or system type.   The
different levels of the independent variable, in this case
long and short or A and B, can be combined with the variable
subjects in two ways. Every subject can provide scores from
all the levels or conditions, or each level can be
represented by a different group of subjects who only
provide scores for that condition. The former design, where
one can make comparisons between conditions within each
subject's scores, is said to be a within-subjects design.

The latter, where this is not the case and one has groups of subjects, is said to be a between-subjects design. Examples of data from these two experimental designs are given in Table 5.3.

Each type of design has its advantages and disadvantages. Within-subjects designs can be more efficient than between-subjects designs because you get more information from each subject you test and each subject acts as his own control. It may be necessary to run a large number of subjects in a between-subjects design before a stable picture of what is happening emerges. However, even with a between-subjects design a large effect should be apparent after running seven or eight subjects. Between-subjects designs score over within-subjects designs in that they are much less liable to order effects and range effects. Consider the experiment on menu length as a within-subjects design. Clearly the two experimental systems will have elements in common and it is likely that there are practice effects so that whichever task is performed last will be performed better (although it is also possible to get order effects due to fatigue). In an attempt to control this, one might have half the subjects use System A then System B and half System B then System A. However, this will only be effective if the practice effects are symmetrical. If, for example, practice on System A is useful when you use System B but not the other way round then the result may be seriously biased. Some statisticians argue that this kind of range effect, where doing one task affects how you do another, is always a possibility and within-subjects designs should never be used. This is probably an extreme position but care should be taken when using within-subjects designs. The menu length experiment, for example, should be done as a between-subjects design.

When using a between-subjects design you must ensure that the groups selected are matched or are randomly selected. If, for example, subjects are allowed to select which group they perform in, or even if the whole of one group is tested before the other, there is the strong possibility of bias.

5.6 SUMMARY

'Know your user' is a commonly quoted slogan. The message of this chapter is that you will only achieve such knowledge by systematic study of the users' behaviour. This may take various forms including user performance measures, interviews, protocol analysis and so on. Behavioural data can be utilised as observations which indicate how the system is used and where its strengths and weaknesses lie. Alternatively in the context of a controlled experiment it can be used to answer specific questions.

Effective experimental design is a relatively straight forward matter as long as one is aware of the different variables and factors which may affect the outcome of the experiment. Whenever you are designing an experiment and whenever you read about someone else's experiment, you should always be trying to think of alternative ways of explaining the results. If you can think of the alternative explanation is generally possible to control it out. Variables can be controlled by fixing them at some representative level (e.g., distraction due to noise) or declaring them as random variables and then sampling from some representative population (e.g., subjects). If your experiment has an independent variable (e.g., menu length) then the appropriate design must be selected (within- or between-subjects). Finally dependent variables (what you measure) must be selected to capture the aspects of the task you are interested in. It is often a good idea to use several dependent variables to measure different aspects of performance (e.g., time taken, number of errors, rated ease of use).

5.7 FURTHER READING

For a useful treatment of experimental design including suggestions about how to format a report on an experiment see Robson (1973). Robson is writing for psychology students. An alternative which may be more closely tailored to the needs of designers and engineers is Shneiderman's book (1980). His chapters 1 to 3 are relevant to this chapter.

For further information about psychometric tests and attitude measurement see Anastasi (1982). Shaw (1980) explains how to use repertory grids.

CHAPTER 6

Statistical Evaluation of Behavioural Data

Andrew Monk

6.1 INTRODUCTION

Chapter 5 explained how to collect behavioural data. One
unfortunate characteristic of behavioural measures, in
comparison with physical measures, is that they are much
more subject to chance influences. Within a group of
subjects there will be differences due to background,
experience, age and so on. Even within the performance of a
given subject there will be variations due to uncontrolled
changes in the environment, minute by minute changes in
alertness and so on. It is thus advisable when reporting
some measure of central tendancy, such as a mean performance
time, also to report a measure of dispersion such as the
variance or the range of times. This allows the reader of
the report to estimate the precision of the result.
    When it comes to assessing the results of experiments a
similar problem arises. Given there is some chance variation
in the results, any difference observed between experimental
conditions could be due to these chance fluctuations rather
than the experimental manipulation. Inferential statistics
of the kind described below allow us to test against this
possibility.

FUNDAMENTALS OF
HUMAN–COMPUTER INTERACTION

6.2 TESTING FOR DIFFERENCES BETWEEN MEANS

Rationale

Any experiment will have some chance element to it. For
example, consider the experiment described in Chapter 5, the
aim of which was to compare two systems. System A is
controlled by making choices from menus of a certain length.
System B works on the same basis but uses more, shorter
menus to achieve the same result. Let us say that a
between-subjects design is used, so one group of subjects
uses System A and the other System B. After a suitable
amount of practice both groups are given five specific
problems to solve and the total time taken is measured.
Subjects are selected to be representative of the population
of potential users of the systems.

To assess the effect of the manipulation of menu length
we need to compare the solution times for the two groups.

TABLE 6.1 Two sets of Hypothetical Results. The scores are
solution times in seconds. Each score is contributed by a
different subject.

A.	Group I	Group II
	623	367
	791	276
	798	548
	562	418
	752	391
	651	452
Mean	696.2	408.7
B.	Group I	Group II
	312	1276
	456	142
	1548	330
	125	303
	561	131
	1175	270
Mean	696.2	408.7

The individuals within each group will differ in a number of ways and so will their scores (time to solve all the problems). In a sense they have been chosen to do so as the groups are supposed to be representative. Thus when we compute a mean score for each group there is always the possibility that the means differ, not because of our manipulation but by chance. Table 6.1 gives two sets of results. Both have the same mean scores but it is clear that only case A. is likely to be a reliable finding. In case B. the variability within the groups is very large, in fact easily large enough to account for the difference between the groups.

The null-hypothesis

The business of inferential statistics is to quantify the above arguments. This is done by computing the probability that the result obtained (or one that is in some sense better) could have arisen by chance. If that probability is very small then the result is said to be 'significant'. This computation is achieved by setting up a 'null-hypothesis' which is in effect a definition of what we mean by chance.

As another example take an experiment where users are exposed to a white on black CRT display as well as an equivalent black on white CRT display. The subjects in this experiment are simply asked which display they prefer. A reasonable null-hypothesis for this task would be that each subject has an equal probability of choosing each display. On that basis one can see it is a relatively simple matter to compute the probability of say 10 out of 10 subjects choosing the black on white display. The probability is small (<0.002) and so we can reject the null-hypothesis and accept that the result 10 out of 10 is a reliable one.

The computation required for our 'menu length' experiment is different but the logic is the same. This time the null-hypothesis is that there is no effect of system type on the scores. All the variance in the scores is assumed to arise from the subject variables. This variance can be estimated from the within-group variance. Using certain statistical techniques it is then possible to estimate the probability that the difference between groups arose from this same source of 'error' variance.

Significance Levels

Having computed the probability of getting our result, or
something better, assuming the null-hypothesis is true
(i.e., by chance) the next step is to decide whether that
probability is small enough for us to reject the
null-hypothesis. Arbitrary levels are set for this purpose,
if the probability is less than this the result is said to
be significant at that level. The critical levels are known
as significance levels. In behavioural science the most
commonly used significance level is the .05 level. That is
if the probability of getting your result, or something
better, by chance is less than .05 the result is deemed
reliable; otherwise it is not. The significance level
represents an error rate. If you habitually set a
significance level of .05 then in five percent of your
experiments where the manipulation really had no effect you
will wrongly conclude that there was an effect. Of course,
if one sets a very high significance level to avoid these
false positives one runs an increasing risk of making
errors in the opposite direction and rejecting real results.
The .05 level has been arrived at by balancing the costs of
the two kinds of errors. If, as is likely, these costs are
different in your situation then a different significance
level may be used. Returning to our menu length example, it
may be that System A is already well established and is
being used in a number of your installations. In that case
one would want to be sure that the difference in performance
between systems A and B was large and could not be
attributed to chance before changing over to system B.

What Test to Use

Three statistical tests are listed below. They have been
chosen because they are simple to use and make no strong
assumptions about the nature of the dependent variable.
Which test you use depends primarily on the experimental
design.

(i) Mann-Whitney U test-
Used for between-subjects designs where there are two
groups of subjects. The dependent variable must be a
score of some kind that can at least be ranked.

(ii) Wilcoxon Matched Pairs Signed Ranks test-
Used for within-subjects designs where each subject gives
you two scores, one for each of two experimental
conditions. The dependent variable is a score of some
kind so that the differences can at least be ranked.

(iii) Sign Test (also known as the binomial test)-
Used when each subject can be classified as supporting
or not supporting your hypothesis. Useful as a quick
check but it may ignore a lot of the information you have
collected.

Procedures for performing the tests will be found in
Robson (1973). More complicated designs are beyond the scope
of this chapter. Some reference books are given in the
bibliography.

6.3 CORRELATION

The tests given in the previous section are for comparing
experimental conditions. A rather different kind of
statistic is needed to measure an association or
correlation. Consider an experiment to see how easily
operators can adapt from one system to another. Each
operator is presented with the new system and after some
suitable amount of practice his performance is measured. Let
us say that as well as this score we also have some measure
of his familiarity with the old system, say the number of
months he has used it. Figure 6.1 is a graph representing
this data. Each subject is represented by a point giving
his performance and experience. The cloud of points is
elliptical and its major axis has a negative slope. This
indicates that in general the more experience with the old
system you have the worse you are with the new one.
Pearson's product-moment correlation, signified r, will
quantify this trend. If r is near to 1 there is a strong
positive relationship. If it is near to -1 there is a strong
negative relationship. If it is near to 0 there is no
relationship. The significance of r depends on the number of
subjects as well as the strength and refers to the
probability of getting a relationship of the same sign.
    There are all sorts of pitfalls to be encountered when
interpreting correlations. The three most common are given
below:

(i) Attributing causality - You cannot attribute
causality on the basis of a correlation. Take the example

above, it is not possible to say that experience with the
old system caused difficulties with the new one because
there is always the possibility there is some third
factor causing the difficulty which is correlated with
experience (for example, age).

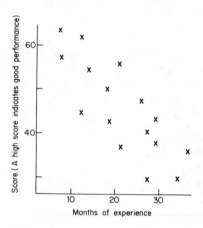

FIG. 6.1 Scattergram of experience on old system against
ability to use the new one.

(ii) Drawing strong conclusions from small numbers of
subjects - Correlation coefficients are notoriously
unreliable when the number of subjects is small. Be wary
of accepting any thing more than the direction of the
correlation unless you have at least 40 subjects.

(iii) Confusing significance with strength - The
significance of a correlation depends on the number of
subjects as well as its strength. With large numbers of
subjects quite small correlations are significant. This
only means that the direction of the correlation is
reliable. The strength of the correlation is given by r.
For most purposes, anything over .6 is a strong
correlation.

If in doubt contact an expert. There are particular problems inherent in interpreting correlations when there are several dependent variables.

6.4 SUMMARY

Statistical tests for assessing the reliability of differences between means and a test of correlation have been discussed. These tests allow one to determine the significance of a result. Significance is achieved if the probability of getting that result, or better, by chance is less than some arbitrary significance level.

6.5 FURTHER READING

Robson (1973) can be recommended as a cheap and easy-to-read text on the principles of experimental design and statistics. All the tests he covers are described with step-by-step procedures accompanied by worked examples. He covers all the tests mentioned in this chapter and a few more. As an alternative to Robson try Shneiderman (1980).

For further technical detail, including tests for use with experimental designs more complex than those considered here and in Chapter 5, consult Kirk (1968) or Ferguson (1981).

CHAPTER 7

Example of an Experiment: Evaluating Some Speech
Synthesisers for Public Announcements

John Waterworth and Antony Lo

7.1 INTRODUCTION

Background

British Telecom are involved in a broad range of human
factors research concerned with making the process of
man-machine interaction as successful and effortless for
users as possible. Access to information-providing systems
by means of speech-based interaction is of particular
interest to us, because this permits users to communicate
directly with information bases by means of an ordinary
telephone. Keyed input or automatic speech recognition,
combined with synthetic speech output from the computer,
provide the means of communication. These services are
principally aimed at the general public, so that no
expertise in computer interactions can be assumed to be held
by users. This means that very close attention must be
directed towards 'the user interface'. We have conducted
several experimental studies to maximise the effectiveness
of voice-based interactive services. These have included
the design and evaluation of complete systems (actual
existing systems and simulated services), as well as more
specific studies on particular aspects of speech synthesis
and recognition. Chapter 13 provides a review of some of the
work in these areas.

This chapter describes two experiments that examined the

89

use of synthetic speech in the context of an interactive
train timetable service. The first compared the performance
of several different synthesisers, while the second focussed
on the effects of synthesiser speaking rate.

Description of Synthesisers

The machines chosen for comparison were all 'formant
synthesisers'. Rather than attempting to simulate the
physical characteristics of the human vocal tract, such
devices embody rules which specify the values of amplitude
and frequency parameters in an attempt to reproduce the
sound spectra of speech in terms of the first few major
resonances of the speech signal (i.e., the 'formants').
Chapter 12 section 12.3 describes how these systems work.
Three of the machines (Votrax CDS-II, Telesensory
Prose-2000, and Microspeech-2) were 'text-to-speech' devices
that take ordinary English typed input and convert this, by
the operation of rules, into synthetic speech output. The
other machine (referred to here as VB-1), was specially
developed to support the target application and was only
capable of uttering a very limited repertoire of messages
appropriate to this service. A human voice was also
included in the trials to provide a basis for assessing
performance.

The principal reason for conducting this investigation
was dissatisfaction with the performance of the custom-built
synthesiser (VB-1) in terms of the quality of output and its
inherent inflexibility. If the same machine were to be used
for other services the preparation of a further vocabulary
set for each would have to be commissioned. Text-to-speech
synthesis, on the other hand, is extremely flexible and the
same device could readily be used for a range of different
services. This obviously imparts both cost and time
benefits, not least because it allows text data-bases
prepared for other purposes to support voice-controlled
interaction.

The three text-to-speech synthesisers were representative
of the range of available products at the time of the study.
Microspeech-2 is a relatively low-cost device operating on
fairly unsophisticated rules. The Votrax machine is rather
more sophisticated, but neither this nor the Microspeech
attempt anything like realistic intonation production. The
Prose-2000, on the other hand, appeared later, and uses much
more complicated rules automatically to structure the
delivery in what is claimed to be a fairly natural pattern
of intonation and pronounciation.

7.2   EXPERIMENT ONE - METHOD

Because of the strictly limited vocabulary of the VB-1 synthesiser, it was necessary to restrict any tests to the words this machine could utter. An alternative approach would have been to use a standardised test where the message content is balanced and controlled. This would have meant having the test vocabulary specially commissioned at considerable expense. Also it was felt that the results would be more applicable to the target service if the actual messages encountered by users of the system were used, as general intelligibility tests are relatively insensitive for detecting deficiencies on a particular vocabulary. It was decided that each subject would experience all the messages. Message identity was thus used as a within-subjects variable, so that variance on message scores arising from differences between subjects would be eliminated by each subject acting as his own control on this factor. Because it would not be possible for a subject to be exposed to the same message more than once, because of memory effects, each subject heard only one synthesiser. That is, synthesiser identity was a between-subjects factor.

Subjects

Sixty-five subjects from the British Telecom Human Factors subject panel at Ipswich took part in the study. The panel consists of volunteers from the general public, selected at random from the electoral roll. In this experiment there were 33 males and 32 females, ranging in age from 16 to 64 years.

Apparatus

Test messages were played from a cassette tape recorder, through a standard telephone hand set via a mixing unit, and amplifier, and a bandpass filter which realistically reproduced the characteristics of a normal telephone line. Subjects' responses were recorded on another cassette recorder.

Materials

Materials consisted of the 17 test messages to be used for the timetable service (see Table 7.1), recorded on tape

TABLE 7.1 Test messages used in both experiments.

---

1.   This is British Telecom's train timetable service for principal intercity trains between Ipswich and London, Liverpool Street.

2.   Do you require advice to use this service? For yes, dial 1, or for no, dial 0.

3.   You will be asked a series of questions, to repeat any question dial STAR, to get advice on any question dial SQUARE.

4.   Do you wish to travel from Ipswich? For yes, dial 1, or for no, dial 0.

5.   Do you wish to travel from London? For yes, dial 1, or for no, dial 0.

6.   Do you wish to enter your estimated departure time from London? For yes, dial 1, or for no, dial 0.

7.   Do you wish to enter your estimated arrival time at Ipswich? For yes, dial 1, or for no, dial 0.

8.   Using the 24 hour clock, please enter the time you wish to depart from Ipswich.

9.   Using the 24 hour clock, please enter the time you wish to depart from London.

10. Using the 24 hour clock, please enter the time you wish to arrive at London.

11. Using the 24 hour clock, please enter the time you wish to arrive at Ipswich.

12. Sorry, you have dialled incorrectly.

13. This service gives arrival and departure times for Ipswich and London, Liverpool Street, only.

14. To repeat the question dial STAR, for advice dial SQUARE.

15. Sorry, you have dialled incorrectly, Do you wish to enter your estimated arrival time?

16. Sorry, you have entered the time incorrectly.

17. The time must always be entered as a four digit number.

cassettes. A 500ms tone (1100 Hz) was recorded at the end
of each message to indicate positively to the subject that
the message had ended.

Rate of speaking was matched to the VB-1 (130 words per
minute) in the case of the Votrax and Microspeech-2.
However, because of time constraints the Prose-2000 was run
at its default rate of about 160 w.p.m. The real voice
was at a 'natural' announcement-reading speed of about 180
w.p.m. Fifteen different random orders of the 17
messages were prepared (see Table 7.2).

TABLE 7.2 Random ordering of the 17 test messages in
Experiment 1.

							Random Orders								
	1	2	3	4	5	6	7	8	9	10	11	12	13	14	15
Messages	3	16	5	15	8	16	12	1	4	3	3	7	5	3	13
	8	8	10	10	1	3	13	3	3	14	7	10	13	7	9
	5	14	9	5	11	13	2	17	7	6	9	13	10	8	12
	15	3	4	7	13	12	16	7	15	11	1	16	8	4	16
	12	9	3	16	17	6	14	13	5	12	8	4	12	15	4
	7	17	16	8	2	9	7	10	9	4	17	15	3	10	2
	17	11	1	14	16	17	3	5	2	13	16	2	2	13	8
	16	10	8	11	4	5	4	9	14	17	4	12	9	11	4
	9	6	11	1	6	1	15	8	10	9	10	17	1	16	15
	14	15	7	6	5	8	17	14	1	7	14	3	14	17	17
	10	5	12	17	3	15	10	6	16	1	2	9	11	9	6
	2	13	14	13	10	7	5	4	13	16	6	14	15	11	5
	13	1	6	4	9	4	6	15	17	8	11	5	4	14	11
	6	2	13	3	14	14	8	12	11	10	13	16	17	5	10
	11	7	15	2	7	2	11	16	8	15	15	8	16	2	7
	1	4	17	9	12	10	9	2	6	5	12	1	6	12	3
	4	12	2	12	15	11	1	11	12	2	5	11	7	6	1
Subjects	1	2	3	4	5	6	7	8	9	10	11	12	13	14	15
	16	17	18	19	20	21	22	23	24	25	26	27	28	29	30
	31	32	33	34	35	36	37	38	39	40	41	42	43	44	45
	46	47	48	49	50	51	52	53	54	55	56	57	58	59	60
	61	62	63	64	65										

Subjects were told that they would be played a series of
messages through the handset, that the messages originated
from a prototype train timetable service, and that after
each message they should try to repeat back into the handset
as much of the message as they could recall. They were also
forewarned that they might find that the voice sounded a
little strange.

The messages were arranged in 15 different random orders,
and each subject experienced one of these orders, to

approximately balance out message order effects. Subjects
were randomly assigned to voice type, with the constraint
that each of the 5 voices was heard by 13 subjects.

After hearing all 17 messages, and completing their last
response, the subjects were asked their opinions of the
speech they had heard in terms of the following 5 points:

    i)   Pleasantness
    ii) Acceptability
    iii) Intelligibility
    iv) Length of messages
    v)   Any other comments

7.3 RESULTS

Scoring

Responses were scored by taking the number of correct words
per message, irrespective of order, and calculating the
percentage of words correct for each message. This is a
fairly arbitrary way of scoring but avoided high scores
being obtained merely as a function of message length. The
absolute values are not meaningful, because of inevitable
transcription errors and the particular way in which the
experiment was conducted. However, they do provide a basis
for comparing performance between synthesisers and between
messages.

Effect of Voice Type

Mean intelligibility scores for each voice type are
presented in Figure 7.1. The Prose-2000 was the most
intelligible of the synthesisers (80.3%), followed by the
VB-1 (69.4%), Votrax (63.3%), and the Microspeech-2 (13.7%).
The results were subjected to a two-way (5 voices x 17
messages) Analysis of Variance. This indicated significant
main effects of voice type (p .001) and message identity
(p .001), and a significant interaction.

Because of a suspicion that the effect of voice was
entirely due to the very low level of scores with the
Microspeech-2, another Analysis of Variance was conducted
without including these scores. Voice type was again found
to be significant, confirming the effect of this variable on
performance even without the influence of Microspeech.

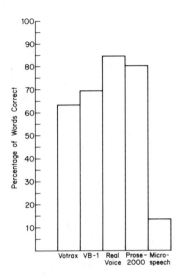

FIG. 7.1 Percentage of words correct for each voice tested in Experiment 1

Effect of message

Figure 7.2 illustrates how subjects fared on each message for each of the voices. As already mentioned, Analysis of Variance indicated a significant effect due to choice of message.

That is, messages differed in terms of intelligibility. As can be seen from Figure 7.2, the pattern of scores across the various messages differed between voices. This was reflected in the significant interaction effect of message by voice. Five within-subjects Analyses of Variance were performed, one for each voice type. All were significant, thus confirming that message identity had a significant effect on every voice tested.

From Figure 7.2 it appears that all voices, except the Microspeech-2, followed a broadly similar pattern on the different messages. A major factor affecting performance is likely to be the length of the message. Even with the real

voice, the longest message (22 words) would place
considerable demands on short-term memory (STM) capacity,
and it has been suggested (Luce et al., 1983) that synthetic
speech increases the demands on encoding and/or rehearsal in
STM (see Chapter 13 section 13.2).

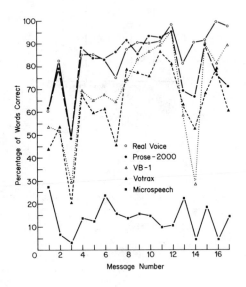

FIG. 7.2 The effect of message for each voice in Experiment 1

With the Votrax, messages 1, 3, and 7 were worst, with
mean intelligibility scores of 21%, 44%, and 46%
respectively. These were amongst the longest tested,
suggesting 'rehearsal' problems as a possible source of

difficulty.   Additionally,   message 3   does   not   have
predictable (in this context) words such as "Ipswich" and
"London", but does include the more obscure (to timetables)
"star" and "square". The worst examples with the VB-1 were
messages 14 and (again) 3, with scores of 29% and 30%
respectively. Although relatively short, message 14 does
contain "star" and "square". With the Prose-2000 and the
real voice, only message 3 (the longest) caused serious
problems with an intelligibility score of 49% for both.
With the Microspeech-2, differences between individual
messages were masked by the overall low level of
performance.

Subsidiary Analyses

Subjects were chosen to be representative of a broad range
of ages.   It seemed possible that older subjects would
experience greater difficulty with synthetic voices than
younger individuals, perhaps because of hearing loss or
reduced memory capacity. Many of the younger subjects
suggested that their older relatives would not be able to
cope with the synthesised speech. Subjects were categorised
into 5 age groups (under 20, 20-29. 30-39, 40-49, 50-64
years)and a one-way Analysis of Variance was carried out to
examine the effect of age. This showed no significant
differences in performance due to age. In fact, the effect
of age-related hearing loss, which is known to start with
high frequencies and work its way down (Deatherage, 1972),
would be minimised here because of the absence of high
frequencies in telephone transmission. Also, Hartley et al.
(1980) report findings which suggest that STM capacity is
not reduced in older subjects unless the task is extremely
demanding.   So it appears that, despite some subjects'
intuitions, age of listener is not a significant factor in
performance on this sort of task.
     Figure 7.3 illustrates the effect of practice on the real
voice, the Prose-2000, and the Votrax. There is some
improvement with repeated exposure, although this is
relatively slight.
     The least natural-sounding voice of the three, that of
the Votrax, exhibits quite dramatic improvement over the
first 6 trials, whereas for the real voice and the
Prose-2000 this is only evident on the first couple of
exposures. With unnatural-sounding speech there does appear
to be an 'acclimatisation period', where subjects are
getting used to both the queer-sounding voice and the
unusual situation in which they find theselves. With the

more natural-sounding speech there is a much reduced 'acclimatisation' effect, because natural speech is already familiar. Whatever the voice, once the 'acclimatisation period' is over further exposure to more speech alone does not bring significant benefits, confirming the findings of Marshall (1982).

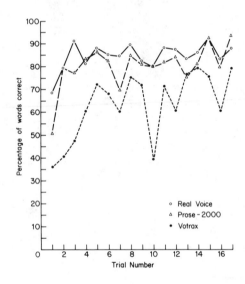

FIG. 7.3 The effect of practice for the real voice, the Prose-2000, and the Votrax.

Subjective comments on the voices revealed some aspects not brought out by the intelligibility analyses. The real voice drew very little comment, but 11 subjects thought the messages were too long. The Prose-2000 was generally well liked, although individual comments ranged from "very pleasant indeed" to "not easy to listen to - a bit grating". The VB-1 was judged as anything from "very nice" to "pretty horrible" in terms of pleasantness, and from "generally unacceptable" to "not too bad" on acceptability. Similarly, the Votrax was seen as "a nice pleasant and helpful tone" or "absolutely awful" depending on the listener. Many subjects thought the Microspeech had a pleasant tone, but was totally incomprehensible. Ascribed accents of all machines varied widely and included Chinese, Indian, Jamaican, American, Geordy, etc.. The same voice was often described as being of different regional origin depending on the listener. This obviously makes it difficult to predict how individual users will react to new synthetic voices.

7.4 CONCLUSIONS FROM EXPERIMENT ONE

The Prose-2000 (80.3% of words correct) compared very favourably with the real voice (84.8%), while the performance of the Microspeech-2 was unacceptably poor. The special-purpose character of the VB-1 , which was specifically designed for high quality output on these messages , was not reflected in subjects' performnce with this device. This suggests that a good quality text-to-speech synthesiser, with the enormous inherent flexibility such devices possess, might well be acceptable for information services of this type. Many subjects commented on the "flat tone" of even the best device, however, so that improved intonation rules may be a prerequisite of full acceptability.

Speaking rate was a confounding variable in the present experiment, since rates varied between voices in an uncontrolled way. Because of this, and the possibility that rate of presentation could be used to improve the intelligibility of synthetic speech, Experiment 2 explicitly examined the effect of rate on the human recognition of synthetic speech.

7.5 EXPERIMENT TWO

Method

The method used was basically the same as that used for
Experiment 1.   The VB-1 synthesiser was used, and the main
aim was to examine the effect of rate of presentation of the
17 messages (Table 7.1) on subjective performance and
opinion. It was thought that a rather slower delivery might
assist listeners to assimilate the presented information.
The machine allowed 6 rates to be selected (63, 82, 103,
121, 130, and 150 words per minute), and these were used as
a between-subjects factor. Forty-eight subjects (25 males
and 23 females, range 16-64 years) took part in this
experiment with groups of 8 subjects experiencing each of
the 6 different rates of presentation. Messages were once
again a within-subjects variable.

Results and conclusions

Figure 7.4 illustrates the effect of rate on intelligibility
scores for the 17 test messages. From this it appears that,
rather than enhancing performance,fewer words were correctly
reported back with the slower rates of delivery. A one-way
between-subjects Analysis of Variance revealed that this
effect was not significant, however. Age effects were also
examined and, as in the first experiment, were not found to
be significant.
      The conclusion from this experiment was that rate of
delivery did not affect intelligibility of the VB-1
synthesiser, and performance thus cannot be improved by
manipulating speed of speaking within the range provided by
this device. It is possible that a broader range of speeds
would have had a greater effect, but the trend revealed in
Figure 7.4 suggests that even extreme manipulations would
not have improved reception of the messages. A
within-subjects design might have been preferable, as it is
possible that the effect of rate was somewhat swamped by
variance between individuals. A within-subjects analysis of
the effect of message revealed a highly significant effect,
as in Experiment 1. Subjective comments generally suggested
that the faster rates were preferred. This is perhaps
partly due to the fact that these more closely approximated
to a natural delivery rate.

7.6 SUMMARY AND GENERAL DISCUSSION

Taken together, the results from these two experiments revealed that the choice of synthetic voice can have a profound effect on how well information is received by listeners, and that a poor voice cannot be compensated for by slowing the delivery rate.

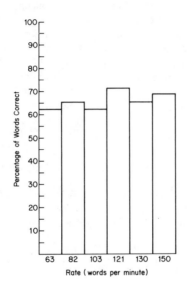

FIG. 7.4 Percentage of words correct for each rate in Experiment 2

The special purpose synthesiser that had been selected to
present information to users of the target service was shown
to be inadequate, and another, more flexible device was
found to be more acceptable. Objective scores revealed that
this machine was almost equivalent to natural speech and
subjective comments suggested that with some improvement to
the intonation characteristics it could be fully acceptable
for a service of this type.

Content of messages was found to have a very significant
effect in both experiments. This clearly points to the need
to select the vocabulary for informative announcements very
carefully.   In particular, unusual or otherwise
unpredictable words are likely to be less well identified
than words which are expected within a particular context.
The interaction effect of voice by message (Experiment 1)
shows that machines differ in the words which they can utter
successfully.   This means that it is essential to test
performance on a set of items that is representative of
those to be used for the target application. The other side
of this coin, however, is that the results obtained are
probably not readily generalisable to other message sets and
devices.

7.7 FURTHER READING

For further examples of experiments on this subject, see
Waterworth (1983).   For general references on how to design
and report experiments see, Chapters 5 and 6.

PART THREE

THE USER INFERFACE

It should be clear from the preceding chapters that this section is not going to lay down rules, which if followed guarantee that the resulting system will be 'user friendly'. The conclusion drawn in the chapters that follow is that there are no such rules. However, the designer with specific problems will need specific answers. How are they to be provided? First, it is to be hoped that the preceding two sections of the book have furnished the reader with a way of formulating questions about the user interface which facilitates user-centred design. Secondly, though the chapters in this section do not prescribe rules they do point out examples of the problems commonly faced by the user and suggest measures which may alleviate them. Much can be done towards improving user interface design simply by considering these examples and the principles they suggest. While there is no set of existing principles general enough to be applied to a wide range of applications yet specific enough to answer precisely the questions asked of them, devising a design tool of this kind is a clear priority for the future.

Chapter 8 by Reid contains the basic information a designer needs about the hardware devices available and how they can be used. This can be thought of as a low level analysis of human-computer interaction: what basic activities can the user engage in and how can information be displayed? A higher level analysis is needed to structure the human-computer dialogue. This more cognitive approach is introduced and illustrated in Chapter 9 by Hammond and Barnard. At this level of analysis one is mainly concerned with the user's internal model of the task. Essentially the problem is to design a system which fits the user's expectations. This means having a system which can be conceptualised in a reasonably straightforward manner and then inducing the user to form the right conceptualisation. An interesting approach to this problem is described by Thimbleby in Chapter 10. He advocates the use of 'generative user-engineering principles'. These principles can be used to contrain the design and at the same time provide a way of communicating the nature of the system to the user.

In Chapter 11 Kofer indulges in some speculation as to what the future may hold by telling a story, set in 1992, about a family buying a house. This chapter has the serious purpose of pointing out the problems to be solved in the design of the automated office.

Chapters 12 and 13 consider communicating with machines

using speech. In the first part of Chapter 12 Bailey
describes our vocal and auditory apparatus. This background
knowledge allows us to specify the nature of the speech
signal and has implications for the design and effectiveness
of devices for speech recognition and synthesis. The
capabilities and limitations of these devices are then
reviewed. Chapter 13 by Waterworth considers how speech can
be used in human-computer dialogue. The problems presented
to the user communicating with a computer via speech are in
many ways different from those faced by the user
communicating via a visual display and a keyboard.
Waterworth explores these differences and how the
limitations of currently available devices can be
circumvented.

Chapter 14 by Alison Kidd introduces the reader to the
new problems posed and the new possibilitites made available
by expert systems.

CHAPTER 8

Work Station Design,
Activities and Display Techniques

Pete Reid

8.1 INTRODUCTION

The potential range of hardware available to the designer of
an interactive system is considerable. The user may
communicate information to the machine via a keyboard,
numerous kinds of pointing devices or even speech.
Similarly, there are many different methods by which the
designer can have the machine communicate information to the
user. Add to this the large number of ways of structuring
the human-computer dialogue and the choice facing the
designer is enormous.

   In point of fact, few designers are given this amount of
choice. Practical constraints, "political" considerations
and precedents will constrict the choice considerably.
Whether there is a large choice or not, it is important that
a designer knows the advantages and disadvantages of the
alternatives, from the point of view of the user. Human
factors considerations can be used to justify breaking with
precedents and to optimise the design within given
constraints.

   This chapter catalogues some hardware devices for input
and output along with user activities and display methods
which can be used to structure the human-computer dialogue.
Each device or method has its advantages and disadvantages
which should be considered when choosing between
alternatives and when incorporating them into the user
interface.

FUNDAMENTALS OF
HUMAN–COMPUTER INTERACTION   107

Much of the chapter takes the form of recommendations which have been culled from the large research literature. References to this literature are given in section 8.7.   It was not possible to give details for all these studies and the reader is advised to look at the relevant literature when seeking an answer to a specific question. The problem is that a result obtained in one context is unlikely to generalise to another very different context.   The recommendations should be treated as guidelines, i.e., pointers to possible problems, rather than hard and fast rules.

The chapter covers input and output devices and then input activities and display techniques.   It does not consider speech input and output which are the subject of Chapters 12 and 13.

8.2 INPUT DEVICES

Table 8.1 summarises preferred input devices for the range of input activities considered by Newman and Sproull (1979). Picking is where a user has to select a choice from several alternatives.   Positioning involves specifying or changing the position or orientation of a displayed object, often a cursor.

TABLE 8.1 Preferred input devices for different input techniques. Highest preferences are to the left and lowest to the right, with equal preferences separated by '/'.

Picking:	mouse, joystick/ tracker ball, light pen/ touch screen/ soft keys, function keys.
Positioning:	mouse, joystick/ tracker ball, light pen/ touch screen, cursor keys.
Numeric input:	numeric key pad, alphanumeric key pad, tablet.
Text input:	alphanumeric key pad, tablet (limited input only).
Drawing:	tablet, mouse, light pen.
Digitising:	tablet.

Digitising is where the user enters a series of discrete coordinates to represent a continuous piece of graphical information. Newman and Sproull may be consulted for descriptions of the devices discussed.

The mouse is good for picking and positioning. Some researchers also favour this device for drawing. It is pushed along a flat surface next to the display. Moving it right moves the cursor right, moving it away from the operator moves the cursor up the screen. It can have integral selection keys making it a self-contained input device. However, it does require an adjacent flat surface and cannot be very robust due to its trailing cable. The joystick (or joypad) is also an effective device for picking and positioning, though many investigators prefer the mouse. Building a joystick into the keyboard gets round some of the problems of the mouse. Tracker balls, sometimes known as rolling balls, have also been found to be effective in this kind of context, more so than the "cursor rollers" and "thumb wheels" they have largely superseded.

The light pen and touch sensitive screen can also be used for picking, positioning and drawing tasks. They both suffer from the fact that the best position for viewing is further away than the comfortable position for pointing. This is especially true for colour displays. In addition, the light pen has a trailing cable, can be affected by dirty screens and depends on suitable ambient lighting levels. Touch screens cannot give very high resolution. However, they are particularly suitable for applications where a keyboard is undesirable or where the environment is too hostile for the other forms of input device. Touch screens are subject to problems arising from dirt being carried on to the screen and parallax if the device is not mounted on the screen itself.

Soft keys are unmarked keys placed around the display screen whose function is indicated on the screen. This makes it possible to change the function of the key depending on the context it is being used in. Function keys which are dedicated to a particular task have fixed labels and are usually mounted with the rest of the keyboard. This is generally thought to be an advantage as the user can maintain a comfortable viewing position and does not have to keep changing position to reach the display as he has to with soft keys. The most commonly found function keys are the cursor positioning keys, usually marked with arrows. A mouse or a joystick permit much faster movement and for that reason are in general to be preferred.

There is some advantage in using a numeric key pad for purely numeric input as compared to using a typewriter-like

keyboard. Some researchers have designed alternatives to
the "QWERTY" alphanumeric key pad but generally only for
very specific applications.

8.3 OUTPUT DEVICES

This section summarises the main features of the common
interactive output devices suitable for use in workstations.
Note that whilst only interactive devices are described,
there may well be the need for some form of hard copy
output. Since the range of hard copy devices is quite
extensive and very dependent upon the required application,
they are not described in this chapter.
    There are two main forms of interactive output devices:
the vector CRT display and the raster display.

Vector Display

Vector displays produce images by directly controlling the
electron beam across the phosphor, thus enabling "pure"
lines to be drawn (i.e., smooth rather than ragged lines).
They are available in two forms - storage tubes, where the
CRT itself acts as the display memory, and refresh tubes,
where the CRT is continually refreshed from a display file
memory located in the device. The storage tube device does
not support selective erasure and so the complete screen has
to be cleared in order to carry out any modification that
would involve removing part of the displayed image.
    The refresh tube device uses a display file which
contains descriptions of all the components (i.e., vectors)
used to construct the displayed image. Typical vector
displays are monochrome only (commonly green) and are
capable of very high resolution (e.g., 4000 x 4000 points).
A disadvantage of vector displays is that they commonly have
very few built in facilities and thus the user has to
"drive" the device at a very low level. In some cases this
can include the forming of any text to be displayed.

Raster Display

These are based on bit map frame buffers where each pixel
(picture point) is represented by a unique memory location
in the frame buffer. Each memory location may require from
one to sixteen bits depending on the facilties provided
(e.g., number of colours). Raster displays can be

monochrome or colour and are capable of high resolution, a raster display needs very large quantities of memory and display processing power (these requirements can make high resolution raster displays very expensive).

Raster displays often support many useful high level facilities such as vector generation, complex shape generation (triangles, rectangles, circles, arcs, polygons, etc.), shape filling (enabling any polygon to be filled with a specific colour and/or pattern), rectangular independent windows, zooming ("blowing up" selective parts of the image), monochrome and colour text display with attributes such as blinking and protected fields.

A disadvantage of raster displays is that they tend to produce "ragged" rather than "smooth" lines. A technique known as "anti-aliasing" is available (both in software and hardware) which uses related colours (or grey scale shades) to cause a blurring of ragged edges. Thus the user sees what appears to be a smooth line rather than a ragged one. Anti-aliasing increases the apparent resolution of raster display images. This technique tends to be expensive in both display time and equipment costs and so is available in a few devices only.

Summarising the above, it can be seen that vector displays are capable of the highest resolution, but are inflexible in an interactive environment and incapable of displaying multiple colours. In contrast, raster displays are only capable of lower resolutions, but provide many facilities, allow the use of colour and are most suitable for use in an environment where rapid changes of display are required.

8.4 FACILITY OR FEATURE SELECTION TECHNIQUES

Choosing Items From a Menu

Menus have been recommended for occasional and novice users as they reduce the amount of information the user needs to remember. They also serve the useful function of limiting, to a well defined set, the responses the user can make. In addition, menus are particularly appropriate where a system offers a small set of facilities. Their disadvantage is that, particularly for the more experienced user, they may be ungainly and long winded. As well as being frustrating this can lead to problems navigating through complex systems. An often quoted example of this navigation problem was the feature selection mechanism offered in early versions of Prestel.

The user of a dialogue constructed with menus is faced
with two basic problems: finding the item in the menu which
he or she wants (this includes the problem of understanding
different items in the menu) and knowing where he or she is
in the system and thinking ahead to the next menu or menus
(i.e., navigating).

There are a number of measures the designer can adopt to
help the user. Problems finding the right item can be
alleviated by careful design and testing of the content and
ordering of menu items. It is important that their wording
and the order in which they are displayed corresponds to the
user's expectancies (see Chapters 9 and 10). The user's
selection should be confirmed visually on the display,
especially if there is a delay before the selection is
activated.

Navigation can be made easier by providing "where am I",
"go back one level" and "return to start" facilities. It is
also possible to include facilities to allow a user to
compose a set of selections as a single action. This may
simply be a case of allowing the user to "type ahead" or may
be more sophisticated such as allowing the user to by-pass
the normal hierarchy rules on occasion for example by
pointing at the required destination on a "system map".

There may be some advantage to making available a number
of ways of choosing menu items. Thus for example users may
be able to move a cursor to the item chosen or alternatively
enter a number corresponding to that item. This caters for
the different styles of usage preferred by different users.
It is of course important that the system is consistent so
that when one method is available the other is always
available too. Also care must be taken to ensure that users
learning the system understand that the two alternatives are
functionally equivalent.

Linear Command Language Specification

A command specification approach has been recommended for
applications having a large number of possible facilities
and for experienced users. There is much more to remember
and users tend to forget the commands available or their
syntax. Spelling mistakes and other "finger trouble" can
also lead to problems. However, common problems with
command specifications can be alleviated by providing
on-line help and using mnemonic command names (see Chapter
9).

Different kinds of help may be required at different

times, for example, "Help, tell me about the system" as
opposed to "Help, I am in trouble". If the system attempts
to correct spelling the "corrected" spelling should be
offered to the user for verification. Other measures which
have been tried with varying success are: "variable
verbosity" in system prompts, abbreviation of command names,
flexible syntax and keeping a log of user interactions which
can be rerun.

Hybrid Systems

A hybrid approach may be adopted for systems that can be
subdivided into a small set of major options, each of which
may consist of a large set of sub-options. Such systems may
be implemented with a menu-based structure at the outermost
level while within any sub-system, the facilities are
selected using a command based structure. The hybrid
approach allows the designer easily to divide a system into
major components and yet allows for a flexible and extensive
set of facilities to be available within each of these
components.

Another common hybrid approach is to provide a menu-based
system with command specification offered as an "override"
facility. In such systems it is common to find that menus
are only displayed upon demand from the user (unless the
system is operating in "novice" mode when menus are always
displayed). Hybrid systems run the risk of being
'inconsistent' (see below) and need to be designed with
great attention to detail (see also Chapters 9 and 10).

General Considerations

There are several measures that can be applied to facilitate
the use of any feature selection or specification system:

  (i) Provide an "undo" facility - users often make
  mistakes; having reduced the possibility of this, ensure
  that the user can recover from mistakes easily (and
  rapidly).

  (ii) Provide system descriptions (preferably on-line);
  this is particularly necessary for command-based systems,
  but is still important in menu-based systems.

(iii) Make sure that the system is consistent; i.e., if a similar or identical action is carried out in more than one place, ensure that the method required and form of interaction is the same.

Nievergelt, 1982, has a good discussion on the problems associated with inconsistent user interfaces. This point is further expanded upon in Chapters 9 and 10.

8.5 DISPLAY TECHNIQUES

Display techniques are concerned with both the physical form of displays and the methods used to represent information. The following sections describe recommendations and techniques relevant to (a) making it easy for users to find a specific piece of information, (b) making it easy for users to understand a specific piece of information, and (c) using multiple display windows.

Simplifying The Task of Locating Displayed Information

Several studies have been carried out into visual display layout. The following is a summary of the recommendations made as a result of these studies.

(i) Avoid overfilling the screen. Twenty-five per cent full is considered to be the maximum above which the background "noise" reduces the ability of the user to locate and recognise information.

(ii) Use the upper right hand quadrant of the screen for exceptional information (e.g., emergency alarms). Danchak (1977) reports that users are more sensitive to changes in the upper right hand quadrant than either of the left hand quadrants. Users are least sensitive to changes in the lower right hand quadrant. (Note that this recommendation presupposes that the user is not looking at any particular part of the screen, if this is not the case, i.e., the user is watching a particular display area, then emergency information should be displayed in the centre of the user's field of vision).

(iii) Use mixed case words rather than all capitals words, i.e., some leading capitals with the rest of the word in lower case (see Chapter 2). This recommendation can be generalised to say that different parts of the

display should be made as well differentiated as possible
by the use of such techniques as colour, typefaces and so
on. Care should be taken when choosing words which have
special meanings in the context of the system (e.g.,
command names). Such words should be short and fit the
users' expectancies (see Chapter 9).

(iv) Design the layout so that the user's eyes fall
naturally on the next item of information. Many
researchers have shown the importance of reducing the
head and eye movement of the user. For example, if the
user is an experienced typist, they will tend to be
viewing the display screen rather than the keyboard.
Therefore, status information may be best displayed at
the bottom of the screen (to be least obtrusive).
However, if the user is a "two finger typist", status
information would be best displayed at the top of the
screen (since the user will probably require newly typed
information to be displayed at the bottom of the screen,
i.e., near to the keyboard).

(v) Use time or blink coding to attract attention.
Several studies have shown that this is very good for
attracting attention, but for the same reason can become
very distracting. In particular, many blinking items can
have a very detrimental effect on performance. Users
should be able to acknowledge a blinking item and cancel
the blinking effect. Use a single blink rate of
approximately 2-3Hz with a minimum "on" interval of 50
msec. Colour can also be effectively used for
"highlighting" and aiding visual search (see Green, Sime
and Cornah, 1979).

Simplifying the Understanding of Displayed Information

People can make very fine distinctions between
simultaneously present stimuli. For example, if two patches
of colour are displayed next to each other very small
differences in hue, saturation or brightness can be
detected. On this basis one might conclude that we can
distinguish many hundreds of different colours. On the
other hand, if we try to teach somebody arbitrary meanings
for a range of colours the position is different. It is
difficult for people to learn arbitrary meanings for more
than about seven values of a unidimensional scale.

This has been found to be the case for a number of different scales, for example, colour, size, brightness, loudness and so on (Miller, 1956).

If the display elements for which arbitrary meanings are being learned vary on more than one unidimensional scale, for example, hue and size, or hue brightness and size, then this limit goes up, though not additively. Thus, if you can learn seven different sizes and seven different brightnesses you will be able to learn more than seven brightness-size combinations but not forty-nine as you might expect.

In general a display will contain information coded in arbitrary ways. To take a concrete example, different colours may code for different elements in a budget which has been expressed as a pie chart. In this case quantity is coded by area/angle and the meaning of the different elements by colour. The areas/angles are simultaneously present for comparison so relatively fine distinctions can be made. However, the associations between the colours and the different elements of the budget may have to be learned and it is important not to overload the code by having too many different elements. Of course, if there is a key simultaneously present on the screen the problems can be alleviated to some extent.

There are many ways of coding information on visual displays; each has its advantages and disadvantages. The following is a list of the main information encoding techniques together with advantages, disadvantages and the maximum number of distinct levels usable for reliable absolute identification of a unidimensional stimulus.

(i) Position coding, i.e., assigning meaning depending upon display position, is very commonly used and is effective on displays with a low information density.

(ii) Length coding, i.e., assigning meaning according to the length of an item, is poor for identification and requires a reasonable amount of display space, but it is good for ratio comparisons. Probably only four to six levels should be used with this technique.

(iii) Size coding, i.e., assigning meaning according to the relative sizes of items, is poor for identification and requires a considerable amount of display space. However, it has a greater impact than length coding. A maximum of five levels should be used with this technique.

(iv) Angle or inclination coding involves assigning meaning depending upon the angle (relative to some axis) at which an item is displayed. This can be as good as position coding, but over-use can produce a confusing display. As many as twenty-four levels may be used with this technique.

(v) Colour coding is better than size, angle or shape for identification purposes, and easier to locate than alphanumerics. It is good for labelling, especially when used as redundant recoding (i.e., recoding some already displayed information in order to reinforce a user's understanding). Of course, users must know how colour is being used, preferably providing a displayed key. Apparently arbitrary assignments of colour can be counter productive. Using colour to encode values on a scale (e.g., temperature) presents problems as, unlike a grey scale for example, there is no obvious subjective scale of colour. When using colour, care should also be taken to avoid unpleasant visual effects, for example, after images (retinal image retention due to excessively intense coloured patterns) and "vibration" (apparent movement of image due to use of complementary colours). One should also bear in mind that approximately 8% of the male population and 0.4% of the female population are colour blind; see Chapter 1. A maximum of eleven levels should be used with this technique. However, the maximum number of distinct colours that can be easily attributed with meaning (unaided) is only five. A final justification for the use of colour is that users appear to prefer colour to monochromatic displays. Several studies have reported that there was a marked preference for colour displays even though in some circumstances there was no measurable advantage in terms of user performance.

(vi) Brightness and texture coding are poor substitutes for colour coding, except where value coding is required. Then a grey scale can be quite effective. Most users can readily understand the relationship between a grey scale and a quantative scale (e.g., temperature). Line and surface texture (e.g., line style, hashing) can be useful for separating similar items. However, brightness coding can interfere with other coding techniques such as colour. A maximum of four levels should be used with these techniques.

(vii) Symbolic or alphanumeric labelling will almost
always be required and careful use of labels can enhance
a display. Numeric data is best displayed in tabular,
rather than linear form and all alphanumeric information
should be displayed horizontally if possible.
Alphanumeric coding uses a small amount of display space
and may be used to supplement other coding techniques.
However, alphanumeric information is less easily located
than colour coded information.

(viii) Shape coding is where the meaning of an item is
suggested by geometric shape or pictorial representation.
Geometric shape coding requires a medium to high
resolution display device and users often have to
memorise the shapes used and their meaning.   Pictorial
(e.g. iconic) shape coding requires a high to very high
resolution display device, but can be more representative
of the intended meaning and so require less memorising. A
maximum of 15 levels has been suggested for geometric
coding and 30 for pictorial coding.

Several studies have shown that the careful use of
diagrams can greatly improve the user interface. The main
disadvantage of diagrammatic representation is that it tends
to require a large amount of display space. The use of
multiple display windows, discussed below, can alleviate
some of these problems.

Multiple Display Windows

A technique available with the advent of rapidly refreshed
high resolution displays is that of "multiple display
windows". This enables the designer (and user) to subdivide
a single physical display screen into several logical
display screens represented as rectangular display windows.
    Previous work in the use of this technique has tended to
concentrate on aids for software production and maintenance.
However, the technique is becoming more widespread with the
introduction of office systems such as the Xerox Star and
Apple Lisa.
    Multiple display windows are a useful way of dividing the
display according to logical structure. Thus, for example,
different windows may display different "views" of the task.
The user then can move from one part of the task to another
simply by transferring his attention to another window.
Windows not currently being used can be shrunk or otherwise
put aside. If menus overwrite one another in overlapping

windows the result is to provide a record of what menus have
been used. These techniques all require reasonably large
screens or the size of individual windows will be reduced to
an unreasonable extent. Also the use of multiple windows in
sophisticated manipulable displays is a relatively new
technique. We need to know much more about the pitfalls
which lie in wait for the unwary designer (see Chapter 10,
section 10.5).

8.6 SUMMARY

Input and output devices should be chosen to fit the
particular application they are to be used in. This means
that the designer must consider (a) the environment in which
the equipment is to be used (e.g., "how robust need it
be?"), (b) the kind of users it will have (e.g. are they
skilled typists?) and (c) the kind of task they will use it
for. Only when all these factors are considered can a
satisfactory choice be made.

Choosing the method by which a user selects facilities or
features using a particular input device is also dependent
on similar factors. The main alternatives are menu driven
systems and linear command language specification. Both
have their advantages and disadvantages depending on the
application. More important, both can be made more
effective by the addition of certain facilities such as
"undo" or on-line help and by careful attention to detail.

Display techniques must be geared to making it easy for a
user to find the information required as well as to make it
easy to understand once found. Choosing a particular layout
and methods of coding information for the user requires
careful consideration of the display as a whole. Coloured
displays and diagrams have a lot to recommend them.
Multiple display windows can also be useful.

8.7 FURTHER READING

The ACM Computing Surveys special issue (March 1981)
considers aspects of human-computer interaction and several
of the papers are relevant to this chapter. Newman and
Sproull (1979) is a useful book though some of it is
somewhat dated now. Another useful book is Schiff (1980)
"Perception: An Applied Approach"; see particularly the
chapter on "Perception Through Pictures and Symbols". Other
useful reviews can be found in Dallimonti (1980) and Engel
and Granda (1975).

Detailed Reference

As was indicated in the introduction to this chapter the designer is advised to refer to the literature directly where possible as many of the principles stated above may depend very much on the context in which they are applied. In many cases much more specific recommendations can be made if the context is well defined and matches that in which the research was done. To make it possible for the reader to access this literature a referencing system different from that used in other chapters will be used here. Subject areas from the chapter are listed as well as some additional headings. Each subject is followed by one or more numbers which refer to references in section 8.8. These references will also be found in the alphabetical list at the end of the book.

8.2 Input Devices
Tasks input devices are used for: 1 - 3
Specific devices - Mouse: 3 - 11
                   Drawing with a mouse: 8
                   Joystick: 1, 3, 5, 6, 11 - 15
                   Lightpen: 1, 3, 11, 14, 16, 17
                   Touch sensitive screen: 3, 13, 15,
                                             18, 19
                   Tablet, 1, 3, 11
                   Tracker/Rolling ball: 1, 3, 11
                   Cursor keys: 6
                   Alphanumeric keys: 3, 11
                   Cursor rollers/thumbwheels: 11
                   Function keys: 3, 11

8.3 Output Devices
Vector and raster displays: 1
Anti-aliasing: 66

8.4 Facility or Feature Selection Techniques
General references: 11, 22, 37 - 40
Use of menus and command based systems in -
                   Text editors: 5
                   Information systems: 15, 20 - 22
                   Programming systems (including syntax
                   driven editors, debuggers and
                   documentation aids): 7 - 9, 18, 23 - 30
                   Computer aided design and manufacture

8.8 REFERENCES

1. Newman, W.M. & Sproull, R.F. (1979).   Principles of
    Interactive Computer Graphics (2nd Ed.). McGraw-Hill,
    New York.
2. Foley, J.D. & Wallace, V.L. (1974). The Art of Natural
    Graphic Man-Machine Conversation. Proceedings of the
    IEEE, 62(4), 462-471.
3. Foley, J.D., Wallace, V.L. & Chan, P. (1981).   The
    Human Factors of Graphic Interaction - Tasks and
    Techniques. George Washington University, Washington
    DC.
4. Myers, B.A. (1980). Displaying Data Structures for
    Interactive Debugging. Xerox Parc Report CSL-80-7,
    Xerox Palo Research Centre.

5.   Embley, D.W. & Nagy, G. (1981). Behavioral aspects of text editors. ACM Computing Surveys, (Special Issue: The Psychology of Human-Computer Interaction), 13(1), 33-70.

6.   Card, S.K., English, W.K. & Burr, B.J. (1978). Evaluation of Mouse, Rate-Controlled Isometric Joystick, Step Keys and Text Keys for Text Selection on a CRT. Ergonomics, 21, 601-613.

7.   Teitelman, W. (1977). A Display Oriented Programmer's Assistant. 5th International Joint Conference on Artificial Intelligence. Cambridge, Mass. (pp 905-915)

8.   Kay, A.C. (1977). Microelectronics and the personal computer. In Morrison, P. (ed.) Microelectronics: A Scientific American Book. W.H. Freeman, San Francisco. (pp124-135)

9.   Kay, A. (1980). SMALLTALK. In: Guedj, R.A., ten Hagen, P.J.W., Hopgood, F.R.A., Tucker, H.A. & Duce, D.A. (eds.) Methodology of Interaction. North Holland, Amsterdam (pp 7-11).

10. Irby, C.H. (1974). Display Techniques for Interactive Text Manipulation. National Computer Conference 1974. (pp 247-255).

11. Engel, S.E. & Granda, R.E. (1975) Guidelines for Man/Display Interfaces, TR 00.2720, IBM, Poughkeepsie, N.Y.

12. Herot, C.F. (1980). A Spatial Graphic Man-Machine Interface. S. Lavington (ed), Information Processing 80, Amsterdam, North Holland. (pp1039-1044)

13. Donelson, W.C. (1978). Spatial Management of Information. SIGGRAPH '78 Proceedings, 12(3), 203-209.

14. Stockenberg, J.E. and van Dam, A. (1975). STRUCT Programming Analysis System. IEEE Transactions on Software Engineering, SE-1, 384-389.

15. Herot, C.F., Carling, R.T., Friedell, M. and Kramlich, D. (1980). A Prototype Spatial Data Management System. SIGGRAPH '80 Proceedings, 14, 63-70.

16. Spence, R. and Apperley, M. (1982). Hierarchical Dialogue Structures in Interactive Computer Systems. IEE International Conference on Man/Machine Systems, Manchester.(pp 11-15)

17. Zimmerman, L.L. (1967). On-Line Program Debugging - A Graphic Approach. Computers and Automation, 16(1), 30-34.

18. Kramlich, D., Brown, G.P., Carling, R.T. and Herot, C.F. (Pers. Com.). Program Visualization: Graphics Support For Software Development.

19. Usher, D.M. (1982). A Touch-Sensitive VDU Compared With A Computer-Aided Keypad For Controlling Power Generating Plant. IEE International Conference on Man/Machine Systems, Manchester.(pp250-252)

20. Newell, A. (1977). Notes For A Model of Human Performance in ZOG. Dept. of Computer Science, Carnegie-Mellon University, Pittsburgh.

21. Newell, A., McCracken, D.L., Robertson, G.G. and Akscyn , R.M. (1982). ZOG and the USS CARL VINSON. Computer Science Research Review, Carnegie-Mellon University 1980-1981, (pp 95-118).

22. Brown, J.W. (1982). Controlling the Complexity of Menu Networks. Communications of the ACM 25(7), 412-418.

23. ETH (1982). Source Code Debugger for Modula-2 Programs. Edgenossische Technische Hochschule Zurich.

24. Archer, J. (Jr) and Conway, R. (1981). COPE: A Cooperative Programming Environment, TR 81-459, Cornell University.

25. Bamford, R.J., Weller, D.L. and Williams, R. (1979). Source Code Generation Method Utilizing A Programmable Graphics Display System. IBM Technical Disclosure Bulletin 22, 2493-2495.

26. Boarder, J.C. (1981). The Graphical Parallel Programming Language LZ. Sixth Annual Microprocessor Workshop on Microprocessor Applications, Liverpool.

27. Boarder, J.C. (1980). Graphical Programming For Parallel Processing Systems. Internal Report Oxford Polytechnic, Oxford, England.

28. Smith, D.C. (1975). PYGMALION: A Creative Programming Environment. AD-A16811/2, Stanford University.

29. Yarwood, E. (1977). Toward Program Illustration. Technical Report CSRG-84, Computer Systems Research Group, University of Toronto.

30. Medina-Mora, R. (1982). Syntax-Directed Editing: Towards Integrated Programming Environments. Ph.D. Thesis, Dept. Computer Science, Carnegie-Mellon University, Pittsburgh.

31. Jones, P.F. (1978). Four Principles of Man-Computer Dialogue. CAD Computer Aided Design 10(3), 197-202.

32. Nesslage, R.L. (1976). The Design of a User Interface For a Color, Raster Scan Graphics Device. AD-A28442/2, Naval Postgraduate School.

33. Sturt, J. (1982). Raster-Scanned Colour Meets CAD. Systems International(GB) 10 (11), 39-42.

34. Hayes, P.J. (1982). Cooperative Command Interaction Through The COUSIN System. IEE International Conference on Man/Machine Systems, Manchester (pp 59-63)

35. Witten, I.H. (1982b). An Interactive Computer Terminal Interface Which Predicts User Entries. IEE International Conference on Man/Machine Systems, Manchester (pp 1-5)

36. Alvi, M.A., Daskalakis, C. and Powner, E.T. (1982). The Design of Man-Machine Software Interfaces. IEE International Conference on Man/Machine Systems, Manchester(pp 6-10).

37. Thimbleby, H. (1978). A Note on Menu Selection. Computer Bulletin 2(18), 20-21, 23.

38. Davies, D.W. and Yates, D.M. (1978). Human Factors in Display Terminal Procedures. In Inose, H. (Ed.) Evolutions in Computer Communications, North Holland, Amsterdam (pp 777-783).

39. Gaines, B.R. (1981). The Technology of Interaction - Dialogue Programming Rules. International Journal of Man-Machine Studies 14, 133-150.

40. Nievergelt, J. (1982). Errors in dialogue design and how to avoid them. Proceedings 1982 International Zurich Seminar on Digital Communications, Zurich, March, 1982 (pp 199-205). (Eidgenossische Technische Hochschule (ETH), Institut fur Informatik, Zurich, Switzerland).

41. Danchak, M.M. (1977). Alphanumeric Displays for the Man-Process Interface. Advances in Instrumentation 32, (ISA Conference - Niagara Falls, Oct. 1977 part 1, pp 197-213).

42. Danchak, M.M. (1976). CRT Displays for Power Plants. Instrumentation Technology, 23, 29-36 (October).

43. Tinker, M.A. (1955). Prolonged Reading Tasks in Visual Search. Journal of Applied Psychology, 39, 444-446.

44. Morse, A. (1979). Some Principles For The Effective Display of Data. SIGGRAPH '79 Proceedings 13, 94-101.

45. Hodge, D.C. (1962). Legibility of Uniform-strokewidth Alphabet: I. Relative Legibility of Upper and Lower Case Letters. Journal of Engineering Psychology 1, 34-46.

46. Schiff, W. (1980). Perception : An Applied Approach. Houghton Miffin Company, Boston.

47. Morvis, J. G. (1979). Using Color in Industrial Control Graphics. Control Engineering (July).

48. Dallimont, R. (1980). Principles of Design for Man-Machine Interfaces in Process Control. In

Man-Machine Interfaces for Industrial Control, Control Engineering (April)(pp 13-34).

49. Hansel, C.E.M. and Stafford, E.M. (1982). Optimum Colour Specifications For Use in VDU Based Systems. IEE International Conference on Man/Machine Systems, Manchester (pp 157-159).

50. Truckenbrod, J.R. (1981). Effective Use of Color in Computer Graphics. SIGGRAPH '81 Proceedings, 15(3), 83-90.

51. Christ, R.E. (1975). Review and Analysis of Color Coding Research for Visual Displays. Human Factors 17(6), 542-570.

52. Carlson, E.D., Giddings, G.M. and Williams, R. (1977). Multiple Colors and Image Mixing in Graphics Terminals. IFIP Congress 77 7, 179-182.

53. DeMars, S.A. (1975). Human factors considerations for the use of color in display systems. NTIS (NASA-TM-X-72196), NASA, J.F. Kennedy Space Centre.

54. Smith, S.L. and Goodwin, N.C. (1971). Blinking Code For Information Display. Human Factors, 13(3), 283-290.

55. Smith, S.L. and Goodwin, N.C. (1972). Another Look At Blinking Displays. Human Factors 14(4), 345-347.

56. Miller. G.A. (1956). The Magical Number Seven, Plus or Minus Two: Some Limits on Our Capacity For Processing Information. Psychological Review 63(2), 81-97.

57. Sproull, R.F. (1979). Raster Graphics For Interactive Programming Environments. SIGGRAPH-ACM, 13(2), 83-89.

58. Herot, C.F., Brown, G.P., Carling, R.T., Friedell,M., Kramlich, D. and Baecker, R.M. (1982) An Integrated Environment For Program Visualization. In Schneider, H.J. & Wasserman, A.I. (eds.) Automated Tools For Information Systems Design, North Holland, Amsterdam, 237-259.

59. Akin, O. (1981). Efficient Computer-User Interface in Electronic Mail Systems. Working Papers in User-Computer Interface, Carnegie-Mellon University.

60. McCann, C. (1978). Graphic Display Interaction. Part II. Information Structure and Basic Functions. AD-A055403/0, Defence and Civil Inst. of Environmental Medicine (Canada).

61. Rowson, J.R. and Salama, B. (1978). Virtual Displays, Electronic Displays, London.

62. Frei, H.P., Weller, D.L. and Williams, R. (1978). Graphics-based Programming-support System. SIGGRAPH-ACM, 12(3), 43-49.

63. Green, T.R., Sime, M.E. and Cornah, A.J. (1979). GUIDO: A software tool to help the average

programmer. MRC Social and Applied Psychology Unit
Report (MRC Social and Applied Psychology Unit, Dept.
of Psychology, University of Sheffield.)

64. Hebalkar, P.G. and Zilles, S.N. (1978). TELL: A System
For Graphically Representing Software Designs. IBM
Research Report RJ2351(31523)9/22/78, IBM Research
Laboratory, San Jose, California.

65. Ng, N. (1978).   A Graphical Editor for Programming
using   Structured   Charts.   IBM   Research   Report
RJ2344(31476)9/19/78, IBM Research Laboratory, San
Jose, California.

66. Leler, W.J. (1980).   Human Vision, Anti-aliasing, and
the Cheap 4000 Line Display. SIGGRAPH '80 Proceedings
14, 308-313.

CHAPTER 9

Dialogue Design:
Characteristics of User Knowledge

Nick Hammond and Philip Barnard

9.1 INTRODUCTION

When people with little or no expertise in computing learn
how to use an interactive software package, they must
typically acquire a good deal of new knowledge in order to
achieve their task objectives in an efficient and effective
manner. They must, for example, learn new ways of
organizing their tasks. Thus, correcting a manuscript using
a word processor as opposed to a typewriter requires rather
different work practices. They must also acquire knowledge
about the operations performed by the system ("How do I
remove a portion of text?"), the circumstances in which the
operations can and cannot be invoked ("Can blank lines be
removed?") and what their consequences are ("Are gaps closed
up?"). In order to invoke the operations, they must learn
to communicate with the system via the interface dialogue.
This in itself requires an understanding not only of the
dialogue syntax but also of how the domain of application is
represented in the computer, in terms of system objects,
their attributes and their relationships. Not least, if
users make errors, they must learn appropriate recovery
procedures.

A Strategy for Research

In this chapter we shall illustrate some of the characteristics of the knowledge and understanding which users call upon in learning to use interactive systems. These illustrations will be drawn from a series of studies we have carried out over the last few years, and include both field observations and laboratory experiments of user performance. The strategy we have adopted is summarised in Figure 9.1. It draws on the experimental, observational and practical techniques of previous research traditions, and to these are added conceptual techniques appropriate to the analysis of user knowledge and cognition. The overall strategy is intended both to increase our scientific understanding of these abilities and to provide practical information for interface design.

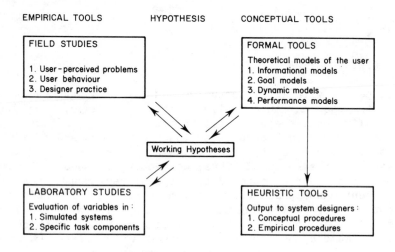

FIG. 9.1 Research strategy: relationship between empirical and conceptual tools.

Within this strategy, observational techniques ("field studies") are used to identify sources of problems at the user interface and to help formulate working hypotheses concerning their underlying causes. These working hypotheses are then evaluated by reference to user performance with simulated interactive systems which allow systematic manipulation of characteristics of the interface itself ("laboratory studies").

The data provided by this kind of experimentation indicate that human performance at the interface results from a subtle interplay of many different underlying factors. These must be interpreted with great care, and there are unlikely to be many simple yet firm guidelines of a cognitive nature for the designer to follow. Accordingly, the strategy calls for a set of conceptual tools for interpreting user behaviour. These form a set of "models" of what the user knows and how users' mental processes call upon that knowledge in their conceptual behaviour ("formal tools"). Again, these models in their full scientific form are likely to prove complex, and are unlikely to be "user-friendly" for systems designers who are not specialists in psychology. In consequence, provision is made in the strategy for the construction of a set of more practical tools for designers to use in the course of system development ("heuristic tools"). These tools translate the technicalities of cognitive psychology into heuristic methods for posing design questions, for determining practical answers in a context-sensitive way and for providing simple empirical techniques for validating design decisions.

This chapter concentrates on the empirical component of the strategy shown in Figure 9.1, and will illustrate the kinds of findings obtained with field studies and laboratory experiments. Section 9.2 will consider some of the characteristics of user learning suggested by field studies of actual system use. In examining these characteristics, we will emphasise general aspects of learning across the different types of knowledge which users must acquire. Section 9.3 will consider evidence from laboratory studies and will focus on a much narrower range of issues associated with learning, specifically those concerned with the learning of command dialogues. We will finish with some comments on the broad constraints on the development of application tools.

9.2 FIELD STUDIES OF SYSTEM USE

The Systems and Users Studied

The evidence to be discussed was derived from three studies of commercially-available interactive systems. The systems were chosen to illustrate different forms of user interface. All were designed for use by personnel with no special

computer training. The first (DB) is a relational database
manipulation and enquiry system. Communication with the
system is achieved by means of a command-language interface
using quasi-mathematical notation to perform operations on
tables of data. Five users of varying experience with the
system performed a number of pre-defined tasks thought to be
typical of everyday usage. Evidence from this study has
been discussed in Hammond, Long, Clark, Barnard and Morton
(1980) and full details of the system together with users'
performance protocols can be seen in Hammond, Long, Clark,
Morton and Barnard (1980). The second system is a business
graphics utility (BG), allowing entities such as line
graphs, bar charts and pie charts to be prepared on a colour
terminal. Communication is via an hierarchical structure of
menu panels incorporating a variety of dialogue styles.
Evidence was collected from the performance of seven novice
users, each observed learning the system for between three
and ten hours. Details of the study are reported in
Hammond, MacLean, Hinton, Long, Barnard and Clark (1983).
The third system (WP) is a word-processing facility designed
for use by secretaries and typists. Communication with this
system made extensive use of abbreviated command "codes".
Evidence on system use comes from the performance of five
novice users each using the system for about eight hours.
Further details may be seen in Hammond, Hinton, Barnard,
MacLean, Long and Whitefield (1984). The initial sessions
for systems BG and WP were based on training courses in the
form of user manuals supplied by the manufacturer. Users
were encouraged to produce a verbal commentary on what they
were doing.

Range of Knowledge Required for System Use

In this section we illustrate potentially important classes
of knowledge required in system learning and use. Figure
9.2 summarises some of these in schematic form   (after
Morton, Barnard, Hammond and Long, 1979). Some classes of
knowledge can be inferred from the nature of the demands of
the task and the system. This 'primary knowledge',
indicated by double borders in Figure 9.2, is required for
successful use of the system and one could imagine an
idealised user who would rely purely on primary knowledge.
As well as having information about the problem in hand, the
user would have to know about physical aspects of the
interface (e.g., how to use the keyboard), about the
interface dialogue (e.g., type "delete" to remove a file),
about the nature of the operations performed by the system

(e.g., what the consequences of "delete" are) and finally about the way aspects of the particular problem area (e.g., word processing) are represented in the computer.

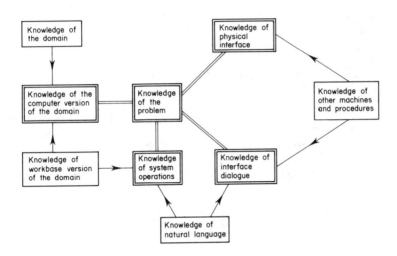

FIG. 9.2 Knowledge required in an interaction. The blocks with double boundaries, connected by double lines, indicate primary information use by the ideal user; other blocks and lines indicate secondary sources of interference and facilitation.

With any real interaction, however, the user will call upon secondary sources of knowledge (boxes with single borders in Figure 9.2) in order to infer primary knowledge which is lacking or uncertain. During learning, these sources of secondary knowledge will exert a strong influence on performance. For example, a user's knowledge of natural language may or may not be compatible with the attributes of the system dialogue, and hence may facilitate or interfere with the learning process. The user will also bring to the interaction general knowledge of the task domain (e.g., editing documents involves textual changes of certain sorts), knowledge of the non-computer "workbase" version (e.g., use of typewriter and correction fluid) and perhaps knowledge of other systems. The next two subsections illustrate the influence on performance of missing primary information and of interfering secondary information (for further examples see Mack, Lewis and Carroll, 1983;

Nickerson, 1981; Norman, 1981).

Parenthetically, it is important to remember that interactive systems are used within organizational and social contexts. While the case studies reported here attempted to reduce the influence of these contextual factors, we have explored elsewhere how potent they are in determining the way the system is viewed and how effectively it is used (Long, Hammond, Barnard, Morton & Clark, 1983).

Examples of Missing Primary Information

The influences of these various classes of knowledge on performance are not typically independent; for example, a poor knowledge of the problem in hand may well influence the learning of the dialogue structure and content, or problems with physical aspects of the system, such as keying, may compound difficulties with more conceptual levels of activity.

Keying was, in fact, a major source of error with all three systems. For example, one user of DB, after typing the command line:

$$*t<-<:s:age<20:>people$$

comments: "Now definitely the worst thing about this is the amount you have to use the shift key." In this example, ten of the 21 transitions between one character and the next involved a change from shift to non-shift or vice versa. Over half of all keying errors observed with the system were instances of the correct key pressed in the wrong shift. Similar examples come from system WP, where all users experienced considerable difficulties operating the SHIFT and SHIFT LOCK keys. Inability to "learn" these somewhat mundane aspects of the interface caused significant increases in problem solution time, and the need to allocate excessive time and attention to keying appeared to degrade planning activity.

Moving to problems arising from knowledge (or lack of it) of the dialogue itself ("representation of the interface dialogue" in Figure 9.2), examples abound in the case studies for all three systems. Thus, one user of system DB is working on the question "What is the precise average age of all the entries in the block called PEOPLE?" After commenting "Right, what is the average age of all the entries? (...) I'll have a go at that", he types:

```
*t<-avg(age,people)
```

The correct solution requires the arguments in the reverse
order: AVG(PEOPLE,AGE). The user's problem here is easy
enough to see. It is more natural to ask "What is the
average age of the entries in PEOPLE?" than "What is the
average for entries in PEOPLE of their ages?". The natural
language representation led the user to put the arguments in
the wrong order.

A more abstract level of knowledge concerns the
conceptualisation of system operations and entities
("representation of system operations" in Figure 9.2).
Thus, users tend to group aspects of the system in ways that
will help them organize their own actions and understand
those of the system. For example, both BG and WP allowed
the user to enter "data" - numbers or text - directly onto
the screen. With both systems, users had problems with the
relationship between information on the screen and its
representation "inside" the system. The default assumption
seemed to be to equate these: once information is on the
screen, it is in the computer; once it has been removed from
the screen, by deletion or overtyping with blanks, it no
longer exists. Unfortunately, this variant of the "What You
See Is What You Get" principle failed to predict system
behaviour in many contexts; for example in system BG,
indirect commands were required to modify numeric data.
(See Chapter 10 for further discussion of this principle.)
Thus one user of System BG, in attempting to remove a column
of numbers by overtyping them with blanks, was utterly
perplexed by the refusal of the system to carry out her
request. In fact, the numbers could only be removed by
typing a one-letter command in a special field on a
different menu panel. The "what you see..." principle had
been inappropriately reinforced in a prior example in the
training course (discussed below: see Table 9.1). The user
induced an abstraction or "model" of this aspect of the
system, appropriate in one context, and attempted to apply
it over a range of other dialogue contexts.

The relations between possible user tasks ("workbase
version of domain" in Figure 9.2) and system function is a
key aspect of interface design. With two of the systems, DB
and BG, users performed a range of typical tasks, and many
difficulties relating task goals to system function were
observed. These involved misunderstandings of how the total
set of functions in the system was structured, of how
task-relevant information was organized and of precisely how
the functions were to be instantiated. One user of BG,
while creating a line graph, wished to change the colour of

the axis lines. From the top level menu (with menu options
labelled "Chart Type", "Data Groups", "Chart Heading",
"X-Axis", "Chart Layout", "Data Color, etc." and "Chart
Notes"), she chose the option "Data Color, etc." This panel
allowed specification of attributes (including colour) of
the data lines, but not of the axis lines. Neither studying
the on-line "help" information nor searching the adjacent
panels (concerning "Chart Layout" and "Chart Notes") could
solve her problem. She eventually conceded defeat. Her
mistake was to assume that "Data Color, etc." defined a main
branch of the menu tree dealing with colour, subsequently
dividing into subsidiary branches for each of the types of
object to be coloured. In fact, the primary split was
between different types of objects, each with separate
branches for specifying colour and other attributes of the
object in question. The user should have returned to the
top level menu and selected the option "X-axis". In this
example, the structure of the user's existing knowledge of
the domain of graph-plotting task goals - an assumption of
the primacy of colour - failed to match the organization of
the task information in the machine.

Examples of the Influences of Pre-Existing Knowledge

Studies of the design process indicate a strong tendency
amongst designers to base preliminary task analyses on the
logical structure of the domain rather than on potential
users' knowledge and goals (see Gould & Lewis, 1983;
Hammond, Jorgensen, MacLean, Barnard & Long, 1983). This
may, of course, be appropriate in many circumstances, and
especially where use is frequent. However, two of the
systems investigated here, DB and BG, were intended for
occasional use. The example concerning colour, cited above,
is an instance of interference from pre-existing knowledge
of the task domain. The message for the designer is not
simply that the menu hierarchy is wrongly structured, since
the evidence comes only from a single user, but rather that
users are likely to assume alternative structures and
accordingly run into problems. A solution in this instance
might be to allow alternative routings within the hierarchy
or alternative dialogue forms, such as keyword entry.
    A further example in system BG concerns navigation around
the large menu hierarchy, and involves interfering
"knowledge of natural language" (see Figure 9.2). A single
function key, called "END", allowed users to retrace their
steps; each time END was invoked, the system returned to the
previously encountered menu panel. This was clearly

described in the training course. However, several users chose this function very rarely. Instead, they pressed a "HOME" key, displaying the top menu panel of the hierarchy, and then re-entered all the choices needed to route down to the desired menu panel. Evidently, the reason was that users were troubled by the normal English meaning of the word "end". Witness the users' comments in de-briefing interviews after the session: "'End' is a funny term to have called it (...) You imagine that 'end' would mean finish a particular process, and if you pressed it, then you would be back to square one. It was something you definitely wouldn't have used unless you had finished what you had been doing." Likewise, another user comments: "I think of 'end of the whole thing', and I think of 'the end product'."

For these users, the normal meaning of "end" not only failed to share semantic features with the action of returning to the previous menu, but it also suggested further actions, ones that they did not want to be performed. The choice of term can only be understood by reference to the implementation concept of "ending" a process at the current level of the hierarchy in order to return to the one above. Here, therefore, the users' prior knowledge - natural language semantics - is seen to interfere with performance.

The Acquisition of New Knowledge

The previous sections have illustrated some of the classes of knowledge listed in Figure 9.2. We now turn to the more active processes of knowledge acquisition. In the initial sessions with an interactive system, the user may face an imposing barrage of new information. People adopt a number of strategies for coping with this initial burden in learning. One strategy is to become highly selective and goal-directed, only taking on board those aspects of the system relevant to the immediate task. Thus Young and Hull (1982), in noting how Viewdata users "fail" to read important information on display frames, hypothesised that users' current goals govern their immediate expectations and hence their strategies for searching information.

The field studies contain many examples supporting the hypothesis that initial learning is strongly directed by the user's immediate goal. If the information encountered cannot be used to satisfy the task in hand, it tends to be ignored. Moreover, this is particularly so in the early stages, when the user may have no suitable framework in which to integrate new information. An example comes from

system BG.   Early in the training course, the user who is
new to the keyboard is advised to refer to an appendix
describing keyboard and display facilities.   Two methods of
control of the cursor are clearly described: movement to
adjacent character cell positions by means of a set of MOVE
keys (up, down, left, right), or movement to an adjacent
input field (a screen location where input will be accepted)
using a number of TAB keys.   The latter was usually the more
efficient means of moving the cursor.   Despite the fact that
all the users read these descriptions, two of them failed to
use the TAB keys until the observer intervened in a later
session.   The reason for this was straightforward: at the
point where reference was made to the appendix, the panel
displayed on the screen contained only one input field.
When the users tried any TAB key, the cursor moved to the
"next" (i.e., the same) input field, its position remaining
unchanged.   These users presumably inferred that the TAB
keys had no observable effect on cursor control.   However,
the MOVE keys operated as expected, and therefore satisfied
the users' immediate goal of moving the cursor.   On the
basis of the hypothesis of goal-directed learning, only
information concerning the MOVE keys was assimilated.
Interestingly, one user happened to be displaying a
multi-field panel while she read the appendix.   She learned
how to use only the TAB keys, and had subsequent problems on
those occasions when the MOVE keys were required.   The point
here is that the immediate goal was to find out how to
control the cursor; users were not concerned with the finer
points of which sort of control was required when.   Learning
one method that "worked" was sufficient to satisfy this
goal.

Another strategy adopted by users to cope with a heavy
learning load is to extrapolate from early examples to new
situations.   Thus, Mack, Lewis & Carroll (1983) have noted
the predilection of novice users for forming explanations
for system behaviour on insufficient evidence, explanations
which they are subsequently loth to reject or modify.   Table
9.1 illustrates part of the training course for system BG.
In this example, the manual is instructing the user on the
consequences of making an error in the context of a panel
which expects numeric rather than alphabetic input.   The
example seems clearly written and users negotiated their way
through it with little difficulty.

TABLE 9.1 Example of interaction between user, training
manual and system.

Manual	User types	System
If you type an invalid value it will be turned to red. Type A after the ==> sign. (It will be green.) Press ENTER. The A is turned red, and a message is displayed.	A ENTER	A green "A" appears. "A" changes from green to red, a warning beep is heard and the message INVALID INPUT is shown.
Overtype the A with a blank, using the space bar. Press ENTER. The message is erased and you return to where you were before.	[space] ENTER	The red "A" disappears. The error message disappears.

From their verbal protocols and subsequent performance,
it was apparent that users extrapolated two important pieces
of information from the exercise. The first was a concept
along the lines that "red means it's wrong, green means it's
right". The second related to the use of the space bar to
erase information on the screen; this suggested that a blank
could generally be used as a rubout key. (This also
reinforced the "what you see..." principle discussed above.)
Unfortunately, both these "knowledge fragments" were only
partially correct, and both caused users subsequent
problems. Since the hardware allowed the colour of fields
on the display to be changed only when the ENTER key (or a
special function key) was pressed, at any one time there was
not necessarily a one-to-one mapping between colour and
correctness. Thus, while the user was in the process of
changing a number of input fields on the screen, some fields
might be green and some red. Some of the green fields might
contain valid data and some might contain invalid data
(typed since the last ENTER and not yet checked by the
software). Moreover, some of the red fields might contain
invalid data and some valid data (cases where the field had
previously given rise to an error and over which the user
had now typed a correct value, remaining red until ENTER was
pressed). This caused confusions, at least until the user
had understood when the colour of fields could be changed.

Even after this, users made remarks such as: "I know that field looks red, but it's really green".

The knowledge fragment concerning the use of the space bar as a "rubout" key caused more far-reaching problems. We can pursue the illustration cited earlier of the user attempting to delete a column of numbers. She first tried removing them by overtyping them with blanks (successfully) and then pressing ENTER. The column remained blank, but an error message "INVALID INPUT" was displayed. Since in this system it was not possible to exit normally from a menu panel when an error state was present, the user tried to re-enter the numbers over the spaces in order to clear the error. She was amazed to see the numbers she typed appearing in red rather than green, violating her assumption that new values were always shown green and could only subsequently be changed from green to red. This caused her to attempt further bizarre explanations of the meaning of green and red fields. Her misunderstanding arose through a combination of the incorrect knowledge which had been initially formed by the exercise in the training manual. The spaces which had overtyped the original numbers were, in fact, rejected as invalid by the system and hence turned "red" (though remaining invisible). Typing over the "red spaces" resulted in her subsequent input being shown red, at least until the next press of the ENTER key. This user's difficulties, then, stemmed from plausible but inappropriate extrapolations from experience gained in working through the exercise in the training course.

The above example illustrates a further aspect of knowledge acquisition that was a common feature of user learning in all three systems. This is that much of the information acquired in early stages of learning is in the form of relatively independent knowledge fragments or packages. This contrasts (but is not necessarily incompatible) with the view held by some designers that user learning is much improved by the provision of a "unitary model" for the system (Hammond et al., 1983). Often, such knowledge fragments will be correct, resulting in appropriate user action. However, when fragments are incorrect, they can inter-relate to cause errors which are difficult for the user to interpret. Thus, the combination of partial misconceptions held by the user in the above example not only made it difficult for her to recover from the error state, but also resulted in her arriving at a yet more wayward explanation of the system's behaviour, rather than learning from her mistakes. It is our impression that much of the early learner's performance is dominated by intertwined misconceptions of this type.

Forms the User's Knowledge May Take

The examples above demonstrate that users rely on a variety of forms of knowledge during the interaction. Some knowledge (single-bordered boxes of Figure 9.2) will exist already within the user's memory, such as the meaning of words (e.g., "end") used in the course of the dialogue. Other information will be encoded in procedural form: for example, which keys are to be pressed in order to move the cursor. Yet further information is likely to be of a more abstract and conceptual nature: an example is the status of screen information in relation to information in the system. These different sources of knowledge enable different sorts of inference to be made about the system and its use. It is unlikely that such diverse information is integrated into a unitary "user model" in any global sense. Rather, the picture that emerges is of a diversity of structure, in two senses. First, users rely on a variety of types of knowledge: procedural and conceptual knowledge are two examples. Secondly, the examples suggest that users' knowledge, at least during early stages of learning, is "packaged" into relatively independent fragments, each with a restricted sphere of applicability. Each fragment can be seen as a partial "user model" in itself.

Young (1981), in analysing users' models of pocket calculators, differentiates between task-action mapping rules and conceptual models. A model based on task-action mapping rules consists of a collection of procedures or actions to be performed in order to reach certain task goals. Thus, the knowledge fragment of a user of system BG "overtype with a space to remove a value from the screen" would be an example of a task-action mapping rule. Evidence from these case studies suggests that such rules may at times be loosely organized in a hierarchical or nested fashion. Simple "molecular" rules may enable users to achieve highly specific subgoals, or they may become chained into a more extended procedure for achieving more "molar" goals. Also apparent were more heuristic task-action mapping rules such as "If in doubt, press ENTER" (in systems DB and WP) or "When lost, return to the HOME panel" (in system BG) which specify recovery or clarification procedures.

In contrast, the form of knowledge embodied in conceptual fragments concerns the relationships amongst system entities. The fragment can be used to infer what action to take in a particular circumstance, and may focus either on the function provided by the system or more on the organization and layout of system information. Also evident are information structures of a more hybrid kind, including knowledge of both system entities and the task domain or other non-computer knowledge. For example, information about dialogue components, such as a set of command terms, is likely to include both system knowledge and non-computer knowledge.

A further form of user knowledge which has received attention in both computing and psychological literature is that of analogy or metaphor (e.g., Carroll & Thomas, 1982; Du Boulay, O'Shea & Monk, 1981; Halasz & Moran, 1982; Tourangeau & Sternberg, 1982). Analogies may be specific or general. An example of the former is their use in pictograms in icon menus (Lodding, 1983). None of the systems described here used specific analogies in this way. However, it is clear from users' verbal protocols that they saw general analogies between the computer system and non-computer devices: "I'm still feeling I'm sitting at a typewriter, that's my hangup." What influence, if any, this knowledge had on performance is less clear. Many errors with system WP could be interpreted as inappropriate extensions of the typewriter analogy: for example, attempting to use the space bar to move the cursor or inappropriately pressing the "required new line" key at the end of every screen line. However, these errors might just have been due to reliance on highly practised procedures (the users of WP were all experienced typists) rather than on a general conceptualisation of the system as a superior class of typewriter.

Halasz and Moran (1982) have argued that analogies are almost always insufficient to explain the operation of a computer system. They may give an overview, but they fail to provide detailed information for the user on what to do. This is not to say that analogies are not powerful communicative devices and hence useful in teaching concepts during early learning. An example comes from a user discussing system DB:

"This is the way I explain it to my staff. We take a copy of our file we want to interrogate... and we dump it in a bucket, say it is a dustbin if you're using a very, very large file like I am. Now that turns out to be your workspace. Well, what happens is as soon as you log on to the system you in fact take a copy of your dustbin and you move it into another dustbin of equal size... so that you end up with your dustbin three-quarters full even before you start manipulating your data... You are able to scour out of your dustbin all the information you didn't want, and pour it back into your first dustbin. Generally in the end you get garbage out of the dustbin anyway."

   This example describes in a memorable way the notion of a
file as a limited container. However, the analogy will be
of little benefit to the user in terms of the details of the
interaction with the system, for example on how exactly to
"scour" unwanted information for the "dustbin". Analogy
seems to derive its major utility from its communicative
function in capturing one or more salient features rather
than by allowing detailed prediction. Chapter 10 discusses
the use of analogy further.

Accessing Learned Knowledge

Once users have formed appropriate knowledge fragments, they
still have the problem of accessing the right one in the
right context. In some cases, the difficulty arises because
the user is unable to identify the appropriate context, a
source of error discussed by Huckle (1980). One user of BG
wished to remove a misplaced heading ("Average Daily
Sunshine") from her graph. She correctly accesses the
appropriate display panel for specifying the heading, and
then types "d" over the heading (which now reads "dverage
Daily Sunshine"), hoping it will disappear. The reason for
this strange action is that the command "d" (for delete) is
used elsewhere in the system, for example for removing a row
or column of numbers from a table. However, its use is not
appropriate for headings, where the "what you see..."
principle holds. Although the user knows about the two
methods of deletion, she has failed to differentiate the
contexts in which they are used.
   A second type of failure to access the right knowledge
results from the tendency to "run off" well learned
procedures with insufficient monitoring of the current
context. Thus one user of DB, half-way through typing a
command string requiring an unusual ordering of elements,
realised he had made an error and commented: "I've done it
again because I've forgotten... I'm always doing that, when
there's one block you go straight into the operator."
Evidently, he had accessed the more commonly used procedure.
He needed no prompting to correct his error. The knowledge
was there, but, seemingly, he could not mobilise it at the
right time. These classes of error could be reduced by
reducing the numbers of system and task contexts or by
providing appropriate cues signalling the context.

Conclusions from Field Studies

The evidence presented is based on a small number of users interacting with a smaller number of systems. As with any observational study of this sort, claims have the status of hypotheses which require more rigorous investigation. Given this caveat, some general points can be made. In communicating with interactive computer systems, as in dealing with many other complex tasks, it seems that people call upon a diverse range of knowledge and skills. No single or unitary user model would seem to be able to capture this diversity. However, where unifying principles or local models are appropriately abstracted, they may help to guide learning. Different representations allow different inferences to be drawn, and relatively distinct fragments of knowledge can be used to deal with different aspects of the interaction. For novice users, at least, prior knowledge will have a marked influence on their conceptualisations of the system. In order to cope with new information during early stages, learning may be highly selective and be driven by immediate goals, and users may form explanations for system behaviour on insufficient evidence. One consequence is that early examples in documentation are extremely potent, and should be both designed with discretion and evaluated on potential users. Following initial learning, users may fail to differentiate between environments and hence perform actions correctly but in the wrong contexts. In any one interaction, then, the particular information called upon and the particular strategy used will depend on the user's predisposition, on his understanding of the current state of the system and task as well as on the nature of the dialogue itself.

As well as allowing general conclusions of this sort, the studies also suggest more specific hypotheses concerning the influences of particular classes of user knowledge on performance. We can illustrate these by reference to Figure 9.2. First, consider the influence of the user's knowledge of natural language on the interface dialogue. The hypotheses that the order of elements in natural language will influence command entry follows from the instance of a user of DB ordering a command sequence on the basis of the utterance "average age of all the entries in the block people". Likewise, the hypothesis that knowledge of the every day meanings of command terms will affect developing knowledge of the system operations follows from the difficulties to users of BG caused by the term "end". Performance was also influenced by knowledge of other machines and procedures. The expectation that system BG should respect the "What you see..." principle is an instance of such knowledge: the display of information on a machine normally reflects its internal state. We can therefore hypothesise that the user will expect syntactic and semantic consistencies within the system which are compatible with their prior knowledge. Prior knowledge of the "workbase" version of the task also had its role in influencing how the user viewed the way task information was organised in the system. An example is the user who expected "colour" to be a high-level node in the menu structure of system BG. In addition, the content of early examples (e.g., "red means error") had their influence on subsequent knowledge of the system operations and dialogue.

9.3 EXPERIMENTAL STUDIES OF SYSTEM USE

The preceding section illustrated how different forms of user knowledge determine the course of dialogue exchanges, and how working hypotheses concerning the causes of difficulties and attributes of the learning process can be formulated. The wider research strategy (Figure 9.1) made provision for these hypotheses to be investigated further in systematic laboratory studies. These studies manipulate aspects of the user interface and monitor the consequences of these manipulations on user performance. The objectives of this type of study are to elaborate the working hypotheses and to develop a theoretical understanding of user behaviour. These in turn will support the development of principles of user cognition which can be applied in the design of future systems.

In order to perform such laboratory studies, it is necessary to meet three practical criteria. First, a laboratory study must have face validity: a working interactive dialogue has to be implemented in a realistic task environment. Nevertheless, for many purposes the experimental system can be simplified, so long as it represents a sample of the full range of the real system. Second, the laboratory system must allow manipulation of characteristics of the user interface. This may require the interface to be constrained in order to restrict and manage the number of variables which could potentially influence user performance. Third, the system must allow appropriate behavioural measurement, such as of times for performing dialogue exchanges, for errors committed and for frequency of referral to additional information ('help'). These should allow the description of user strategies and how often they are recruited. Without such detailed

measurement, specific results are often interpretable in
only the most general terms.

This section will illustrate how systematic manipulation
of interface characteristics in experiments can reveal major
differences in user performance. These performance
differences provide additional clues to the factors which
complement and extend the evidence from field studies. The
range of coverage in this section will be more restricted
and will concentrate specifically on the properties of
different types of user-computer dialogue.

As in the preceding section, we will illustrate points by
reference to a number of studies. In each of these we have
monitored the performance of novice users in the initial
stages of learning interactive systems. The studies
systematically manipulated variables concerned with command
structures and vocabularies under different styles of
dialogue. The individual experimental manipulations were
based in part on prior analyses of interface attributes and
in part on the products of the field studies. For example,
in the preceding section we illustrated difficulties arising
from structural aspects of dialogues, such as with the
ordering of elements in a command string with system DB or
the organization of menu panels in system BG, and from the
content of the dialogue, such as with the interpretation of
command terms (e.g., "end" in BG) or of system objects
(e.g., data entry fields). We also illustrated the
influence of the content of early examples or instructions
on later performance (as in BG).

Dialogue Style, Structure and Content

For many dialogues, the exchange of information can be
characterised in terms of its 'style', 'structure' and
'content'. We shall use the term style to refer to
differences in the character and control of the information
exchange. The use of command languages, menu selection,
question-answering, query-by-example, and analogue spatial
control, represent different styles of dialogue. In the
case of question-answer dialogues the computer system may
"control" the dialogue by asking the user a particular
question requiring a more or less constrained response. In
contrast, with a command-oriented system the user may
"control" the dialogue by issuing a command to which the
system responds. Obviously, the primary locus of dialogue
control may change within a particular exchange - as, for
example, when a user issues a command and the system
responds with a sequence of prompts requesting parameter

information. The critical point is that we need a concept such as dialogue style in order to characterise the nature of the communicative demands imposed by dialogues of different types.

The concepts of dialogue structure and dialogue content will be used in a straightforward way. We shall use the term structure to refer to the formal description of dialogue elements in terms of their constituent structure together with their ordering within and between dialogue exchanges. Likewise the concept of dialogue content will be used to describe the semantics of the information exchanged - in terms of the user's general knowledge of the nature and consequences of computer representations and actions.

The style, structure and content of human-computer dialogues are areas in which the decisions of software designers often have a major positive or negative impact on the usability of their products. One obvious result of the move towards user-friendly systems is a demand on behavioural research to establish guidelines for taking decisions concerning the style, structure and content of human-computer dialogues for different applications and user populations. Questions which frequently arise include: is it more appropriate to use a menu-oriented system or a command-oriented system for this application or that user population? (Style); how should we order the elements of dialogue? (Structure); or, what kind of command vocabulary is appropriate? (Content). We shall argue that simple answers to questions of this sort are unlikely to be forthcoming. The reason for this is that human cognition is remarkably flexible. Obviously, factors such as the style, structure and vocabulary will undoubtedly all have consequences for ease of use. However, as the observational studies indicate, the detailed consequences depend not only on the formal properties of the dialogue itself but also on the detailed 'cognitive context' in which a particular exchange occurs.

Cognitive Context

The term context has had many different uses in psychology and linguistics (e.g., Clark & Carlson, 1981). Our use of the term "cognitive context" represents an attempt to move the emphasis of analysis away from approaches which focus on isolated attributes of the explicit dialogue. Rather, we would prefer to see the emphasis move towards an analysis which focuses on user cognition. Thus, the cognitive context of a dialogue exchange includes mental representations and cognitive processes relating not only to the explicit structure and content of the dialogue but also to the general cognitive demands imposed by the system. These include information extracted from the wider task environment, the specific question or problem motivating an exchange and the cognitive strategies mobilised in the course of learning, use and remembering.

The experiments which follow examine relationships amongst these and similar factors concerned with the structure and content of dialogue exchanges. Each of the illustrations will focus on different aspects of the cognitive context in which the interaction between user and system is carried out. Fuller details of the individual experiments are reported in Barnard and Hammond, 1982; Barnard, Hammond, Morton, Long and Clark, 1981; Barnard, Hammond, MacLean and Morton, 1982; Hammond, Barnard, Clark, Morton and Long, 1980; Hammond, Morton, Barnard, Long and Clark, in preparation.

Experiments 1 and 2: Cognitive Context
in Command-Argument Sequences

A style of dialogue, particularly common in certain types of text and file manipulating applications, requires users to enter a command verb such as DELETE or INSERT followed by one or more arguments, such as the entity to be deleted and the place it is to be deleted from; for example DELETE <FILENAME> <DIRECTORY>. Our first illustration is drawn from a series of studies designed to examine the effects of alternative ways of structuring this type of command string. One hypothesis suggested by the observational studies is that the arguments should be ordered in the same way as they would be in natural language. An alternative hypothesis is that a consistent ordering, where the common argument either always comes first or always comes second, might be most effective.

In the task used in these experiments "coded messages" had to be decyphered. This required the manipulation of the messages using various commands. All the commands referred to a common argument, a "message-identifier". In a real system such as a text editor the corresponding common argument might be a line number.

Table 9.2 illustrates two different ways of ordering the command strings used. The examples on the left hand side have the common argument consistently in the same position, in this case as the first argument. In the experiment different groups of subjects had the common argument

consistently first and consistently second. The examples on
the right hand side of Table 9.2 use the "natural language"
principle of placing the direct object of the command verb
before the indirect object, such as SAVE (the) message (in
the) file and DELETE (the) digit (from the) message. With
this kind of rule the position of the common argument varies
from command to command. The use of a simple positional
rule, then, provides a way of minimising demands on the
user's memory for order. In contrast, placing the direct
object immediately after the command verb might increase
demands on the user's memory for order but would have the
advantage of being compatible with users' natural language
predispositions. Obviously it is not possible for most
command sets to use both principles at once - they conflict.

TABLE 9.2 Two possible ways of ordering command strings
when all the commands involve a common argument.

	Common Argument First		Direct Object First
SEARCH	Message Id, File Number	SEARCH	File number, Message Id
TRIM	Message Id, Segment size	TRIM	Message Id, Segment Size
REPLACE	Message Id, Code number	REPLACE	Message Id, Code number
INVERT	Message Id, Group Size	INVERT	Group Size, Message Id
DELETE	Message Id, Digit	DELETE	Digit, Message Id
SAVE	Message Id, Reference no	SAVE	Message Id,Reference no

(Message Id = Message Identifier)

We studied these alternative principles in a laboratory
task which required users to decode secret messages by
issuing a sequence of six commands. Figure 9.3 shows an
example display. The system prompted the user as to which
command to issue next by highlighting the required command.
Thus the users' task was relatively simple - they had to
remember the identity of the arguments required for each of
the six commands and the order in which the arguments were
to be entered.

During training (as in Figure 9.3) users were also given
information about how to enter the arguments. Following
training, if they couldn't remember what to do, they could
display the instructions again. The number of times "help"
information was consulted provided one measure of how
quickly they were learning. Times and errors were also
logged. We compared the two forms of positionally
consistent rule for placing the common argument with two
rules involving variable placement of the common argument.

```
*** ATHENE DECODER ***

--------------------------------------------------------------------
 Search        Trim        Replace      Invert      Delete      Save
--------------------------------------------------------------------
 Invert groups of characters in the message
 (Specify group size and message identifier)
 --) invert group size, message identifier (ENTER)
--------------------------------------------------------------------
 Message identifier: 33   Code number: 19   File number: 5   Groupsize: 3
--------------------------------------------------------------------
                        Current message state
      GEPUSA :S5A5EHT SNO5T5R EMO5A UGU5TSR* FE5ERE5CN 5E4
--------------------------------------------------------------------
 invert 3 33

--------------------------------------------------------------------

--------------------------------------------------------------------
```

FIG. 9.3 Experiment 1: Example display.

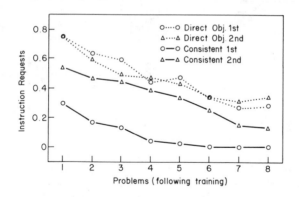

FIG. 9.4 Experiment 1.: Use of instructions ('help').

These involved the "natural" language principle of placing the direct object immediately after the command verb: VERB direct object, indirect object (DO 1st); or its less "natural" inverse: VERB indirect object, direct object (DO

2nd). The data for instruction requests following initial training are given in Figure 9.4. Data for times and errors showed similar patterns.

Essentially, what these results show is that when the common argument occurred in the first position, performance was generally superior compared with the other three types of structure. The important point is that having a consistent argument position enhanced performance when the common argument came first but not when the common argument came second. Thus, we cannot attribute enhanced performance solely to better memory for argument order as a consequence of the presence of a clear positional rule for the common argument.

There was no average difference between the command sets involving the natural language "compatible" order of placing the direct object first and the "incompatible" order of placing the direct object second. In this case natural language compatibility did not appear to enhance learning relative to its inverse. Possible explanations of these results are considered in more detail in the full report (Barnard et al., 1981).

```
------------------------------ATHENE DECODER------------------------------
Command options: append  erase  fill  help  list  prepose  regroup
                 replace  reverse  select  substitute  unite  update
--------------------------------------------------------------------------
Zone:    1-Western Europe    2-North America    3-Communist block
Source: Washington  Day: Tuesday    Security: Restricted    Code value:

Command list enters the city names in the source column
Command is: list table-number zone-number (ENTER)


        Table 10              Table 11              Table 12
  Transmission wavelengths   Adjustment values     Code values

  :Source Mo Tu Th Fr Sa Su:  :Mo Tu Th Fr Sa Su:  :Mo Tu Th Fr Sa Su:
  :1:     -  -  -  -  -  - :  :-  -  -  -  -  - :  :19 84 10 66 31 27:
  :2:     -  -  -  -  -  - :  :-  -  -  -  -  - :  :41 60 45 76 34 57:
  :3:     -  -  -  -  -  - :  :-  -  -  -  -  - :  :15 62 97 71  4 79:
  :4:     -  -  -  -  -  - :  :-  -  -  -  -  - :  :44 38 18  9 55 83:

  list 10 2
```

FIG. 9.5 Experiment 2: Example display.

The structure of the command string clearly exerted a major influence on the ease of using our simple interactive system for decoding messages. But if such findings were to be translated into guidelines for ease of use we would want at least to ensure that structural findings would generalise to other situations. Accordingly, in a second study we again contrasted the two rules involving a consistent position for arguments common to subsets of commands. However, in this second study, the users' task was made more complex in three respects: the user was required actively to select commands rather than being prompted by the system; the command set was expanded from six to twelve and the system was made operationally more complex - the user modified some code tables before going on to decode the message (see Figure 9.5). It was assumed that these changes would force the users to remember not only argument indentities and order but also the command operations themselves (for full details see Hammond et al., 1980 and 1984). As with the previous experiment, prompts were given during initial training but were available only by explicit request (a "help" command) during the later trials.

TABLE 9.3 General and specific commands.

Command Term		
General	Specific	Argument Labels
USE	LIST	Table no, Zone no
CALL	SELECT	Table no, Source no
GET	FILL	Table no, Wavelength
CHANGE	REPLACE	Table no, Adjustment value
TRANSFORM	SUBSTITUTE	Message no, Code no
RESET	REGROUP	Message no, Code no
EDIT	ERASE	Message no, Element no
MOVE	PREPOSE	Message no, Element no
PERMUTE	REVERSE	Message no, Segment no
RELATE	UNITE	Message no, Segment no
MODIFY	UPDATE	Message no, Security rating
INSERT	APPEND	Message no, Security rating

In this experiment there were no inconsistent command orders but instead two different command sets were compared. For each type of argument structure half the subjects had a command set of relatively specific verbs such as "LIST, ERASE, REPLACE", as had been the case in the earlier

experiment.   The other half of the subjects in each
condition had a command set of more general verbs such as
"USE, EDIT, CHANGE".   The more specific verbs implicitly
provide more semantic information concerning the nature of
the operations they perform (see Table 9.3).

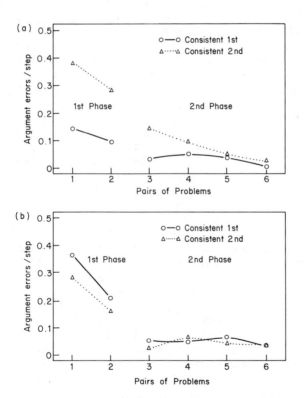

FIG. 9.6 Experiment 2: Argument errors for (a) specific
command terms and (b) general command terms.

Some results from this experiment are shown in Figure 9.6. With the specific command vocabulary (Figure 9.6a), we again found an advantage for placing the common arguments in the first argument position.   However, the main advantage was confined to initial training where the prompts were present (Pairs 1 and 2).   As soon as our users were required to select commands for themselves, the effect of the structure of the comand string diminished rapidly.   When the general command verbs were used (Figure 9.6b), there were no statistically reliable advantages for placing the common argument first.   In short, the kind of structural effect observed in the first experiment appears to be restricted to a context in which the system is prompting or guiding the user over which command to enter, and then only a system employing a relatively specific command vocabulary.

In certain respects these results are reminiscent of early psycholinguistic research where effects of the structural complexity of sentences disappeared when semantic or contextual cues resolved ambiguities. However, the fact that the findings of the experiment do not generalise across all task conditions should not be taken to mean that the users' behaviour is unsystematic or unprincipled. It simply means that any coherent analysis of the usability of different forms of dialogue structure must take into account an analysis of the cognitive demands of the task being performed.   In short, the cognitive context differs between the experiments. For example, command selection and the use of a general command vocabulary could be interpreted as requiring additional active mental processing of the more semantic aspects of the way in which the interactive system works. According to some theorists (e.g., Craik & Lockhart, 1972) this would result in a more elaborate memory trace which would have different consequences for performance than tasks which emphasise purely structural learning.   The fundamental point is that these consequences can only be understood by reference to the cognitive context in which a dialogue exchange occurs rather than to a simple analysis of the formal properties of the command structure. In the case of the data we have illustrated, the cognitive consequences derive in part from attributes of the dialogue style (the extent to which a user is prompted) and in part from its detailed structure and context.

Experiment 3: Cognitive Context in Menu Dialogue

The first two studies involved entry of command strings. We have obtained similar kinds of influences of task demands and entry order with a style of dialogue in which users select command verbs and objects from menus. From these studies we shall focus on illustrations of how information available to users in a task context can bias their performance. Users were required to answer a sequence of preset questions on the basis of information stored in a data base. The information was structured into a set of objects (FILES, LISTS, TABLES, STATEMENTS, ITEMS) which could be operated upon by an equal number of functions (DISPLAY, COMPARE, DELETE, INSERT, REPLACE).

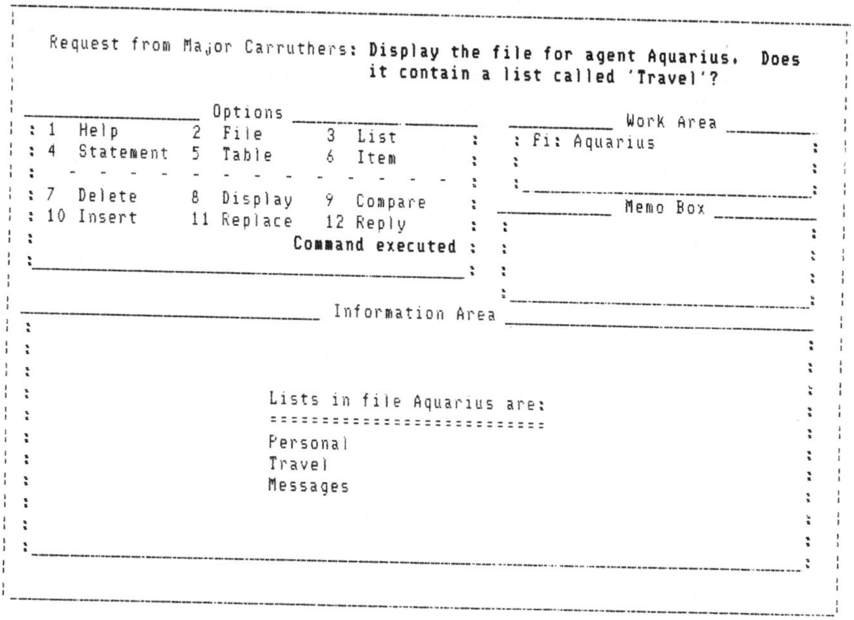

FIG. 9.7 Experiment 3: Example display.

Using these functions and objects, users were asked questions such as "Display the file for agent Aquarius. Does it contain a list called travel?" The question could be answered by selecting a function (e.g., DISPLAY) and an object (e.g., FILE) from a menu. For the first ten questions, the answer would be derived after a single transaction of this type (e.g., DISPLAY FILE). The last four questions were more complex and required two such transactions (e.g., DISPLAY FILE; COMPARE LIST). As with the previous experiments, users could obtain instructional information by selecting "HELP". In one version of this task users were allowed to choose functions and objects in any order from a single unified menu. This is shown in Figure 9.7.

Under these circumstances we manipulated three variables. For half the users the menu was structured with the functions (delete, etc.) above the objects (files, etc.) and for the remaining subjects the objects were located above the functions. Likewise, for half the users the initial experimental "briefing" provided information primarily about the functions (i.e., what you could do with the system). For the other half of the users they were provided with information about the objects (i.e., the organisation of information within the data base). This manipulation is a "content" variable. Additionally, half of the questions for any one subject mentioned the function first (as in the example given above) and half mentioned the object first (e.g., "the file for agent Aquarius should be displayed..."). There were thus a variety of sources of information available to the user which might bias the exact way in which the dialogue would be conducted (initial briefing instructions, menu structure, question structure).

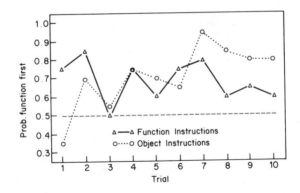

FIG. 9.8 Experiment 3: Probability of entering function first under free menu selection.

Figure 9.8 shows the effect of the content variable provided by the initial briefing instructions. The measure here reflects the order in which the two dialogue components (function and object) were selected. The dashed line indicates an equal probability of specifying either component first.   Since most of the points lie above this line, there is an overall bias towards a dialogue in which the function is selected before the object.   This conforms to normal imperative syntax, as in "close the door". However, this is modified by the briefing instructions. Those initially informed about the objects in the system tend to select objects first, other things being equal.   In addition the cross-over effect (statistically reliable) would indicate that users were learning more about the uninstructed components as experience with the system progressed.

Similarly, other things being equal, users tended to make their first selection from an item in the upper part of the menu and they tended to select as the first element of a dialogue transaction the item mentioned first in the question posed at the top of the display.   Both of these latter findings are consistent with left-to-right and top-to-bottom reading strategies.   Thus, with this free selection style of dialogue, information available in the user's memory from the initial briefing and structure of information on the display both played an important role in determining the dialogue actually selected.

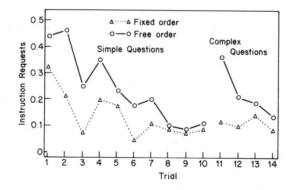

FIG. 9.9 Experiment 3: Use of instructions for fixed and free choice.

In another version of the same task we introduced a formal structure.   The main menu was broken into two and

users were forced to select first from a menu of functions
then from a menu of objects or <u>vice</u> <u>versa</u>.   Under these
circumstances, both initial briefing and the structure of
the   question   had   less   marked   effects   on   performance.
Furthermore,   the   order   of   selection   FUNCTION-OBJECT   or
OBJECT-FUNCTION had virtually no effect on performance.   It
might   have   been   expected   that   the   natural   imperative
ordering of FUNCTION-OBJECT (as in "Close the door") would
have been easier than the less natural OBJECT-FUNCTION order
(as in "The door should be closed"), which conveys a rather
different meaning.   However, as with the experiment using
command argument structures, use of a natural as opposed to
an unnatural order had little effect.

The nature of the task itself had an important effect.
Figure 9.9 illustrates the difference in performance between
the free selection of the first version of the task and the
fixed order of selection imposed in the second version of
the task.   In all cases the same information was entered for
the   same   questions   -   only   the   order   constraint   differed.
The figure shows that users initially required more "HELP"
when they were free to choose functions and objects in any
order.   This difference rapidly diminishes across the first
ten questions, but dramatically reappears when the more
complex   two-transaction   questions   are   introduced.
Apparently, under conditions of free choice the users had
not acquired the same level of knowledge as those in the
fixed   order   of   entry   condition.   The   latter   groups
"transferred" more readily to the more complex problems.

Thus, as with the command-argument experiments, the
demands   imposed   by   the   dialogue   changed   patterns   of
performance.   Under conditions of free choice, contextual
information guided the course of the dialogue, but users
apparently learn less efficiently than when the system
itself has more control over the structure of the dialogue.
It is entirely plausible that when the user has to take
decisions about the order of elements in the dialogue, they
may rely on relatively superficial sources of information
and   knowledge.   On the other hand, when the dialogue order
is fixed by the system, users may have more cognitive
resources available to learn about what the system is doing
- and hence transfer the skill readily to the more complex
problems.   Once again, the structural effects in dialogue
and their consequences appear to depend not so much on the
formal properties of the structure of the dialogue but on
the cognitive context in which the dialogue exchanges occur.

Experiment 4: Cognitive Context and Command Selection

In the previous two sets of illustrations, the main focus was on the ordering of elements in a dialogue sequence. The final illustration is drawn from an experiment in which we looked in more detail at the consequences of using command names with different attributes. We again studied performance with command terms with relatively general meaning and those with relatively specific meaning. Names with relatively specific meaning should provide additional semantic clues as to the precise nature of the function actually performed. The experimental task involved users doing text-editing operations to eliminate errors in well known proverbs. An example display is shown in Figure 9.10.

```
T-------------------------------------------------T
|    _____COMMAND OPTIONS_____         |
|   |  (Type 'help' for further details)  |       |
|   |                                     |        |
|   |  append   cancel    end      fetch  |        |
|   |  front    insert    join     prefix |        |
|   |  rubout   send      split           |        |
|   |------------------------------------- |       |
|   |        TARGET SENTENCE              |        |
|   |   a stitch in time saves nine      |        |
|   |------------------------------------- |       |
|   |   sti tch in a time xpqy aves nine  |        |
|   |   sti tch in a time aves nine       |        |
|   | >  a sti tch in time aves nine    < |        |
|   |                                     |        |
|   |_____|        |
|                                                  |
|           Type your next command:                |
|  join_                                           |
|_____|
```

FIG. 9.10 Experiment 4: Example display.

Users had either a general command vocabulary or a specific command vocabulary and they were also trained under different task conditions. In this chapter we shall only refer to the effects of type of vocabulary. The type of vocabulary did not interact with the nature of the task. The general approach was similar to the previous experiments except that in this study users were tested twice, learning the text editing task in the first session and returning two weeks later for a memory test and a second interactive session.

During initial learning the type of command vocabulary did not influence the average time taken to correct each proverb (Figure 9.11a).

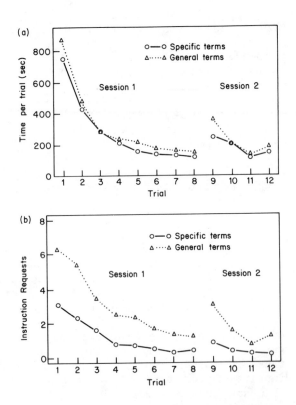

FIG. 9.11 Experiment 4: (a) Time per trial and (b) use of instructions for general and specific terms.

However, users of the general command vocabulary more often requested "HELP" (in the form of a listing of definitions of the command actions; Figure 9.11b). Examination of the more detailed pattern of performance indicated that, although both vocabularies resulted in comparable solution times, users distributed that time in different ways. The users of the general command vocabulary appeared to adopt the strategy of consulting "HELP" very frequently and after brief delays from the onset of any particular problem. In contrast, users of the specific command vocabulary appeared to spend more time actively considering what to do. When these users did decide to consult "HELP" they spent more time over this decision and then, on average, spent more time reading the definitions. Thus, the types of command vocabulary precipitated different strategies for learning. Furthermore, the strategy adopted by the users of the specific command terms resulted in better memory for the command operations two weeks later.

Characteristics of the User and Strategies of Use

The strategy differences were not a function only of the type of command set. In this experiment we also monitored individual differences in the user sample. Two tests were used to classify the individual user - a test in which the users had to derive a word from a definition, such as "To make up one's mind, to resolve or settle a question" (the target is "to decide"). This test probably taps verbal intelligence. The second test was the Cognitive Failures Questionnaire - which was developed to assess failures in everyday life of perception, memory and action (Broadbent, Cooper, FitzGerald & Parkes, 1982). This requires answers to twenty-five questions concerning how frequently the respondent forgets things like names, appointments or what they are currently doing, as well as aspects as their distractibility or clumsiness. Performance on these two tests does not correlate ($r=-.131$). The results of our analysis showed that people who were good at the definitions test consulted the interactive "HELP" facility less often than those who were not so good ($r=-.382$, $p<.01$ for session 1; $r=-.327$, $p<.05$ for session 2). Possibly the smarter people were adopting an active learning strategy. People who were high on cognitive failure also consulted the "HELP" facility less often ($r=-.251$, $.1>p>.05$ for session 1; $r=-.414$, $p<.01$ for session 2). Perhaps this was due to a failure to capitalise on available information.

The fundamental point here is that the different types of

users appeared to be adopting different cognitive strategies which exerted a major influence on the course of their individual dialogues with the interactive system. The different types of command name had an effect over and above these individual differences in cognitive strategy. However, for the most part, the demands imposed by the content of the vocabulary simply seemed to modulate the individual user's predispositions for controlling the exchange of information in a particular way.

Summary of Experimental Evidence

In this section we have described a range of findings which illustrate various effects on usability of dialogues of different styles. The findings confirm that aspects of the structure and content of the dialogue are critical determinants of ease of use.

The fact that there are parallel findings for command entry and menu selection could be seen as encouraging for the development of guidelines such as "natural language characteristics do not necessarily enhance learning" or "fixed structures can enhance learning and performance". However, this would miss the principal implications of the findings. Such summary statements only capture limited aspects of the data. The important implication of these experiments is that the structure and content of the dialogue would never provide a sufficient or complete analysis of usability. The experiments illustrate not only how the effects of structural and content variables inter-relate but also how they depend on other considerations. These include: (i) the precise task demands imposed by the style of dialogue, (ii) information available in a current display, (iii) the specific question or problem motivating a dialogue exchange, (iv) the kind of initial briefing received by users and (v) the kinds of cognitive strategies adopted by users to learn and use the particular type of dialogue. For convenience, we have identified these components as contributing to the cognitive context in which a dialogue exchange occurs. This contrasts with a formal analysis of the attributes of the dialogue which, taken in isolation, would fail to identify major sources of user difficulty.

9.4 APPLICATION OF FINDINGS

Figure 9.1 illustrates a long-term strategy for translating research findings into design tools. Essentially, the strategy has two major requirements. First, it requires means for capturing the characteristics of users' knowledge and cognitive processes and for charting the complex relationships amongst them. Since user behaviour is complex and varied, we have aimed to collect converging evidence from a range of field and laboratory studies. In the above two sections we have focussed on this requirement.

There is a further requirement of the strategy, however. This is to provide means for understanding, interpreting and applying the empirical findings. The results we have reported show that there are not going to be simple guidelines for ease of use based solely on analyses of structure and content of the dialogue. The attributes of the cognitive context in which dialogue exchanges occur must also be taken into consideration. In the longer term, then, user performance will best be predicted by reference to psychological models which take full account of the wider cognitive context, including user's knowledge and cognitive processes (the "formal tools" in Figure 9.1). The evidence reported here, and from many field and laboratory studies conducted elsewhere, forms the basis for the development of such models. Without these models, we run the risk of formulating principles for the usability of dialogue which do not accurately reflect the richness of users' cognitive behaviour.

The immediate demands of system design cannot, of course, wait for such models to be completed and there already exist a variety of heuristic tools which are of direct use to the designer for thinking about task and interface design. For example, one may construct formal representations of the user interface before the design is actually implemented (e.g., Jacob, 1983; Moran, 1981b; Reisner, 1982; Roach & Nickson, 1983). Thus, Moran's "Command Language Grammar" (CLG) proposes a top-down design process in which a conceptual model of the system is first specified and then a command language is created to communicate with it. The CLG aims to describe a putative user's mental model of the system. These techniques can result in a sound basis for system design, but they are only a starting point, and in many instances the designer will still have to rely on less formal decision-making methods (see also Chapter 10).

A further conceptual approach is to use procedures which predict relevant characteristics of user performance in restricted situations, such as in routine text-editing (e.g., Card, Moran & Newell, 1983). Thereby, the effectiveness of alternative putative designs can be compared without actually building and testing the interface. These procedures rely on simplified but detailed models of the user as a processor of information termed "engineering models" or "calculational models". As yet, this approach is only available in certain limited domains, and the models assume practised and error-free performance. Even within these constraints, the models have been criticised, and it has been proposed that more complex models based explicitly on cognitive processes are necessary (Allen & Scerbo, 1983).

These tools, then, are a start in the development of design methods which incorporate critical aspects of the user's knowledge and cognitive processes. In the absence of models which fulfil all our requirements, it is certainly important for the designer to develop a sensitivity to the needs of the user in terms of his cognitive limitations and competence. (That is, after all, one of the aims of this book.) In this spirit, Barnard (1983) has proposed that designers be provided with integrated "packages" of information which can serve as think pieces on particular design issues. These might consist of a psychological principle with exceptions, examples and supporting empirical data. Such integrated sets of information might form the basis of an expert system to support design decisions.

In addition to the use of these conceptual tools, it is often also important to collect behavioural evidence as part of the design process. A number of empirical procedures are available to the designer, for example using observational and experimental methodologies of the sorts illustrated here, or comparing user performance with existing "benchmark" standards (e.g., Roberts & Moran, 1983). The advantages and disadvantages of these will not be discussed here; details can be found in Chapter 5 and the articles referred to above. We will just consider and, we hope, counter some of the arguments raised against empirical testing.

Designers working within commercial constraints commonly raise two objections to empirical tests: testing requires the system to be almost complete, at which stage advice will be too late, and testing takes too long; it is costly relative to its benefits. As Gould & Lewis (1983) point out, the first objection is just not true: one can do a considerable amount of user testing even before a single line of code has been written. Paper and pencil techniques were used to evaluate alternative forms of syntax for IBM's

Query-by-Example system (Thomas & Gould, 1975). Using hybrid computer and human simulations, Gould, Conti and Hovanycez (1983) have extensively investigated characteristics of a "listening typewriter" even though such a device is still well beyond our present technical competence. Such approaches can provide information about components of system use and about user understanding of task characteristics which will help the designer to start off on the right track.

As regards the second argument, it is certainly true that user testing takes time and other resources, but in all too many cases its benefits may not be seriously considered at all (Hammond et al., 1983). Detecting and fixing an unusable interface feature late in the design cycle may take very much longer. With the increasing market for application systems, too much faith in the designer's powers of reasoning and too little in the quirks of user behaviour may be a costly mistake. There are certainly a number of documented cases where user testing with prototypes, and the integration of findings into the final product, have resulted in measurable and large improvements in user performance (see, for example, Savage, Habinek & Barnhart, 1982).

9.5 SUMMARY

To learn to use a complex interactive system, people have to acquire a good deal of new knowledge. They must attempt to organise and to structure their knowledge so that it conforms to the requirements of the system. In the first part of the chapter, we report findings from observational studies of novices learning to use computer systems. The results illustrate the complexity and diversity of human learning; users call upon many sources of information and represent their knowledge in many ways. Both general and specific hypotheses concerning the nature of user knowledge are drawn. In the second part of the chapter, we explore some of these hypotheses by reference to a number of experimental studies of interface dialogue. Taken as a whole, the results suggest that analyses of the ease of use of a system must take into account not only the nature of the interface dialogue itself, but also the detailed cognitive context in which a particular exchange occurs. The cognitive context of an interaction includes the general cognitive demands imposed by the system, information extracted from the wider task environment, the specific question or problem motivating the exchange and the cognitive strategies mobilised in the course of learning and use.

9.6 FURTHER READING

Further information on the psychological aspects of computer dialogues will be found in Bailey (1982), Card, Moran, & Newell (1983) and Shneiderman (1980). The following edited collections are also useful primary sources of information: Green, Payne & van der Veer (1983); Hartson (In Press); Smith & Green (1980) and Thomas & Schneider (1983).

Much of the recent work is reported in the proceedings of three international conferences:

(i)   Human Factors in Computer Systems.   Gaithersburg, MD, March 1982. ACM: New York

(ii)   CHI '83: Human Factors in Computing Systems. Boston, December 1983. ACM: New York. (Issued as special issue of SIGCHI Bulletin.)

(iii) Interact '84: First   IFIP   Conference   on Human-Computer Interaction.   London, September 1984. Shackel, B. (ed.) North Holland: Amsterdam.

CHAPTER 10

User Interface Design:
Generative User Engineering Principles

Harold Thimbleby

10.1 INTRODUCTION

Design is difficult, and the design of interactive computer
systems is especially difficult. This chapter reviews some
of the reasons why. Even though there is no general and
systematic design procedure, consciously knowing some of the
difficulties in the design process will help designers avoid
them.

One way to facilitate design is actively to employ a
"user model". This concept is developed and leads to the
idea of 'generative user-engineering principles'. These
principles are assertions about interactive system behaviour
and have equivalent colloquial forms. Generative
user-engineering principles make a promising contribution to
the design of acceptable user interfaces, because they
effectively bridge the conceptual gap between designer and
user. In its colloquial form a generative user-engineering
principle can be used to help clarify requirements in
participative design, or to explicate documentation. In its
rigorous form, a generative user-engineering principle
provides a constructive higher-order consistency on a user
interface. The principles help the designer avoid most of
the problems discussed in the first part of this chapter.

FUNDAMENTALS OF
HUMAN–COMPUTER INTERACTION

Terminology and Assumptions

This chapter uses the terms "user", "designer" and "evaluator" to indicate roles; the role of a person using an interactive computer system, the role of a person designing it, and the role of a person evaluating it. The user is often an expert in the particular task he is performing, but he is not necessarily an expert in its implementation on the computer. The designer is almost certainly a computer scientist, and is thoroughly familiar with the implementation and technical details of the user interface. Finally, the evaluator examines a system to establish how effective it is in advancing the users' goals. Different people take these roles at different times; for example, it is possible for one person to take on each role in turn. It is also possible for a group of people to design a system, for a group of people to use it, and for a third group to evaluate it. Sometimes the designer is constrained by the user's manager's requirements. The user's manager may or may not be technical; but for our purposes if he is making a technical contribution he is fulfilling a designer role; if he is expressing how the user should be able to work (e.g., by giving a worked example), he is adopting a meta-user role;if he is worrying about the effectiveness of the system he is in an evaluator role.

Take as an example, a designer entering a program. While entering the program he is a user of the program-entry interface. He may then test his program to see if it is adequate to its requirements and specification: he is then an evaluator (in the wider sense of the word). As an evaluator, the designer probably tries to behave as much like the program's intended type of user as he possibly can. We could say most interfaces are designed for 1.2 people (1 designer + .2 of another user). Usually, however, the designer and user are different people and the evaluator's role is not clearly discriminated. Interesting communication problems arise if all three try to participate in constructing an effective user interface. That is what this chapter is about. Because I wish to emphasise that user, designer and evaluator are roles and not people, the terms will be written in capitals in all that follows.

I start with four assumptions, purely to limit the domain of this chapter.

(i)   The DESIGNERs with primary responsibility for technical user interface design decisions are computer scientists or are similarly qualified.

(ii)   The primary USERs who work directly with the
interface are skilled at their job and are naive relative
to the computer implementation of their task.

(iii) The primary concern of our design considerations
is the satisfactory completion of the USER's immediate
task: this excludes from consideration games, high
security applications and many forms of computer-aided
instruction. In these cases we would have to consider
the longer term issues, rather than the moment-to-moment
interaction with the machine.

(iv) Further, that the user interface is separable from
the application. Thus I assume there are essential
qualities of the user interface which can be abstracted
out and separated from the application-oriented tasks,
hardware and social setting of the system.   (Perhaps it
would be more palatable to define "user interface" in
this way and use a wider term such as "man-machine
system" to cover everything else.)

Various inferences can be drawn from these basic
assumptions.   Thus, for example, from (i) and (ii), the
DESIGNERs have no choice but to infer, by appropriate
procedure, the system specification; and the USER will
assume, but cannot verify, the DESIGNERs' success. Similarly
from (ii) and (iii) one may infer that it is not
constructive for implementation concerns to intrude on the
interface. A very trivial example is that a diagnostic such
as 'stack overflow", which relates to an implementation
concern, should not arise in this sort of interface. From
(iii)   we   assume   the   USER   is   responsible   and
self-motivating;in other words we are interested in the
USER's interaction more than his fulfilling a particular
organisational role (e.g., his job description). Assumption
(iv), the abstract nature of the user interface, is somewhat
more radical and deserves further explanation.

What is the User Interface?

The very term "user interface" suggests that there is
something   distinct   from   the   USER   and   the
thing-interfaced-to.   It is useful to distinguish between
the physical and conceptual aspects of the interface. The
physical hardware (keyboard, joystick, display screen, voice
synthesiser and so on) affect the way in which the system
behind the interface may be used, but they do not affect its

conceptual power.

Physical constraints can be significant. For example, it would be very difficult to drive a car using a keyboard - a wheel is superior; similarly a physically handicapped person may require particular types of device to be able to interact at all. But there is a limit of interest. The colour of a workstation, the height of a keyboard and whether a mouse or touchscreen are used do affect the perceived quality of the user interface but, if anything, may serve to disguise important conceptual design problems. It may be useful to define "normal" variations; for example, terminal noise is not a factor affecting the user interface until the terminal becomes abnormally noisy.

Intrinsic in man-machine systems, conceptual problems arise because the machine representation of world knowledge is absolutely minimal and rigid, and most likely only just sufficient to achieve the task in hand. There are three directions for user interface developments to alleviate this problem:

(i) to widen the machine representation of the task and its environment (e.g., expert systems; see Chapter 14)

(ii) to widen the communication bandwidth (e.g., using mice, virtual terminals and so on - as in the Smalltalk-type approach);

(iii) to develop techniques to enable humans to work more effectively given the narrow interface bandwidth and limited world view of computer systems.

It is this last approach which concerns us for the rest of this chapter. It is clear that the available techniques and styles needed to achieve this conflict in some sense and must be constrained by higher level precepts for any high quality user interface to emerge.

10.2 PROBLEMS IN INTERACTIVE SYSTEM DESIGN: MOTIVATION FOR A BETTER WAY

Conventional interface design is not constrained - rather it is bottom-up. User interfaces typically grow by adding unrelated features and no method is used to specify coherent sets of user interface techniques. Features are added because they are locally powerful, and no orthogonal "neat" design theme ever emerges, or if one does, the USER cannot rely on its being uniformly applicable.

This unfortunate situation is the result of a number of influences on the DESIGNER. One strong influence comes from the USER. Presented with even a manifestly bad system, USERs invest a lot of themselves in learning how to handle it just in order to use it all. They then, justifiably, resent any so-called improvements. On the other hand, if there are no precedents there is a "chicken-and-egg" problem. Neither DESIGNER nor USER has a clear idea of what is required until they have a working system, and only then do they really know...

Another problem is the confusion between functionality and ease of use. A system becomes easier to use for a DESIGNER as more capability is added. However, the DESIGNER has a higher threshold for complexity than the USER, especially when the USER is learning. A system becomes harder to use for the USER the more that needs to be learned and, indeed, the more that can be done accidentally.

As has been argued in previous chapters, turning to the human factors literature does not necessarily solve these problems. Technology continues to outstrip any experimental basis, sound experiments are rare and usually highly specific in their terms of reference. DESIGNERs are not, in general, experimental scientists and it is, therefore, very easy for them to over-generalise naively from experimental work and from their own personal experience.

It is usually obvious when an interface fails or is not a total success. Many people can easily say what is wrong with a particular interactive system, from their point of view, and maybe they will even be able to offer hardware or software solutions to the immediate problems the poor design poses. However, such would only be palliatives. The DESIGNER really had needed preventive medicine. Industrial and other realistic time scales are frequently too long for the designer to have several goes at getting it right. Some sort of principles are required to contain the DESIGNER in a top-down way and to allow him to communicate with the USER more effectively. One possible vehicle which might serve this purpose is the user model.

10.3   INTRODUCING GENERATIVE USER-ENGINEERING PRINCIPLES

The User Model

The idea of a user model was discussed in Chapter 9. The user model is the term given alternatively to the abstraction of what a USER is doing, or thinks he is doing,

or what somebody else thinks he ought to be doing, when he
uses an interactive system.

Here we wish to evaluate the concept of the user model as
a tool for the system DESIGNER. If the DESIGNER has access
to a user model, an abstraction of the USERs' requirements
and expected behaviour, this can have a profound influence
on the design. But, the nature of the user model is usually
established experimentally in the context of a working
system (pre-computerised or computerised). The DESIGNER
needs hard facts much earlier than his system will be
working! Most people, when they talk about user models,
envision a sort of hand-waving description of what the USER
is up to. This is obviously a start; it certainly helps
ensure the DESIGNER delivers an approximation. But it does
not have or imply any precise details to answer questions
such as: "What name is best for the consolidate command?"
"What happens when the USER presses 'up' at the top of the
page?" "How should we explain error 56?"

What we know from Chapter 9 is that without specific
guidance USERs will construct their own models of the system
and methods to achieve goals using them. There is no reason
for these models to have any rational, let alone axiomatic
basis: such models will be, at best, ritual 'magical'
systems. When USERs are not computer experts, their models
will be over-complex, difficult to generalise and, most
likely, of a wildly superstitious nature (Weizenbaum, 1980;
Gaines, 1976). And, because USERs may lack appropriate
training, there is no reason whatsoever to assume that their
self-established models are entirely conscious or provide
any foundation for reasoning about the interface issues
which confront them. This last point is important as under
these circumstances it is highly likely that a
computer-naive USER will react very differently, in an
emotional way, than a DESIGNER would. The DESIGNER (often a
computer scientist, of course) interprets unexpected
behaviour in a computer system as an intellectual challenge;
the non-expert, who has possibly struggled against all odds
to acquire what skill that he has, will see unexpected
behaviour as a personal threat, because he is unable to
differentiate a partially subliminal (e.g., pre-verbal)
model from his Self. When his user model is wrong, his
perception is that he is wrong. On the other hand, when a
computer scientist detects a discrepancy, his first thought
is probably that there is a bug, certainly nothing to bother
his self image.

It is now becoming popular to design systems around
somewhat formal user models. Useful as that is, there is a
danger that the DESIGNER will still overlook the emotional

artefacts of human/computer interaction, the very details of
which are abstracted out by a well-defined user model, and
hence the DESIGNER might attach too little weight to the
correct design of the details of the dialogues and their
psychosocial consequences. The DESIGNER may under-estimate
the actual complexity of the interface, possibly
dramatically. The alternative trap is that the DESIGNER may
assume the model is sufficient.
     Nevertheless, an interactive system is 'easy-to-use',
'user-friendly' and predictable if it is compatible with the
user model, more or less irrespective of our definitions.
Thus we can state a categorical principle of the design of
effective interactive systems:

"The DESIGNER is obliged to ensure the USERs have or
construct an appropriate user model."

This is similar to Gaines's (1981) recommendation "Use the
user's model", although the tense of his phrase presupposes
a model.
     This obligation needs a means to operationalise it.
Clearly, in order to ensure the model is appropriate, the
DESIGNER must at least: take account of existing conventions
(the USERs', not the DESIGNERs'!), train local experts,
build in system guidance and help, demonstrate the systems
to USERs, write manuals and devise teaching material,
emphasise inconsistencies and restrictions, implement the
system coherently and so on... by no means an enviable task.
In fact, this is not the best approach, for it assumes that
the user can take in all this information. The design
problem is unchanged; it has just shifted from system to
system-definition.
     The USER needs a brief, catchy, memorable and accurate
maxim (principle) which conveniently expresses a large,
strict subset of the rules of system interaction. Given
this, together with training in explicit reasoning about
interaction, the USER would be provided with a sure
foundation on which to build his user model. The DESIGNER
would then be able to use the same maxim (plus equivalent
reasoning processes) to constrain the system behaviour to be
compatible with it.

User-Engineering Principles

User-engineering principles for the DESIGNER, which are
sufficiently constructive to be used in design, are numerous
and highly task-specific (see, for example, the vast list

being compiled by Sid Smith, 1982). In fact, many such principles appearing in the literature have been derived from very small experiments and it is dubious whether such hypotheses merit promotion to principles. It is unlikely that constructive principles can be generalised or used in combination reliably, certainly not without considerable design experience.

For example, though experiments suggest that unanticipated cursor positioning is faster using a mouse, it is not clear that a mouse will always outperform key-selection for selecting items from a known menu. Principles interact too strongly with USER skill levels, task dimensions (frequency, openness), hardware (e.g., resolution, response times), psychosocial issues (e.g., consequences of USER performance and error), and may even be in mutual conflict. At this level, user-engineering principles can be used no more constructively than as suggestions for particular design features.

The problem with user-engineering principles is that they are too sophisticated for the USER and yet can still be interpreted by the DESIGNER with considerable freedom. What is required is a limited number of "generative" principles. Generative principles should be applicable as theorems over the modules of the system specification to overcome the bottom-up, piecemeal approach of applying conventional engineering principles. They should also be capable of expression in a form accessible to USERs and EVALUATORs. Phrased in lay or colloquial form a generative principle could be used in both requirements specification and in documentation. In the former case it would permit the USER to contribute to higher-order requirements, and in the latter case he could be given an unusually coherent view of it.

The colloquial form must be judiciously chosen; in Carroll and Thomas (1982) the colloquial form is termed a "metaphor" and excellent recommendations are given for their presentation.

We shall use the term "generative user-engineering principle" (abbreviated "guep" below), to distinguish a principle which has a colloquial form and can express design constraints on the overt behaviour of a system. Necessarily a guep has to be compatible with ergonomic guidelines. (Even after implementing a system this can be achieved weakly because simply stating a system property makes the system easier to use.) This new term releases the basic term "generative principle" to be used for specificational purposes where there may need be no ergonomic requirements at all. The idea is not new and appears to have been first used under the 1960s interactive system JOSS, where gueps were termed "rubrics" (Baker, 1967) although no attempts were made to make them either fully user-referenced or properly formal.

To summarise the argument so far, in an ideal world, user interfaces should be designed by collaboration between USER, EVALUATOR and DESIGNER. However, each role has limitations which restrict communication and curtail the emergence of an overall design approach. This chapter proposes using gueps as a "thematic" requirement of the user interface behaviour expressible in task-oriented terms. With them, the USER may have reasonable and well founded expectation; the EVALUATOR can check compatibility of a system against them; and the DESIGNER may rephrase them as theorems over the formal specification. In addition, gueps, as a type of generative principle, impose a high degree of internal consistency which can be checked formally. But what are gueps?

10.4 EXAMPLES OF GUEPS

The purpose of the next section is to show what gueps may look like, rather than to develop them in detail which would be tedious. After all, gueps will only be useful insofar as the DESIGNER can develop specific gueps relevant for the system being designed.

Gueps for concealed information

Information in user interfaces may be concealed by a variety of means, usually with the intention of making the dialogue more rapid, catering for varying levels of USER skill or for 'folding' (i.e., reducing) complex information into less cluttered forms.

Typical mechanisms for concealing information range from the straightforward absence of the information (as in default command operands), forms of abstraction (as in macros or programmable "soft" keys), to symbolic expressions (as in regular expressions). The purpose of the relevant guep is to express constraints on these kinds of mechanisms, and hence improve the chances of designing a consistent and compatible user interface (and, additionally, give the USER an explicit key to the particular form of consistency). The distinction between gueps and user-engineering principles is now perhaps a little clearer: a plausible user-engineering principle might suggest that "defaultable operands should occupy a consistent position" but this is very specific and

has a limited domain. Compare the above with the bases of
gueps presented in Table 10.1, which are widely applicable
and can also be communicated to the USER when presented in a
suitable form.

TABLE 10.1 Some gueps for concealed information.

Principle	Colloquial Form
(a) Only complete instances of syntactic categories can be abstracted or concealed.	Only entire objects are folded. (Ideally, some task orientated term would be substituted for the word 'fold').
(b) Information may be totally concealed locally, but there must be a convention to indicate that concealing has occurred.	One is always made aware of any folding.
(c) Information concealing and information revealing never occur as a side-effect of some other operation.	Objects must be folded by some direct act.
(d) The body of an abstraction is consistently available as an operand.	Folded objects can be used in the same way as unfolded objects.
(e) The abstraction mechanism is conservative and invertible	Folding can always be reversed.

Let us apply the gueps in Table 10.1 to linear command
languages. We may view a default as the USER folding
system-known information. However, the system normally
echoes the command which may remain displayed for some time,
perhaps until it scrolls out of sight. In this case, the
echoed form conceals information from the USER about the
history of the system's actions. Adhering to (b), the
echoed form should minimally indicate that a default has
been assumed. Adhering to (e), the USER should be able to
determine what default has been taken.

Command languages often support abbreviation mechanisms,
e.g., "wild cards" to match sets of operand. The wild card
is part of an expression representing a hidden body, namely

the string of operands it is expanded into for the purposes
of evaluating the command. (e) implies that the USER should
be able to unfold ('expand') and and re-fold ('retract') the
wild card before the command is evaluated.

Macros are a very direct way of permitting the USER
control over abstraction. If we adhere to the suggested
guep (a), the system should impose syntactic constraints on
the bodies of macros. (Most macro interfaces fail to do
this.)

The same gueps can be applied to menu-based systems.
Single-level menus often grow to such size that the entire
range of options cannot be displayed. Unfortunate systems
exist which flaunt (b) and therefore surprise their USERs *flout*
when they select non-displayed choices. "What you see is
what you get." is a guep discussed below which will address
this problem from a different perspective.

If the rest of a menu is folded (for example, by
providing an option 'others'), adherence to (e) suggests
that a function must exist to return to the enclosing menu.
Of course, if the menu is arranged as a hierarchy, (e)
suggests that this 'go back' function is uniformly
available.

"What You See is What You Get"

In simple English, this phrase specifies certain properties
of a user interface which, with a little explanation, may be
used for the USER to develop hypotheses about system
behaviour. The phrase may also be placed on a more formal
base as follows (for a more detailed treatment see Harrison
& Thimbleby, in preparation).

A display can be considered a function **content->view.**
Given some text (as **content**) the display function works out
a **view** - some sort of representation of the text on the
screen. The display function will use various conventions,
especially for formatting characters like tabs, spaces, new
lines, centring etc. Operations on **contents**, such as edits
are **content** transformations (**content->content**) with
corresponding display transformations (**view->view**) to
provide feedback on the outcome of the edits. The "what you
see is what you get" simply requires the display function to
be a morphism of the **contents** and **view** transformations. The
USER can then equally view commands acting on his data
(**content**) or on what he can see displayed (**view**): this may
be non-trivial to specify because in most applications the
display function is a projection with no inverse (partly
because of the formatting conventions), so some 'obvious'

(easy to use) **view** transformations are complex **content** transformations. Indeed, most user interface problems stem from the non-uniform conventions for the display transformation and obscure quoting and meta conventions are introduced. Consequently, a user interface which adheres to the "what you see" guep may well be more consistent and easier to use, but it is very likely to be much harder to implement.

It should be noted that the accepted interpretation of "what you see" by the computer-science community is different from the semantics presented above. Here, we have simply taken a workable phrase and shown how it might be utilised - after all, USERs who are presented with this guep need not know of its original (weaker) connotations. The non-standard semantics are explored and are also applied in other areas such as robotics in Thimbleby (1983b) and the usual interpretation is discussed further below in section 10.5.

"It Can Be Used With Your Eyes Shut"

Being able to use a system 'with your eyes shut' clearly implies a very predictable interface. But if the USER really did shut his eyes, to be able to make effective use of the system, the interface would have to be mode free and indicate diagnostics in a non-visual sensory mode (e.g., audibly) and rapidly, to be synchronised with the occurrence of the error, rather than at the end of a unit utterance in a dialogue. In a keyboarded application this requires per-character interaction and a postfix (or function key) command structure. Already we have quite definite technical constraints consistent with the view of the interface the USER may have been encouraged to elaborate from exactly the same principle. See Thimbleby (1982a) for further discussion.

Gueps for Quoting Mechanisms

Any general purpose system will require quoting mechanisms. For example, a text editor must allow a USER to issue commands and to enter text to a file which, for example, could document those commands. When the commands are entered as documentation, they should not be executed and therefore they have to be quoted, that is, interpreted in some non-command mode. In addition, a text editor would normally provide a command which allows the USER to search

for textual patterns: the patterns will use metacharacters
to construct patterns which may be overloadings of textual
characters. To search for a textual character which is
overloaded requires that character to be quoted.

Perhaps quoting mechanisms most frequently arise where
different input/output devices have different resolutions or
character sets. USERs are confused by the consequent
overloading e.g., '^K' denoting 'control-shift-K', not 'up-
arrow' 'K'. The problem would not arise if there was a
displayable form for 'control-shift-K' compatible with the
keyboard legends. (In this particular case quoting is
implicitly determined.)

Amusingly, an example which was to be included at this
point used the same quoting character as the word processor
used for this book. I wanted a backslash followed by an 'n':
somehow it was printed as newline followed by 'n', although
on the screen it looked innocuous enough! What we saw was
not what we got!

A guep is needed which might express some of the
following constraints: (i) there is one quoting mechanism
which is permanently available (e.g., there is a dedicated
'quote' key); (ii) quoted composite objects become atomic;
(iii) the quoting mechanism superordinates all other
functions.

10.5 A WARNING AGAINST PSEUDO-GENERATIVE PRINCIPLES

There is a class of principle which superficially meets the
given criteria for gueps. Two outstanding examples are the
'desk-top model', that is, the interface should simulate a
USER's desk-top displaying appropriate icons mapping onto
objects which might be found on office desk tops, such as
calculators and spread sheets, and (ii) the "what you
see..." principle as it is conventionally interpreted.

The Desk-Top Model

It will expose the misconception in the desk-top view of
man-machine interaction if you consider the horseless-
carriage period at the beginning of this century. The
initial approach to designing cars followed the obvious
'generative' principle of being compatible with the
functional predecessor. This resulted in machines which
were no doubt familiar and 'easy to use' but which pushed
carriage technology to limits, e.g., in suspension,
steering, coachwork and so on. The principle (not that it

was ever espoused as such) led to the exposure of limitations in contemporary technology - far from constraining it. So far as I am aware the horseless-carriage period achieved no standardisation in the user interface, not even the development of the steering wheel. Similarly, the desk-top approach in office automation leads inevitably to display processing requirements (e.g., to scroll A4 text in real time in arbitrary direction) which is certainly an impetus to technological development but may not be a valid approach to designing a user interface as such.

Amusingly, systems adhering to the desk-top model display a waste paper basket (as the destination for discarded objects)... and what office worker keeps his waste paper basket on his desk?

What You See is What You Get

As conventionally interpreted, "what you see..." implies equivalent resolution for hardcopy and display devices (when there is usually an order of magnitude difference). It may also be taken to imply real-time formatting and screen updates. Again, the principle primarily encourages systems research rather than either an improved user interface or research towards one.

10.6 SUMMARY

After summarising problems in interface design, this chapter introduced 'generative user-engineering principles' (gueps) as a means to design systems which are not only internally consistent but which are compatible with user expectations to a greater extent than is normally possible. The intention has been to demonstrate the potential for higher-order guiding principles which can help bridge the gap between DESIGNERs and USERs.

Generative user-engineering principles are easily understood and used both by USER and DESIGNER in their respective forms. They can be expressed in such terms that

(i) The user interface may be designed top-down, using gueps as guidelines to select appropriate low-level features.

(ii) The USER has a sound basis on which to construct an understanding of the system, even before using it.

(iii) The USER may generalise his knowledge reliably. The USER is confident as to what has happened (e.g., after an error), and does not need debugging skills.

(iv) The USER is encouraged to use his skills fully. Gueps can help enhance the view that what the USER does is real and not abstract. This is especially motivating.

(v) The DESIGNER can use gueps to meet clearly defined USER expectations, often with specific techniques. Often the gueps can be strongly formalised.

Having once suggested a basis for the user model, the DESIGNER is under an obligation to ensure its coherent implementation through careful system design, which should maintain the model as understood by the USER - this approach will entail evaluation and retrospective refinement.

I believe that gueps, plus attention to detail, already provide a constructive approach to the top-down design of effective, acceptable, interactive systems. At the very least, even if a guep is ergonomically unsound, an interactive system explicitly designed around it will have more internal consistency and be more clearly documented than the average interactive system available today.

10.7 FURTHER READING

Palme (1981) is one of the best brief introductions to human issues in user interface design. Engel and Granada (1975) is not the most comprehensive list of guidelines, but is eminently usable because it is brief and is not so daunting as, say, Smith (1982). Gaines (1981) provides higher level approaches, rather than specific rules, for designing dialogues: more expertise is required to make good use of them. An approach such as that developed by Gaines must be used to make effective use of ergonomic guidelines in a total man/machine system. Lampson (1983) discusses computer system design, and his discussion can be very usefully contrasted with views taken in this chapter. Carroll and Thomas (1982) give excellent recommendations for phrasing gueps for the user, and their paper highlights some of the problems USERs will have. They highlight some issues not touched on in this chapter, such as the interaction of gueps and their long term utility as the USER becomes more skilled. Shneiderman (1983) is a clear article which will clarify the advantages of direct manipulation which is a style of interaction particularly amenable to gueps.

Thimbleby (1980) introduces some straightforward terminology
which is intended to help DESIGNERs think more clearly about
USER needs.

CHAPTER 11

Future Uses of Future Offices

G. Reinhard Kofer

11.1 INTRODUCTION

The office can be defined as a place where people deal with information handling tasks. There is no single way of organising an office, neither is there any homogenous stratum of office workers, so the market for office automation is a pluralistic one. Consider, for example, the offices found in a bank. The office of the manager and the teller's booth are quite different and quite different transactions occur in them. This chapter argues that catering for the pluralism of offices is going to be the hall mark of the successful companies of the future in this market.

Many changes in current practice may occur. For example, the office does not have to reside in a given location any more. One can easily imagine droves of businessmen toting suitcase-size computers in the streets of the future. Whatever these changes are, we shall still require service which matches our expectations and needs. The office machinery of the future must cater for a full range of users from the computer naive to the computer sophisticated, and not just some remote group of engineers who designed the system.

Rather than presenting a lengthy ideological harangue, this chapter will take the form of an example. What follows is a story about finding a house for a family in 1992. The first scene takes place in a fixed location office, the second in a spatially-distributed variable-location office.

11.2 SETTING THE SCENE

Meet Mr Selfstart, a highly successful real estate broker in
London. He does not mind operating some of his computers
himself, so long as it doesn't have to be all day long.
Next meet Ms Punkie Newlook, his young assistant. Punkie is
the real innovator in Selfstarts enterprise, but it was
Selfstart who made money out of the sometimes chaotic
creativity by installing a certain amount of order.
Punkie's motto is 'Why bother myself if I can make the
computer bother faster!'.
    Selfstart's speciality is buying and remodelling houses
in decaying neighbourhoods. At the same time he offers help
with banks and credits, accepting authentic old furniture as
interim collaterals.   Just now he is on the telephone
talking to a prospective buyer, Mr Luigi Portobello who has
a wife and 4 children.

P.: "Do you have a house at the approximate price I
     mentioned with a small garden; then my sister could take
     care of the younger children."
S.: "Before I ask the computer, will your sister live with
     you as well?"
P.: "She'd love to, but she has this enormous chestnut
     cupboard from Tuscany, which is her one and only
     treasure. She'll never part with it!"
S.: "That's less of a problem than you might think. If you
     want me to, I can try to find you a house with a big
     room for it. And I can give you a loan on the cupboard,
     if it is a proven antique; then you can afford a little
     bit more garden for the kids."
P.: "Wonderful, but will that cost me a lot of commission?"
S.: "Well, you will have to pay by the computer hour. But
     actually you save a lot compared with other brokers,
     because I only charge a very small minimum fee of £100.
     If you draw detailed plans with my assistant later on,
     it is only £40 per started hour. The advantage of our
     service is that the software that we use has been
     certified. This means that you don't have to submit your
     plans for approval by the CEBR (Commission for Enforcing
     Building Regulations) and that will save you time and
     money. Will you be consulting us then, Mr Portobello?"
P.: "Yes. Is tomorrow afternoon convenient?"
S.: "Yes, perfectly, if it is after 3pm. Please bring along
     the downpayment of £100 in cash. We guarantee you one

hour of consultation for that plus written documents for
bank negotiations, etc.   And don't forget to bring the
exact dimensions of this cupboard! See you tomorrow and
thanks for calling."

Conclusions to be Drawn

One of the uses of an effective office in the future will be
to turn out more profit by addressing more customers in a
more flexible way than your competition can afford to. This
is true only if your system displays ease of use and error
stability - so let us see why Mr Selfstart could go about
his business with such selfconfidence.

How Selfstart and Newlook Learned the Business

Many years ago, Mr Selfstart discovered that he would be out
of business remodelling houses if he remained with manual
paper work. The ecomomy wasn't all that good, so people
took a long time to decide whether they would take a house
or not. All his time went into planning and replanning and
his capital sat idle, while the interest rate went up.
Luckily he still had some money left on his accounts from
the good days. So, rather than replacing his oldest lorry,
he decided to buy a multifunctional computer that could
present both text and graphics.   In those days, Punkie's
father worked for him as an accountant and volunteered,
together with a friend of his, to add some programs to the
new computer. (In the process that friend became so wealthy
that he was able to start his own company, DATA BRICKS, and
Punkie's father joined the company the following year.
Selfstart does not mind because he receives a 10% royalty
for every copy of the program sold.)
    The essence of these programs was that drawings of
buildings were composed of parts or groups of parts, and
that these entities could be associated with arbitrary
descriptive data which in turn could be related to the
cost-model software that came with the machine he bought.
So for wealthy customers you could foster their egos by
erecting fabulous buildings in front of their eyes (and talk
up the price ...) and for skimpy customers you could cut out
gimmick after gimmick until the price ceiling was met.   For
Selfstart that was heaven compared to what he had grown up
with. To Punkie it was hell. Each and every time the model
had to be created from scratch. So she pestered her father
to teach her the modelling language at his home terminal.

It was at that time that the business began to flourish.
Every second week or so she worked out another standard
model. Punkie was a genius in discovering similarities.
Selfstart didn't mind, because he quickly found out that
checking whether the standard models were correct cost him
less time than to set them up two or three times manually.
What bothered Selfstart was that, in order to give him
planning permission, the authorities were taking his
computer drawn plans and feeding them into their statics
packages. This was error prone, time consuming and, worst
of all, these guys charged him money for doing a job he had
already done. So in a major business decision, he had all
the programs certified. This was fairly expensive as it
required some reprogramming. However, after this ordeal, he
had the most ergonomic integrated architecture support
package of 1989, and today, in 1992, he still proudly shows
the certificate.

Conclusions To Be Drawn

Given a certain level of flexibility, one use of a future
office is gradually to transform itself into an even more
futuristic one. Innovation is more likely to happen from
the bottom up than from the top down. This is due to the
fact that the pressure for change is felt more directly at
the customer's site than at the vendor's. This means
customizability should be a mandatory component of any major
office systems vendor's long range strategy.

11.3 SCENE ONE – THE FIRST CONSULTATION

It is 3.30 p.m. the next day, the consultation contract is
signed and £100 has changed hands. It turned out that the
cupboard could be separated into two pieces, one of which
was 10.8 feet and the other 19.3 feet wide with a depth of
1.7 feet, an unusually large piece indeed! (Selfstart
didn't even dare to think of the height, an unbelievable 8.4
feet in the middle turret ...) Putting on his most
convincing facial expression he switched on his largest
MULTIFUNC Screen.

S.: "Mr Portobello, what we do now is to search the current
    sellers' catalogue for a room larger than 12.5 feet by
    21 feet, ignoring for the moment the exact positions of
    doors and windows. As you see, there are 15 entries,
    which I will list now."

(Small photographs of the houses appear on the screen)
P.: "Fabulous system you have here, but the houses all seem to be mansions which I couldn't possibly afford."
S.: "Don't worry, that was just the beginning! What is your price limit?   £400 for interest and repayment per month and you have £12000 existing capital. How old are your children? All below 12 years."
P.: "Amazing, two of the mansions remain on the screen!"
S.: "And there is a reason for that!   As you see in the explanation windows, one has a deteriorating roof, but it does not need a complete repair immediately.   So in 6-8 years your children might do the work for you. This is a very experienced program that scouts for hidden capital as well. The other one has a moisture problem - let us see, where?"

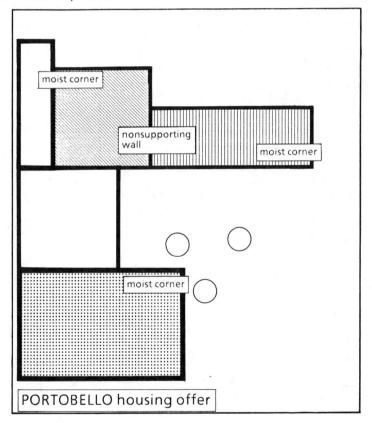

FIG. 11.1 Floor plan as displayed on MULTIFUNC screen.

(Selfstart depresses the DETAIL button and a floor plan fills the screen.   The floor plan is shown in Figure 11.1)

S.: "Well, that is not so good, the corner by the trees will remain moist unless you spend a very large sum, and even if we break out the non-supporting wall we still have a moist corner near your valuable cupboard. I propose we forget about this particular house and search for houses where two rooms combined would satisfy the space requirement. So we input: non-supporting wall out gives room longer than 30.1 feet.   Now let's see what comes out."

P.: "When I make my own final plans with your assistant will she tell me what I can look for?"

S.: "Yes. She laid the groundwork to these programs and handles them even better than I do. The rationale of usage is deliberately straightforward. The database we are searching gives you houses as they are right now and with their current prices. If anybody modifies the house or hidden damage is discovered, the database is updated. You specify the changes you would make in simple terms, one after another. The System then knows what the house would look like after all the changes and selects accordingly.   Also it tells you what the modification would cost."

P.: "So how do you work this machine?"

S.: "Well, if you want to do something to an object, for instance a wall, you simply touch it and a little menu window will pop up which tells you what can be done at a reasonable cost.   You yourself cannot do anything but accept one or more of the menu proposals, but my assistant, Ms Newlook, can do much more. You just have to explain to her what you want."

P.: "Just out of curiosity - what could I do to a wall except breaking it out altogether?"

S.: "Just the normal things. You could fortify it for big loads on the level above, or you could put in windows or doors - the program usually has more ideas than I can tell you off hand ..."

P.: "Before I forget, at the moment my sister has this cupboard in a former attic which has been very nicely converted to a flat. Did we search for attics?"

S.: "No, we didn't. So I enter in addition: add attics or other non-primary rooms, same sizes as before. Thanks to your idea we now have 23 houses instead of 17!   Do you want to separate the boys and the girls?"

P.: "Yes, indeed. I want to give the two boys one room and
    the same for the girls.   And there should be two
    bathrooms and a bedroom ..."
S.: "... which brought us down to seven houses already!
    Let's talk about your wife a little - does she prefer to
    shop in the neighbourhood or does she have a car as
    well?"
P.: "We don't have a car at all, so we need a subway station
    close by or a day and night bus line."
S.: "Fine, that leaves three houses now!   I'd also like to
    point out that we are getting close to the end of the
    first hour today. Unless you want to spend more money
    right now, I will print out the plans for you and before
    you come back I recommend you visit the locations. To
    see the houses from inside will cost you by the hour
    again, and I will have a portable computer with me to
    keep track of modification costs. Is that OK?
P.: "Yes, no objections and thank you for your assistance so
    far!"
S.: "Fine. Ms Newlook will hand you the printouts and draw
    your attention to peculiarities, if any.   I have to
    leave now. We hope to hear from you again soon."

Conclusions To Be Drawn

First, note the amazing frankness and directness of the
exchange.   Businessmen will not change into angels just
because data are easily accessible - but with precise
control of data and their ownership it is possible to
negotiate with greater speed and smaller margins of safety.
Secondly, we see that the computer's role doesn't differ all
that much from the human ones. The computer portrays a
capable partner, rapidly displaying facts, causes and
consequences. Not all computers are equal though.   This
particular one, having high image resolution , was more or
less tied to a building.   It would have been too power
consuming, too heavy and too fragile to be moved frequently.
Also, since photos of objects can be shown on the screen,
this computer must have access to a high bandwidth
communication channel or a large volume archival storage.

Remodelling Begins

Mr Portobello had his own notion of "time is money" and
decided to stay.   He agreed with Ms Newlook that he would
study the floorplans for half an hour, then select his

favourite house and begin to remodel it under her
supervision. She established a credit line for him and then
went back to her other work.

P.: "Do you have a moment?"
N.: "I'll be right with you - what is the code for the house
     you want to consider?"
P.: "Here is the plan; you can copy it".
N.: "Very well then, the house is locked for any other
     transactions now.   Have a play with it!   And don't
     forget, your current credit gives you a maximum of one
     and a quarter hour of computer time.   If you don't
     complete, we save your data for up to one month, free of
     additional charge.   You can also take the data home on a
     small cassette; that is £2 however - which we will
     reimburse if you bring it back undamaged."
P.: "Can I move the staircase over here?"
N.: "You start with ambitious moves, don't you?   We have to
     remove this wall ...   Oops, why is the machine yelling
     at me?   Oh, it was an essential wall ...   So we have to
     reinforce the ceiling first - my goodness, do you see
     what that will cost you?   Wait a minute, where these two
     rafters meet we could change the old wall to a
     freestanding concrete pillar ...   So here is your new
     staircase.   What will you do with that enormous empty
     space?"
P.: "That's exactly my problem, Ms Newlook!   I hope to place
     this cupboard there.   I will sketch it for you.   Can you
     get this into the computer?"
N.: "With difficulty, yes. I will declare it as individual
     pieces of furniture and then mark it as inseparable
     assembly.   What do you store in this giant thing by the
     way?"
P.: "Various foreign wines, books, garments and suchlike."
N.: "Tell me where the heavy things are.   Eventually we must
     support from the basement."

To cut a long story short, after one hour of simulator work,
the house looked right and the price was still manageable.
An available subcontractor had been located, and a bank
credit plan was at hand.   Both agreed to make a perspective
view of the remodelled house and to show it to Mrs
Portobello on Friday.

Conclusions To Be Drawn

A future office is not only a data repository but also a
simulation laboratory.   The result of such simulations will
be considered decisions as well as added insight into the
intricacies of a financial or technical domain.   The
author's opinion is that this is by far the most important
new use - genuinely new, because nothing like it ever
happened outside of our heads before.   That society which
most efficiently and decidedly uses this information
generation principle will have enormous advantages.

11.4 SCENE TWO - ON LOCATION IN CAMDEN TOWN
FRIDAY MORNING THE NEXT WEEK

Mr Selfstart had arranged that all parties to the deal would
meet in the house for a final discussion of all technical
and contractual issues.   So a mason and a carpenter were
there, as well as a pipelayer and an electrician. FRIENDLY
BANK had an assessor ready to drive over in 10 minutes, and
Mr Portobello brought along his wife Elena.

S.: "Now that we are all here, let me explain to you, Mrs
     Portobello, what we will do.   The house you see is a
     little bit run down, but it is very spacious and the
     backyard will make a beautiful garden. It is massively
     built which will help with the extensive remodelling
     your husband has proposed."
P.: "Do you have both old and remodelled plans of the house
     in your portable computer?"
S.: "Yes, I do. And the current owner has allowed us to use
     his DATAPHONE, so in case we decide to proceed
     differently, Ms Newlook at my home office can take down
     additional details.   I cannot picture-edit on this
     machine - it has a very coarse resolution screen -   but
     I do have online labour cost information, so when our
     four skilled craftsmen give their estimates, we can
     arrive at the final price offer right here while we are
     still together."

Conclusions To Be Drawn

Another very important future use of future offices will be
to get factual much earlier than we are used to today.   "No
sooner said than written" might be the business style to
come.   This will mean it will get harder to develop second

thoughts. The computer owning businessmen will thus automatically become the moderators of discussions, and may even prepare the course of discussion by pre-arranged sequences and combinations of electronic documents. Notwithstanding that probable development, it will be the task of the large software vendors to offer enough basic software for functional completeness. So a very indirect future use of future customizable office software will be to find out, in the first place, what it might be that real businessmen need. With ever faster telecommunication technology, rapid exchange of requirement and solution will be a market of its own.

Meanwhile Inside The Portobellos' Future Home

The carpenter: "Looking at your plan, Mr Portobello, you put
   a pillar below the middle platform at this stair here,
   but later cover it up entirely with shelves. For the
   same price or less, you could have walls for a small
   stowage area beneath a concrete stair support, and the
   sturdy rafters could be the raw materials for the urgent
   repair needed in the attic."
Portobello: "What shelves?   Oh, you mean the chestnut
   cupboard we made this entire modification for!"
   To his wife: "Well, dear, would you rather have that? I
   think this is an excellent use for the remaining space."
Selfstart: (after perceiving the silent approval) "So, I
   will enter it in the cost model: 'Save pillar material
   and construction, replace by wall support for lower
   stairs, add door, no frame, give 8 yards of rafter to
   free supplies'. Savings computed are £235. Estimated
   masonry value is £150, labour only. Everybody agrees?"
Mrs Portobello: "Can we have bigger windows upstairs?"
Selfstart: "Where exactly? Here! Well that might affect
   the stability of the walls. I would have to link into my
   main computer for stability analysis at £30 per hour.
   Is that alright with you Mr Portobello?"
The electrician: "Before you do that, Fred, I'd better tell
   you that the middle window as it is supposed to be now
   will get in the way of the main power line. On the
   other hand, I'd advise you to install new cabling for
   fire safety anyhow."
Portobello: "Since it's somewhat dark up there, we will
   invest the £30. Please dial up your main computer!"

Conclusions to be drawn

The portable computer is quite nice, but without readily accessible high performance backend servers you only get half of its potential. The real office of the future is (a) the multilocation workstation together with (b) fully electronic (or electro-optic) document and program exchange plus (c) powerful central computers (privately or publicly held) for all those tasks that are numerically or otherwise more demanding. Thus we need both the powerful local workstations like the MULTIFUNC where Punkie Newlook works and the cheap communication front end devices the hardware and software for which are still in the process of being invented. All major vendors are convinced of this 'trilogy' and are gearing their efforts towards that goal.

A Last Look At The Portobello Deal

S.: (speaking via the DATAPHONE) "Hello, Punkie, we have an important modification to the Portobello home: if you read my memory here, you'll get data for new window locations. One of the windows will interfere with electrical cabling. Ignore that and have your new program optimally recable the house, please!"

N.: "Sorry, my recabler doesn't work for such complicated shapes yet. I will partition the problem as I see fit, do the rest manually and will retransmit the results. As soon as I can"

P.: "I assume that will take her 10 minutes at least. Could we compute a cost estimate locally or not?"

S.: "Certainly! £950 for materials and £650 labour cost for the windows. For the price of the cabling I'll have to wait for the main computer."

P.: "Maybe we should not overextend ourselves, dear. If the old cabling is a fire hazard it ought to be fixed, naturally. But the windows can wait some years, can't they?"

S.: "If I may interfere, yes, they can wait at no change of cost in planning since the old window areas are all inside the new ones, and the cabling is based on the data for new ones."

N.: (via the DATAPHONE speaker) "Can anybody hear me?"

S.: "Yes, but I don't see any cabling costs yet - what's the problem?"

N.: "That is exactly why I am interrupting you! There seems to be a very old fashioned boiler in the future kitchen which will waste a lot of energy and it gets in the way

of the new cabling, too ... Could you please check?"
The pipelayer: "I'll have a look.   I will be right back".
N.: "Also, with the safety cabling I put in, there is a
considerable reduction in the cost of fire insurance."
The pipelayer to the Portobellos: "Unless you want to start
a pub or restaurant of your own, I would advise you to
sell the boiler.   It is in excellent shape but of no
real use in a private home.   With the price you ought to
get, you will almost get a small new one - and don't
forget the energy savings!"
P.: (via the DATAPHONE) "Ms Newlook, please take out the big
old boiler and put in a standard kitchen one."
S.: "And here comes the price - very attractive indeed!"

The deal was completed, the Portobello family still lives
happily in the house, and Mr Portobello (with the
substantial help of his son, now 16 years old) started a new
business in his basement - VIEWDATA TELEMODELLING.   This
year's earnings, somewhat to the dismay of Elena, didn't go
into the windows but instead into the brandnew MULTIFUNC
model.

11.5 SUMMARY

The prediction made is that offices of the future will be
both more diverse and more flexible than present ones.   The
successful entrepreneurs will be those who can find or
create a new market for their services so office information
processing equipment must be easy to adapt to new uses.
    The role of the computer will change to something more
similar to the human roles of adviser and informant.   Also
the availability of electronic document and data exchange
will change the form of business transactions and the rate
at which they take place.
    Finally, the chapter sees an important place for portable
computers which can be linked to more powerful central
computers.

11.6 FURTHER READING

This chapter draws on some of the speculations contained in
John Naisbitt's (1984) 'Megatrends' while a further
introduction to the technology hinted at in this chapter is
available in Kofer (1983) which also contains more detailed
references to the relevant literature. Alternatively, try
Shneiderman (1983) and Otway and Peltu (1983).

CHAPTER 12

Speech Communication:
The Problem and Some Solutions

Peter Bailey

12.1 SPEECH AS A MEDIUM FOR COMMUNICATION

The ability to understand and produce spoken language is
acquired naturally and without effort by most people during
the first three years of life, and through exposure and
practice becomes a skill which provides a uniquely efficient
medium for communication. We should note that although most
people can learn to read, they do not do so naturally. It
appears that speech is a code which has evolved to exploit
with great effectiveness our basic anatomical, physiological
and cognitive capabilities, and is therefore an attractive
candidate for study if we wish to discover the most natural
and efficient means for humans to communicate with each
other, or with machines.

Processes in Speech Communication

Understanding and producing speech is typically so
effortless that we have no sense of the processes which
underlie the conversion of an idea to its linguistic
representation in an acoustic wave, or the recovery of the
idea expressed in an acoustic speech wave arriving at our
ears. Yet evidently the representation of the information
in a spoken linguistic message has different forms. We may
consider it in terms of the neural commands to muscles of
the vocal tract, as actual movements of the vocal tract and

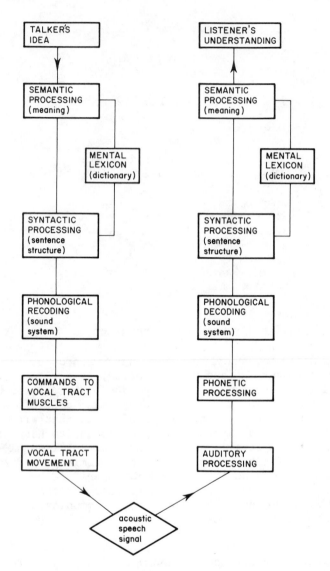

FIG. 12.1 A descriptive model of the speech communication process.

its articulators (e.g., tongue, lips, jaw etc.), as the speech sounds which result, as the patterns of activity in the nerves which carry signals from the ear to the brain, or in more abstract terms as an internal psychological representation of words, their meanings and their syntactic relationships in a sentence. This multiplicity of levels of representation has led to the process of speech understanding being considered as a set of sub-processes, each of which transforms the information in a message from one representation to another. A scheme of this kind is illustrated in Figure 12.1.

Describing speech production and understanding (or any other psychological process) as a set of discrete information-processing stages is convenient because it implies that each stage may be studied relatively independently of the others, but it is important to be aware that this is only a naive descriptive model of the speech process. The model will need to be modified in the light of results from experiments designed to identify and characterise each stage, and we have no a priori reason to suppose, for example, that information processing in the brain proceeds in the strictly hierarchical fashion indicated by the model of Figure 12.1. Nonetheless, modelling psychological processes, often with models expressed in the form of computer programs, can be a fruitful source of ideas for experiment and theory, provided the caveat is observed that psychological models can only be validated by data from psychological experiments.

For the engineer, system designer or computer scientist an attraction of psychological theory is the insight it may afford into highly efficient information-processing strategies which have been refined and optimised by the pressures of evolution. The practical consequences of understanding psychological processes in detail will depend on the task in hand. Knowing how brains understand speech will have implications for those concerned with designing improved systems for speech recognition. Knowing about the processes in and structure of the mental lexicon - how words are remembered and how the meanings of words interrelate - may be more relevant to those concerned with dialogue design than those developing speech recognition systems. At the very least, models of speech communication can serve the important function of clarifying what a brain or a machine must know, and have in common with other brains or machines, for communication to be possible.

The ease and precision with which the processes of speech production and understanding can be investigated depend heavily on their accessibility. The mechanics of articulatory behaviour - the movements of tongue, lips, jaw and soft palate during speech - and the relationship between articulation and acoustics are relatively well understood because both articulation and the concomitant acoustic signal can be observed directly and measured. Similarly, the early stages of auditory perception - mechanical and neural processes in the ear - have been described in some detail (see section 12.2). In contrast, understanding of the more abstract processes assumed to be involved in syntactic and semantic analysis - that is, apprehension of the meaning of a complete utterance, given the meanings of individual words in the utterance - is less well advanced, despite being a focus of interest for a number of disciplines, including psychology, descriptive linguistics, computer science and philosophy.

Between the acoustic speech signal and the relatively central brain processes of sentence understanding lie the processes of most concern here - speech production and speech perception. These have in common a capability to transform between a linguistic and an acoustic specification of a message - that is, speech production generates an acoustic speech wave from an abstract internal representation of the sounds in the message, and speech perception must reconstitute an equivalent internal representation of the message from the acoustic speech wave. Note that, when a talker can be seen, optical information about the message will also be available from lipshapes and gestures. Although in certain conditions - hearing impairment or very high environmental noise levels - this type of information may be very important, it is not normally essential and will not be considered in detail here.

Information in Speech: Units of Analysis

The processing stages shown in the descriptive model of speech communication in Figure 12.1 can be thought of as transforming the linguistic message from one representation to another. The essential information must be preserved at each level for communication to be possible, but it is represented in a more abstract form at higher levels. To be able to analyse the representation of information systematically we need a relatively formal notation which specifies, amongst other things, the unit(s) of analysis at each stage in the model. No such notation exists for the very abstract levels such as those of the talker's idea or the listener's understanding (see Chapter 3 section 3.3 for further discussion of this problem), but for less abstract levels it becomes easier to represent the information in terms of familiar linguistic units.

The elements we consider a spoken sentence to be formed from will depend upon the level of analysis we are concerned with. In syntactic processing, for example, the elements of the message are words, or, more precisely, morphemes - meaningful word stems, prefixes and suffixes that cannot be further subdivided without becoming meaningless. Moving even closer to the peripheral processes of speech articulation and auditory perception, the morphemes can be thought of as consisting of strings of elements which have no independent meaning, but which describe the way the message sounds. Thus we can describe an utterance in terms of its component syllables, or more usefully in terms of the relatively small number of basic sound elements that are needed to construct all words in the language. These are known as phonemes.

Phonemes

An important assumption in conventional taxonomic descriptions of speech is that it can be represented as a sequence of discrete segments, corresponding very roughly to the letters we use in writing. We can define these segments - called phonemes - in terms of the minimal sound change that will change meaning. Thus the English word 'ban' consists of three segments since we can form the words 'pan', 'bin' and 'bat' by changing the first, second and third segments respectively. Similarly, 'sheep' consists of three segments (not five as implied by the word as written), since we can form 'heap', 'ship' and 'sheet'. A phonetic alphabet has been established to represent phonemes conveniently, a version of which is shown in Table 12.1. Note that languages differ in the number of phonemes that are distinctive - about 40 for English and as few as 15 for New Zealand Maori - and some languages, for example Zulu, use rather rare phonemes like clicks. The sound systems of different languages - their phonologies - differ substantially: in Spanish, for example, the final sounds in the two English words 'ice' and 'eyes' are not phonologically distinctive, and in Arabic a distinction is made between the similar sounds at the beginning of the two english words 'keel' and 'call'.

The classification of speech into phonemic segments can be broken down further by exploiting the fact that speech sounds fall into intersecting classes defined by

characteristics of the articulatory manoeuvres we make to
produce them. For example, the sounds /p,t,k,b,d and g/ are
all in the class stop consonant, since they all involve
complete occlusion ('stoppage') of the vocal tract.   Within
the class of stop consonants the sounds /p/ and /b/ are
classified as having bilabial place of articulation, since
they involve closing the vocal tract at the lips, and the
sounds /t/ and /d/ as having alveolar place of articulation
since they involve closure with the tongue tip against the
alveolar ridge behind the upper set of teeth.

TABLE 12.1 Phonemic symbols for transcribing (a) English
consonants, and (b) English vowels.

(a)

p pole	f fine	m my	l lack
b bowl	v vine	n nigh	w whack
t toll	θ thigh	ŋ hang	r rack
d dole	ð thy		j yak
k coal	s sue		
g goal	z zoo		
	ʃ shoe		
	ʒ azure		
	h hack		
	tʃ church		
	dʒ judge		

w water ?

(b)

i heed	eɜ hay
ɪ hid	eɪ high
ɛ head	oo how
æ had	oɐ hoe
ɑ hard	ɪɐ here
ɒ hod	ɪə hair
ɔ hoard	
o hood	
u who'd	
ə herd	
ʌ hug	

A further contrast is made at each place of articulation
between voiced consonants, for example /b/ and /d/, and
unvoiced consonants like /p/ and /t/.   The class of vowels
can be subdivided similarly, primarily in terms of the
characteristic position of the tongue in the mouth, so the

vowels in 'heed' and 'hard' are described as high, front and low, back respectively. These articulatory properties are referred to as phonetic features. Phonemes specified in terms of phonetic features provide a convenient and natural vocabulary for describing the information in speech at its most basic linguistic level.

To acknowledge that phonetic segments and features are convenient descriptors of speech is not to imply that speech is planned or recognised necessarily by processes in which phonemes or phonetic features are functional elements. Clearly the psychological reality of phonemes can be established only by appropriate psychological experiments, and in general the results of such experiments provide some support for an explicit phonemic representation during speech production, but only equivocal support for the perceptual reality of phonemes. However, it is worth noting that descriptions of speech in terms of phonemes and features allow us to state in very economical terms prescriptive rules which express knowledge that language users evidently possess. For example, although generally written with an 's' or 'es', the plurals of English nouns are realised phonetically as /ɪz/ (buses), /z/ (pens) or /s/ (books), depending on the nature of the immediately preceding phonetic segment. This rule can be applied creatively to unfamiliar nouns we have not previously encountered. It turns out to be very laborious to state the rule without assuming a phonetic specification of the message.

Prosody

It is clear that the various means for describing linguistic information considered so far do not represent the full range of information in speech. There is a wealth of extra-linguistic information - sometimes called prosodic or supra-segmental information - which is carried in the way a particular string of words is uttered. Variations in emphasis and emotional content are achieved by means of variation in pitch, loudness and rhythm, and similar variables are employed to carry meta-linguistic cues such as those which facilitate turn-taking in fluent conversation.

In section 12.3 we shall consider how machines can be made to synthesise speech from a specification of the information in the message in terms of the segments - words or phonemes - required, and their supra-segmental - prosodic - properties. The segmental specification has a large effect on the intelligibility of the speech output by such machines, whereas the accuracy of the prosodic specification is a major determinant of whether or not the speech sounds natural. It is worth noting that at their current state of development machines which recognise speech are in general incapable of decoding or using prosodic information, and attempt only to recover a segmental specification of the input as a word or string of words.

12.2 SPEECH ARTICULATION AND RECOGNITION: HOW DO PEOPLE DO IT?

The Vocal Apparatus: Acoustic Theory and Articulatory Dynamics

In its role as a generator of sound the vocal tract can be thought of as a system consisting of an excitatory sound source and a set of filters. When a steady-state vowel is uttered, for example, the vocal cords (in the larynx at the base of the pharynx) vibrate rhythmically, coming together and moving apart to allow a series of puffs of air into the upper part of the tract. The frequency of vibration - the fundamental frequency - is a major determinant of the pitch of the voice. The amplitude spectrum of this periodic sound source consists of a series of harmonics at multiples of the fundamental frequency whose amplitudes decrease steadily with frequency.

As with any object or enclosed air space - consider organ pipes, for example - the cavities of the vocal tract have resonances at frequencies determined by the cavity size. These act together to filter the source spectrum by attenuating its harmonics by different amounts. The peaks in the spectrum so produced are called formants. Different configurations of the vocal tract result in cavities with different sizes and hence different resonant frequencies, so the spectrum of the sound which emerges from the lips varies as the shape of the vocal tract is changed. This is illustrated for three different vowels in Figure 12.2. Think about the shape of your own vocal tract as you produce the vowels in 'heed', 'hard' and 'who'd'. Similar general principles apply when the vocal tract is excited by a noise source produced by turbulent airflow, as in whispered speech or consonants like /s/.

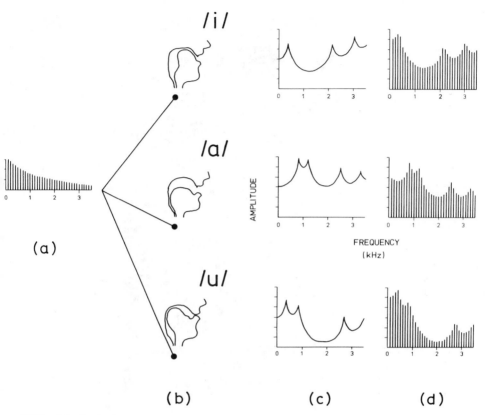

FIG. 12.2 The source-filter model of speech acoustics
(a) the source spectrum for a periodic (voiced) sound, showing the harmonics of the fundamental frequency.
(b) Tracings of mid-saggital vocal tract X-ray photographs during the production of a steady-state vowel.
(c) The effective filter (transfer function) resulting from the resonances of cavities in the vocal tract.
(d) The output spectrum, showing the amplitudes of harmonics modified by the vocal tract filter to give spectral peaks (formants) and valleys.

Measurements of the movements of major articulators in the vocal tract - lips, tongue and jaw - reveal intricate motor patterns, as attending to the antics of your own vocal tract whilst speaking this sentence aloud in slow motion will confirm. The source-filter account of speech acoustics outlined above predicts that all these movements will have acoustic consequences, so we should expect, and find, that

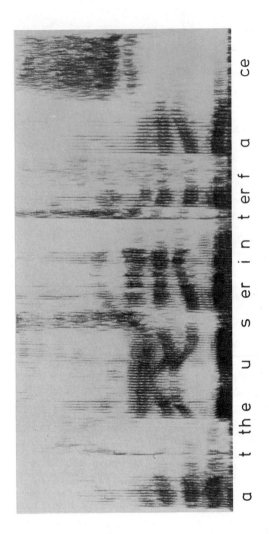

FIG. 12.3 A speech spectrogram (voiceprint) of the utterance
'at the user interface'. Frequency increases up the short
axis and time along the long axis. Intensity (energy)
is represented by the grey scale. High energy time/frequency
coordinates are darker than low energy ones. This spectrogram
was generated by repeatedly scanning the speech signal with a
300 Hz bandwidth analysing filter whose centre frequency was
increased from 80 to 8000 Hz. After appropriate amplitude
compression the output of the filter was written onto a sheet
of current-sensitive paper. Note the absence of acoustic
segmentation corresponding to linguistic boundaries.

steady states are rare in the acoustic patterns of fluent speech. This can be seen in Figure 12.3, a spectrographic representation of a natural utterance. The dynamic properties of fluent articulation are manifest in dynamic acoustical patterns which must be transduced by the listener's auditory system so that critical information is preserved in the internal neural representation of speech in the brain. Some of the characteristics of the auditory system and auditory processing that achieve this are discussed in section 12.2.

We may note finally that this 'source-filter' account of speech acoustics suggests a simple way in which speech can be synthesised. Two sources of excitation - pulses or/and noise - can be fed in specified amounts to a set of resonators with variable centre frequency and bandwidth. Usually controlled by a digital computer, this arrangement allows the time-varying spectrum of speech to be modelled with sufficient precision to produce natural-sounding utterances, but, of course, presupposes that the appropriate types of excitation, amplitudes, frequencies and bandwidths are known for the required speech sounds. This will be discussed further in section 12.3.

Our Auditory Apparatus: An Optimal Speech Processor?

A wide range of physiological and behavioural investigations of hearing has made it possible broadly to characterise the internal neural representation of complex signals like speech after they have been processed by the peripheral auditory system. Contrary to some early theories of hearing, the ear is not simply a microphone which transduces the input signal more or less faithfully into patterns of neural activity. The peripheral auditory system turns out to be a rather sophisticated signal processing device, particularly well suited to preserving and probably enhancing the informationally-rich properties of speech patterns. Thus it behoves those concerned with the optimal form in which speech should be represented internally in a machine to take note of the strategy evolved in the ear-brain system.

Very roughly, the ear acts as an approximately one-quarter octave band-pass filter set with many overlapping filters, making available to later processes a form of running power spectrum. This should not be taken to imply that there exists in the ear a fixed number of discrete filters, but rather that for a given frequency there is a given degree of tuning. The fact that the

bandwidth of the notional filters is specified in octave
terms implies that the degree of tuning decreases with
frequency, so their bandwidths are greater at higher
frequencies. This means that the form of the 'neural
spectrogram' must be rather different from that of the
spectrogram reproduced in Figure 12.3. Conventional
spectrographic analyses of speech use a filter of constant
bandwidth (300 Hz in the case of the examples in the
figures) with the consequence that at high frequencies,
frequency resolution is better than that found in the ear,
whereas at low frequencies the ear is capable of better
frequency resolution than the conventional spectrograph.
This allows the auditory system to achieve adequate spectral
resolution at low frequencies without losing temporal
resolution at higher frequencies. This strategy is well
suited to processing speech, in which phonetic information
is coded in details both of the spectrum envelope and of
short-term temporal coordination.

Some broad generalisations about the major psychophysical
properties of auditory processing relevant to speech are
given in Table 12.2. These are derived in part from
analyses of behavioural responses to sound patterns which
have been manipulated systematically in perceptual
experiments, and in part from analyses of the physical
characteristics of speech sounds. Further details may be
found in Klatt (1980), Moore (1982) and Hawley (1977).
Although it has not been demonstrated formally, it is
generally assumed that speech processed by a device with the
characteristics given in Table 12.2 will be maximally
distinctive, in the sense that the differences between the
input acoustic patterns corresponding to a pair of phonetic
classes will be maximised in the patterns of activity in the
output channels of the device. This is clearly a desirable
feature of the early stage of processing in a speech
recogniser, whether in brain or machine.

**The Nature of Speech: the Relation Between
Linguistics and Acoustics**

Specifying the relationship between linguistic and acoustic
parameters is complex, not just because many speech sounds,
for example stop consonants, are essentially dynamic, having
no static form, but primarily because acoustic analysis
reveals that speech does not consist simply of a sequence of
sound segments corresponding to the phonemes, syllables or
words of the message. Reference to Figure 12.3 shows that
no clear acoustic boundaries exist between segments, and

that in voiced segments particularly, the formant pattern changes relatively smoothly over time. When acoustic discontinuities do occur, for example when the energy drops in a stop consonant or excitation changes for an /s/, they do not coincide consistently with boundaries between phonemes, syllables or words.

TABLE 12.2 Broad psychophysical characteristics of auditory processing relevant to speech.

Overall frequency response:

(a) the frequency range from roughly 260 Hz to 5600 Hz gives maximum intelligibility
(b) the mid-frequency 2-3 kHz region is emphasised
(c) the contribution to intelligibility is greater from low frequency regions than from high frequency regions

Frequency resolution:

(a) auditory filters are capable of resolving frequency components spaced roughly 1/4 octave apart, and are overlapped sufficiently to detect changes of roughly 3-5% in the frequency of spectral peaks
(b) auditory filters are asymmetrical, with steeper high-frequency than low-frequency slopes

Temporal resolution:

(a) events that occur close together in time can be resolved separately if they are separated in time by roughly 5-15 milliseconds, depending on their spectral characteristics

Amplitude resolution:

(a) the dynamic range of the auditory system is over 100 dB, but for speech need only be about 50 dB
(b) changes of roughly 1 dB in the amplitude of spectral peaks are detectable.

The smooth changes between successive segments have an important consequence: the acoustic form of a particular speech sound will depend upon the context in which it occurs. This contextual influence - known as coarticulation - is an inevitable consequence of the way in which vocal tract articulators move to avoid successional discontinuities, and its effects can be seen over time spans involving several phonemes: think about the position of your lips for the /k/ sound at the start of the words 'construe' and 'constrain' when spoken in the middle of a sentence. As we shall see, the existence of coarticulatory effects presents considerable problems for the process of speech perception, although it serves to make speech highly redundant and, as such, resistant to the effects of noise and distortion. Coarticulation also accounts in part for the problems encountered in attempts to synthesise natural-sounding speech by concatenating supposedly context-free exemplars of phonemes, syllables or words into sequences (see sections 12.3 and 13.2).

Attempts to define simple rules for coarticulation have been made in several speech 'synthesis-by-rule' algorithms, which take as input a specification of an utterance in terms of a sequence of phonetic symbols, augmented by extra information about pitch, stress placement, and rate of speech. Acoustic target values for all phonemes are held in a look-up table, and the algorithm computes synthesiser control parameters, including smooth transitional segments between targets for successive phonemes where appropriate. This and other techniques of automatic speech output are discussed in section 12.3.

The planning mechanisms by which the human brain/vocal tract system produces this smoothly coarticulated running speech are poorly understood, although techniques such as cineradiography (X-ray filming), direct fibre-optic observation and electrical recording from speech muscles during vocal tract movement have furnished much information about the style of control that is exercised over muscle systems in speech.

There are other contextual effects which contribute to the complex relationship between linguistic and acoustic segments. Speech is highly intelligible over a very wide range of different rates of utterance: even in noisy environments intelligibility does not start to decrease substantially until speaking rate reaches 160 to 200 words per minute. Figure 12.4 shows two spectrograms of the same phrase spoken at different rates; evidently the acoustic consequences of these changes in rate are very marked, yet the perceptual system is able to detect the same phrase in

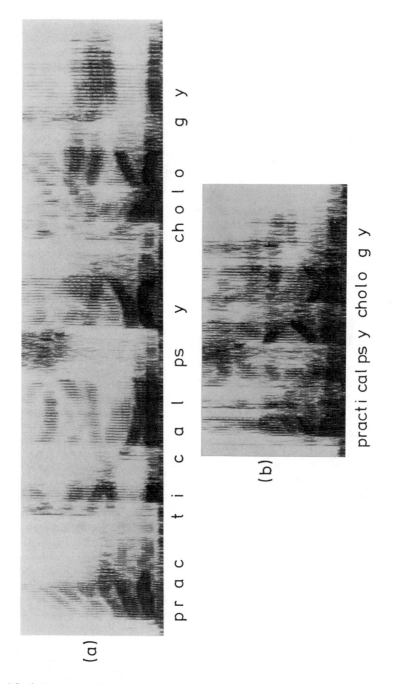

FIG. 12.4 Two spectrograms of the phrase 'practical psychology' spoken (a) slowly, and (b) rapidly. Both utterances were clearly intelligible. Note the extent of articulatory (and hence acoustic) restructuring for rapid speech, manifest particularly in non-linear compression of segment durations.

each case without apparent effort. In fact the vocal tract shapes characteristic of words uttered in isolation are often not reached at all when the same words occur in rapid speech, particularly when the words are unstressed.

Perceptual constancy in the face of acoustic variability is seen also in our ability to understand talkers of widely different sizes - for example, adults and children. As we have noted already, the acoustic characteristics of speech are determined largely by the size and shape of the vocal tract, so small people tend to produce high spectral frequencies (although not necessarily high fundamental frequencies). The same word spoken by different sized talkers will inevitably result in different acoustic signals, quite apart from any differences attributable to idiosyncratic speech styles or different accents and dialects.

We should note also that speech is rarely heard in quiet, anechoic environments. Extraneous noise levels are often high and unpredictable, echoes distort the speech signal, and irrelevant conversations compete for our attention. Error rates for most automatic speech recognition (ASR) systems rise to unacceptably high levels in noise conditions that have almost no effect on intelligibility for human listeners, but little research has been carried out on this aspect of ASR in natural environments.

Finally, we should consider a different level of contextual influence found in running speech. We have assumed that the input to the speech production process is a sequence of phonemes, and there are data, for example from studies of speech production errors, which support this assumption. The phoneme sequence may be supposed to derive from a phonemic specification of words held in an internal dictionary or 'lexicon'. However, the phonemes actually produced (sometimes called phonetic allophones) when words are uttered in a sentence are not always those which define a word in isolation. For example, the words in the sentence 'Did you go?' when spoken in isolation may be written phonetically /dɪd/ /ju/ /goʊ/, but may appear as /dɪdʒʌgoʊ/ when spoken fluently. This process of phonological recoding which occurs in the preparation of an utterance from the stored phonemic patterns of words, is an important characteristic of speech production, and one which, like the other contextual effects introduced above, has major implications for theories of and practical schemes for phoneme and word recognition.

In the foregoing I have emphasised the essential variablility of speech, since it is not intuitively obvious, and it creates some of the major problems in speech recognition. However, not all aspects of the speech signal will be as vulnerable to contextual effects as others. For example, when the vocal tract gets into a position for bilabial stop closure in the consonant at the beginning of the word 'bat', the articulatory constraints are such that at the moment when the lips come apart for the release of the closure, the characteristics of the acoustic signal produced by that manouevre - the 'release burst' - are largely independent of context. As we examine the acoustics at moments in time further from the release, the contextual influence of the following vowel becomes more apparent and the acoustical specification of place of articulation less unique. As we shall see in the next section, different approaches to human speech recognition have differed in the extent to which they emphasise the decoding of contextually-conditioned information.

Theories of Human Speech Recognition

The listener in a conversation is presented with an acoustic signal and has the task of discovering the talker's intention. All of the contextual influences discussed in the previous section conspire to present a seemingly intractable perceptual problem. In running speech there is apparently no clear, unique acoustic specification of a given phoneme or word, yet we extract the message with ease. It is clear that we cannot do this with a simple template-matching strategy, in which input patterns are compared directly with fixed, stored templates representing known phonemes or words. In such a scheme recognition would correspond to the template furnishing the smallest distance score when compared against the input, but context-dependent variability, most notably in this case the variability resulting from changes in rate of speech, will often result in the wrong choice. No fully adequate psychological models have been developed of the perceptual process for speech, despite increasing research interest in the theoretical and practical aspects of the problem. In this section I shall outline some of the approaches that have been used to try to explain human speech recognition performance, and some of the problems they encounter.

One of the most widely cited theories and one that placed heavy emphasis on the variability in speech is the 'Motor Theory' of speech perception (Liberman et al., 1967). This argued that listeners to speech are able to deal with contextual variability because they are equipped with a special speech decoder which can make use of internal

knowledge about the way speech is produced. Underlying this
proposal is the assumption that at some level in the
production process - specifically at the level of commands
to the vocal tract musculature - speech is represented in a
manner which is less contextually dependent than the
acoustic speech signal. Although the motor theory provoked
much useful research, it has found little unequivocal
empirical support, and has precipitated problems such as how
infants, who can typically recognise speech before they can
produce it, acquire the special knowledge about production
required for speech decoding.

An alternative approach which emphasised those aspects of
speech which are not so contextually dependent (e.g.,
Stevens, 1980) has suggested that the perceptual process is
attuned to sample the amplitude spectrum at moments of large
amplitude and frequency change, where the gross spectral
shape can specify place of articulation, for example. This
static sampling strategy will succeed in discriminating
certain phonetic contrasts. However, the fact that it makes
little use of sensitivity which listeners can easily be
shown to have to information carried in acoustical change
over time suggests that it cannot be the whole story.

Central to both the approaches outlined above is the
assumption that speech recognition involves an early stage
of phoneme identification. I have argued above
(section 12.1) that there are good reasons for believing
phonemes to have some psychological reality, but this does
not necessarily imply that phonemes are recognised
explicitly and behave as functional elements in the normal
recognition process. Accordingly, increasing attention has
been devoted to models of speech recognition in which there
is no intermediate stage of phonemic representation between
the output of auditory processing and the stage of lexical
access - the activation of a word in the internal lexicon
corresponding to the input speech pattern. In these models,
word recognition proceeds directly from the neural
spectrogram.

Some of the more successful systems to emerge from a
major initiative in development of speech understanding
systems in the United States (see Klatt, 1977) used
precisely this strategy to recognise words. The HARPY
system, for example (Lowerre and Reddy, 1980), included a
massive network of spectral templates. Pathways through the
network corresponded to all possible words and word
sequences that could be recognised. Word recognition was
achieved by computation of a metric of spectral distance
between the input spectral sequence and paths through the
network that could correspond to the input by adaptive

template matching, and selecting the path with the smallest distance metric as a likely word candidate. The phonetic and phonological knowledge required for this to work was built into the stored network of spectral templates, which had to be pre-compiled at considerable computational cost, so that the on-line recognition process was manageable in something approximating real time.

A variant of this strategy has been offered as a psychological model (Klatt, 1980), but it awaits systematic empirical evaluation. It is worth noting that although direct lexical access from spectra may be possible for known familiar words, it will probably be necessary to incorporate a separate perceptual process with an explicit intermediate level of phonemic representation to account for the perception and learning of new and unfamiliar words. However, the decision strategy that determines which perceptual route a given input will take then becomes a critical feature of the model. Also crucial is how successful a single pre-compiled network will be at recognising the speech of many different talkers in normal environments, since the computational cost of modifying or re-compiling the template network will be very high.

Models of human speech recognition and understanding expressed in terms of computer programs have the considerable merit of being open to operational evaluation, since working criteria can be established to judge their performance. A related attraction is their necessarily explicit formulation of the distinctions and interactions between the different kinds of knowledge the model is assumed to have. For example, it is a matter of common experience that when listening to speech we are greatly helped by knowing, amongst other things, the talker's speech style and the topic of conversation. This 'top-down' information derived from 'hypothesis-driven' processes allows us to develop expectations which can disambiguate or augment the 'bottom-up' information from 'data-driven' acoustic-phonetic analysis of the kind we have considered here. We should expect that the amount of information derived from each will vary with the particular talker, topic and circumstances, so any system which embodies an interaction between the various kinds of knowledge will need to be flexible. A plausible proposal is that data-driven and hypothesis-driven processes converge at the level of word recognition, but this is an active research issue which is unlikely to be resolved simply.

It is likely that this issue of how different knowledge sources can be organised to cooperate efficiently in the recognition process will be a key one in the development of more sophisticated models of human speech recognition, as well as of more effective ASR systems that are not restricted to small sets of known talkers using limited vocabularies.

12.3 SPEECH PRODUCTION AND RECOGNITION: HOW CAN MACHINES DO IT?

Automatic output and input of speech from and to machines can be achieved using several different procedures, each with attendant advantages and disadvantages for a given application. Some of these are considered in the sections which follow.

All depend at some stage upon a capability to convert between an analog and a digital representation of the speech signal and _vice versa_. The waveform of speech, or any other analog signal, can be represented internally in a computer or similar machine by a sequence of numbers - samples - corresponding to the values of the wave from some baseline (usually zero) at a series of regular points in time. The time between successive samples will determine the precision with which the wave is represented, with short inter-sample intervals required to capture the details of high-frequency changes in the wave. Thus the sampling interval will determine the bandwidth over which waves can be represented without distortion. Waves in this sampled-data form (sometimes called 'pulse code modulation' or PCM) can be acquired from appropriately filtered and conditioned external analog signals by use of an analog-to-digital converter, then manipulated, processed, recognised or output using a digital-to-analog converter. Alternatively waves may be computed directly by some algorithm which incorporates rules for wave synthesis, and then output.

Speech Output Using Natural Speech (Concatenation)

One of the easiest ways to achieve automatic speech output is to use a computer system as a sophisticated random-access tape recorder. Recordings in sampled-data format can be stored in memory or on some rapid-access mass-storage device, and played out as required. In its simplest form this strategy is appropriate for applications where a restricted set of potentially high-quality predictable words or phrases is required to provide commands or give information. As discussed by Waterworth in the next chapter (section 13.2), much greater flexibility can be achieved by concatenating stored waveforms corresponding, for example, to syllables or words, and so building up a novel message from a relatively small set of meaningful elements. For the reasons discussed in section 12.2, if only one version of each element is stored the speech will sound unatural, but more natural-sounding speech can be generated if more than one version is stored of elements which can appear in more than one position in an utterance. It may suffice simply to have one version of a word for use at the beginning or in the middle of an utterance, and a different version for use at the end.

Speech quality will be determined by the quality of the original utterances, and by the sampling rate and number of bits per sample. Intelligibility is not improved by sampling at rates greater than about 12 kHz, although sampling rates of 30-40 kHz are required for high-quality sound reproduction, and rates as low as 6 kHz can still be intelligible. To avoid aliasing errors the signal must be low-pass filtered on input and output so that energy at frequencies above one half of the sampling frequency is attenuated by at least 60 dB. A low-pass filter with the highest possible attenuation rate should be used to preserve information in the pass-band. The number of bits per sample influences the ratio of signal power to the power of quantisation noise; 11 bits per sample are required to achieve a signal-to-noise ratio (SNR) of 60 dB ('toll quality'), with an additional 6 dB gain in SNR for each extra bit. Thus, in terms of information rate, adequate representations of speech can be obtained by use of rates between 66 kbits/sec and 440 kbits/sec, depending on the application.

Although requiring only simple software, use of sampled natural speech places relatively heavy demands on permanent storage, and on central processing resources during output. The latter constraint can be avoided to some extent by use of direct memory access (DMA) devices. The demands on storage can be reduced at the cost of a great increase in programming complexity by use of 'adaptive, differential' PCM, which allows the sampled waveform points to be stored using fewer bits by coding only amplitude differences between adjacent points rather than absolute amplitudes, and by changing the quantisation step size as the average signal level changes, so that signals of different amplitudes can be coded using the same number of bits. ADPCM allows the data rate to be reduced to around 20-40 kbits/sec.

Speech Output Using Synthetic Speech

Synthetic speech is appropriate primarily for applications demanding output of unpredictable messages from an unrestricted set, provided there is no stringent requirement that the speech sounds completely natural. Further, given that intelligible messages can be produced with a data rate as low as 0.6 kbits/sec using certain types of synthesiser, synthetic speech output can be particularly useful when storage and central processing resources are limited, and the messages can be stored as pre-processed synthesis parameters.

A speech synthesiser, whether realised in analog hardware, software or, as is increasingly common, digital programmable hardware, is controlled by passing to it a set of parameters which specify the desired state of the synthesiser, and the time for which that state should last. Parameters may be passed at regular intervals - intervals between 5 and 20 milliseconds are typical - or only irregularly when a change in the output is required. The nature of the controlling parameters will be determined by the type of synthesis strategy in use. In this section we shall consider two synthesis strategies: linear prediction analysis/synthesis, and formant synthesis-by-rule.

The parameters for linear prediction synthesis are derived from a linear predictive analysis of natural speech. Linear predictive analysis (or linear predictive coding - LPC) is a procedure which assumes that a given sample of speech can be approximated by a weighted linear combination of the previous m speech samples. The weighting coefficients (called linear prediction coefficients) are determined by minimising the squared difference between actual and linearly predicted speech samples. The value of m is referred to as the 'order' of the filter, and the linear prediction coefficients may be thought of as specifying the filter characteristics for an all-pole model of the vocal tract transfer function. If the filter order is high enough, however, say 12-15, most speech sounds can be represented adequately, including those strictly requiring zeros in the transfer function. In addition to estimating the predictor coefficients, a complete speech analysis must include an estimate of the (log) magnitude of the speech signal and a determination of whether the speech is voiced or unvoiced, and, if voiced, of the pitch period. To avoid quantisation errors, predictor coefficients should be represented by 8-10 bits each, log magnitude by about 5 bits, the voiced/unvoiced decision by one bit and the pitch value by about 6-8 bits. For a 100 Hz frame rate (i.e., parameters updated every 10 msec) a data rate of 10-13 kbits/sec is implied. Speech can be resynthesised from these data most straightforwardly with a direct form filter specified by the predictor polynomial used in the original analysis, excited by pulses or noise as determined by the voiced/unvoiced switch. One attraction of this strategy lies in the fact that since the linear prediction analysis can be entirely automatic, the parameters sufficient for relatively good quality synthesis of a set of utterances can be obtained easily. Texas Instruments' 'Speak & Spell' toy is an example of this approach.

Maximum flexibility in the use of synthetic speech demands procedures which can accept a conventional specification of a message - derived perhaps from printed text by an optical character recogniser, or directly from, say, an ASCII coded text file on a computer system - and compute a corresponding sequence of phonemes or diphones (pairs of phonemes), together with some supra-segmental (prosodic) information about stress placement, pitch and speech rate. This phonemic and prosodic specification of the message can then be passed to a synthesis-by-rule algorithm which incorporates at least some knowledge about the contextual influences found in natural speech (see section 12.2). The algorithm obtains target values of the synthesiser control parameters for each unit in the message from a look-up table, computes smooth transitions between adjacent targets using interpolation rules optimised for speech quality, and outputs the appropriate sequence of synthesiser control parameters for the sound pattern of the message as a whole. An example of this approach is the Digital Equipment Corporation's DECtalk system. Although the output speech from systems of this kind is usually highly intelligible, at the current state of the art it does not always sound natural.

Synthesis-by-rule systems commonly use a formant synthesiser as an output device. Formant synthesisers consist of a set of resonators with variable centre frequency and bandwidth, fed by appropriately shaped periodic and/or noise excitation of appropriate amplitude. They require between 10-30 variable parameters to be specified, according to the complexity of the synthesiser configuration. In general, larger numbers of parameters and more complex synthesisers increase the precision with which natural speech waveforms can be modelled. A typical set of parameters might consist of values for the frequencies and bandwidths of the four lowest formants, the amplitude and rate (i.e., pitch) of voiced (periodic) excitation, the amplitude of unvoiced (noise) excitation, and the frame duration for which these values should continue to be used. To avoid serious quantisation errors formant frequency and pitch parameters require roughly 9-10 bits, amplitudes about 4-6 bits and bandwidths about 2 bits. Target parameter values are normally extracted from measurements of spectral analyses of natural speech, which are often very laborious. Since most speech events can be represented adequately when time is quantised to 10 msec (i.e., 100 Hz), a data rate of roughly 5-15 kbits/sec is implied. In some formant synthesisers resonators are arranged in cascade, thus avoiding the need for explicit specification of the relative formant levels. This serial arrangement of the resonators typically produces good vowels but poor consonants, so a hybrid configuration is sometimes used, with separate branches of resonators for vowels, consonants and nasals. The most flexible formant synthesiser configuration is one in which the resonators are arranged in parallel, although a slightly larger number of parameters must be specified in each time frame, with associated costs in computation time and complexity of controlling software.

   The flexibility afforded by synthesis-by-rule can also be exploited with linear prediction synthesisers, but care must be taken to ensure that interpolating parameters between target values avoids conditions which lead to an unstable filter. One way to avoid the risk of instability is to use reflection coefficients computed directly or derived from the predictor coefficients. Resynthesis with reflection coefficients requires a more complex lattice filter, but has the advantages of unconditional stability and lower susceptibility to quantisation effects resulting from finite word length parameter specifications. Linear prediction synthesis-by-rule systems have been developed using several different basic speech units, notably diphones and words. Imposition of the appropriate prosodic contour for an utterance is achieved effectively by manipulation of the pitch and overall magnitude parameter values and the duration of each time frame, according to rules for intonation patterns and stress placement.

Automatic Speech Recognition (ASR)

Evidently some form of speech recognition system is a prerequisite for a voice-based user-machine interface. At the current state of the art no system exists with capabilities near those of human listeners. However, by careful choice of constraints on the flexibility required for a given ASR application, some useful working systems have been developed. Some of the issues that must be considered in their selection, evaluation and use are shown in Table 12.3 (see Newell et al.,(1973)), and discussed in Chapter 13 (section 13.3).

TABLE 12.3 Considerations in the development, selection and evaluation of automatic speech recognition systems.

Type of speech:	isolated words, phrases, continuous speech
Number of talkers:	single talker, several designated talkers, unlimited
Type of talker:	co-operative, casual, male, female, child
Environment:	sound-attenuating booth, computer room, public place
Channel to recogniser:	high quality microphone, high quality audio, noisy low-bandwidth telephone link
Type and amount of system training:	none, fixed training set, continuous
Vocabulary size:	small (<20 words), medium (<100 words), large
Speech format:	constrained text, free speech
Error tolerance:	high, low

Several commercial ASR systems are available. Most are capable of recognising only isolated words or phrases from small to medium-sized vocabularies spoken carefully by one of a set of designated talkers. Some of the more expensive recognisers can accept continuous connected speech, with words selected from quite large (2000 word) vocabularies, but they are still restricted to use by designated cooperative talkers who have previously trained the system by uttering at least one example of each word to be recognised.

The most common recognition strategy is to pre-process input speech with a band-pass filter, or its digital equivalent, and to compare the filter outputs with each of a set of stored templates derived from a training session in which the talker has uttered a number of repetitions of the target words or phrases. Some rudimentary syntactic constrants are sometimes applied in recognition of strings of connected words. For the reasons discussed in section 12.2 - contextual effects, effects of varying speech rate and style, etc. - choice of the smallest simple distance measure obtained from direct comparison of non-normalised input with all stored templates will not, in general, lead reliably to the correct identification. Great improvements in accuracy can be achieved by applying a non-linear time-warping process to the input (using dynamic programming) to maximise the alignment of input and template. Note that for most small-scale ASR systems, recognition is defined in the limited sense of correct choice of one from n templates, giving rise to one of n outputs from the system.

Substantial research and development effort is being expended on more realistic larger-scale speech recognisers that go beyond identification of single words or phrases and attempt to 'understand' connected speech. For example, within the context of a data-base such as an airline travel guide, the system would perform some action appropriate to the input utterance. This larger objective raises a range of problems, for example, how are the syntactic, semantic and pragmatic facts which facilitate sentence understanding to be represented, and what information needs to be included in the vocabulary about word meanings? One simple strategy for accommodating syntactic and semantic facts into a recogniser is in terms of the transitional probabilities between words within a state diagram representing all possible recognisable sentences. The transitional probabilities reflect, amongst other things, the fact that recognition of an article ('the' or 'a') constrains the candidates for the next word to adverbs adjectives and nouns. Systems incorporating this type of knowledge extensively require substantial storage and processing resources, and are likely to be expensive, at least initially. Further significant developments will depend in part upon improvements in the representation and use of phonetically relevant properties of the acoustic signal (such as amplitude discontinuities and rapid spectral change), in part upon exploitation of phonological and phonotactic constraints such as what sounds can follow what, and in part upon improvements in representation and use of linguistic structure.

Talker Verification and Identification

Systems for voice-based verification of claimed identity,
using techniques similar to those introduced above (i.e.,
LPC analysis and non-linear time warping), have been
developed which are capable of performance with error rates
near zero, reaching only about 4% errors using professional
mimics attempting to imitate the speech of particular
talkers. Talker identification, that is matching the input
with all known talker templates instead of just one, is
somewhat less reliable. The accuracy of these systems
depends largely on the size of the set of potential talkers
and the duration of the input speech sample available for
comparison.

12.4 SUMMARY

Speech is an efficient and convenient vehicle for
communication, being fast, ubiquitous and resistant to
distortion. The information in speech can be represented
equivalently at several different more or less abstract
levels, each with its own units of analysis. Speech
production and understanding by both humans and machines may
be seen as consisting of sets of processes which convert the
information from one representation to another.
Consideration of the form of the information in the
acoustical speech signal makes it possible to identify
several reasons why fully automatic speech understanding by
machine remains a utopian goal. However, investigations of
the characteristics of speech understanding by people are
contributing to improvements in the performance of speech
recognisers, which is already sufficiently good for
real-world applications.

12.5 FURTHER READING

Good general introductions to the issues involved in
linguistic communication are Miller, G.A. ed. (1973)
'Communication, Language and Meaning' and Miller, G.A.
(1981) 'Language and Speech'. For an introduction to speech
acoustics see Ladefoged (1962) or Fry (1979). A general
introduction to speech is Fry (1977) 'Homo Loquens'.
   More detailed coverage of speech production and
perception is to be found in Lehiste (1967), Lass (1976) and
Cole (1980).
   Speech synthesis and recognition are discussed in two

Scientific American articles: Flanagan (Feb, 1972) and Levinson and Liberman (April, 1981). A more detailed review of ASR research is Lea (1980).

The background of speech intelligibility assessment is to be found in Hawley (1977). The theory of digital speech processing is covered in some detail in Rabiner and Schafer (1978). A general treatment of computer-based speech processing and output systems is to be found in Witten (1982a).

A magazine called Speech Technology, for those interested in 'man/machine voice communications' is published quarterly by Media Dimensions Inc (525 E.82nd Street, NY, NY 10028), edited by R.H. Wiggins.

CHAPTER 13

Speech Communication: How to Use It

John Waterworth

13.1 INTRODUCTION

Speech appears to have a number of advantages as a medium of
communication; it is natural, and thus is familiar and might
be presumed to be convenient, and its use with computers
could, in principle, convert every telephone into a low cost
remote terminal. The general public could thus access all
the information and facilities that are now available from
computerised systems by means of the humble but ubiquitous
telephone. Speech also has undisputed advantages in certain
situations where other media are impossible or inconvenient
to use, and for particular classes of users. It can be used
in hostile environments where visibility is limited, and in
circumstances which make it desirable or necessary to have
the hands and eyes free for other tasks (e.g., warning
systems). Similarly, people with visual or physical
handicaps can also take advantage of the medium, as can
illiterates (of which there are currently about 5 million
adults in the UK). Other applications, although
comparatively trivial, are for individuals who prefer not to
use other available means of interaction, and simply for the
novelty value (e.g., 'executive toy' phones, talking coffee
machines, etc.).

Whatever the reason for selecting speech for an
interface, its use will inevitably lead to changes in the
relationship between users and systems. Talking and
listening are activities that are intimately bound to social

FUNDAMENTALS OF
HUMAN–COMPUTER INTERACTION

conventions of interpersonal communication acquired throughout our development. Pressing buttons and viewing displays trigger a rather different set of associations and behaviours. Because of this, man-machine speech communication gives rise to several problems that make this a fertile area for human factors research. As speech is such a natural channel the user will bring to vocal interactions a body of experience and expectation not associated with nonvocal communication. Speech is naturally used for a great many purposes (e.g., 'avoiding worse activities', 'conformity to norms', 'expression of affect', etc.) other than the exchange of factual information (Robinson, 1972). That is, most natural speech is performing functions that are of significance in communication between people (e.g., establishing friendships and relative status, expressing feelings and emotions, telling jokes and telling people off), but which may not be appropriate for person-machine interaction (in the immediate future at least).

Another crucial factor is the temporary nature of speech and the way this interacts with the limitations of human information processing capacity. Speech is ephemeral, it cannot be scanned and so must be held in memory long enough for it to be interpreted and acted upon. But the amount of information that humans can actively retain in this way is very limited, and this limited capacity must often be shared between current cognitive operations. Perhaps reflecting these two characteristics of speech, many conventions have been developed to control the use of speech in natural interactions (e.g., 'opening', 'closing' and 'turntaking' rules; see, for example, Schegloff and Sacks, 1973). These allow speaker/listeners to achieve a fluent interchange by providing ways of controlliing the conversational process itself (i.e., 'encounter regulation'). It may be necessary to take account of these conventions when designing speech-based interactive systems. This would involve providing the system with a model of conversational performance, as well as means for assessing the current status of the interaction.

13.2 MACHINE-GENERATED SPEECH

The speaking clock annnouncements make use of the principle of concatenation (see Chapter 12 section 12.3), mechanically to select the required vocabulary to give the appropriate message every ten seconds. This principle is being extended, in System X exchanges, to the real-time

concatenation of digitally-coded announcements appropriate
to the use of 'Star Services' (such as Short-code Dialling,
Diversion Services, Repeat Last Call, etc.). This method
has the advantage that only a small part of the vocabulary
need be re-recorded to update announcements, each user hears
each announcement from its beginning, and messages can be
tailored to the needs of individual users. Because of these
advantages such a system can also be used for interactive
general information services.

Attitudes and Expectancies

The voice of the speaker used to generate the announcements
has an effect on the attitudes and expectancies of the user
towards the system. The choice of speaker for the
announcement master recordings was the result of preference
tests on members of the public from British Telecom's large
volunteer subject panel at Ipswich. An attempt has also
been made to relate judged preference and ascribed
personality (Cox and Cooper, 1981). In one experiment,
subjects ranked several voices for preference and on 28
bipolar personality scales (for example: 'serene -
irritable', 'intelligent - unintelligent'). Factor analysis
broke the personality ratings down to two main factors -
'agreeableness' and 'assertiveness'. In general, female
speakers were found to have a slight advantage over males on
rated preference, and were marked up for exhibiting
'assertiveness', while men were marked down for exhibiting
this trait. These findings, of course, provide only a very
partial account of why one speaker's voice may be preferred
to another's. The content of announcements is crucial and a
considerable effort was devoted to devising clear and
concise forms of words.
    The perceived quality of concatenated, stored-waveform
speech can be very high. It may be possible to improve this
even further, on the basis of a detailed study of natural
speech prosodics, but the cost of realisation would be high
if, as would probably be the case, this resulted in the need
to store more versions of each concatenation component. The
introduction of a more natural rhythmic structure could be
achieved at minimal cost, however. But we should not
overlook the danger that a very natural delivery could be
mistaken for a live speaker, with all the confusion this
could cause. Recent experiments have shown that the
characteristics of the voice selected for system influence
the way users tend to interact. A mechanical sounding voice
seems to encourage the ascription of a lower level of

intelligence than a more natural-sounding delivery.

Processing Demands on the User

The use of the auditory channel for information presentation to users raises several problems for the dialogue designer. As speech cannot be scanned, information must be held in 'working memory' long enough for it to be interpreted and acted upon. Baddeley and Hitch (1974) suggested that 'working memory' is composed of two components; a very limited-capacity 'articulatory loop', and a 'central processor' which also has some storage capacity. Storage in the 'articulatory loop' is thought to be limited to about 3 items, and can be utilised without making substantial demands on the processor. Baddeley and Hitch found that processing tasks such as verbal reasoning, prose comprehension, and free-recall learning were impaired when more than 3 items were held in working memory but not when 3 or fewer items were stored, because in the latter case only the articulatory loop was involved. A later study demonstrated that the 'articulatory loop' seems to be limited in time, rather than number of items, accommodating only as much material as can be articulated in about two seconds. In contrast, the 'central processor' is probably item- rather than time-based (see Baddeley, 1976). Chapter 3 provides an account of hypothesised human memory stores and their characteristics.

We have examined the impact of these human limitations on the assimilation of auditory information using, for example, 'menus' of varying size and conceptual complexity. In one study, two information systems using auditory menus were compared. A simple system, providing information on a very restricted problem domain, did not give users difficulty. Here the menu structure was very clear; there were no overlapping categories or tree structures to introduce a problem solving element into the task. An auditory version of 'Prestel', on the other hand, proved very difficult for users to cope with. They often asked for repeats of menus and were often unable to work out the structure of the menus while retaining the options in memory. That is, the problem solving and memory requirements combined seemed to cause the capacity of users' 'working memories' to be exceeded. The same 'Prestel' menus in the visual modality would probably not have caused problems. The visual menu can be scanned repeatedly, so that the memory load is reduced, and visual cues such as colour can provide pointers to the menu structure, thus alleviating the problem solving requirement to some extent.

The presentation of digit strings, by concatenated speech, presented particular problems. Comparison of the short-term retention of automatically announced digit strings, with those spoken by a human operator, indicated inferior performance with the former. A study was conducted (Waterworth, 1983) to investigate the effect of timing and intonation on users' preferences and memory performance with digit strings. We found that memory performance could be improved significantly by increasing the duration of pauses between sub-groups of digits within a string, confirming the work of Grusec (1976), although preference ratings were not affected. Conversely, using a more sophisticated, and natural, pattern of intonation improved subjective preference significantly, but did not influence memorability. Nor were there effects of interactions between timing and intonation, although these factors are known to interact in natural speech production (Pike, 1945).

An alternative to the machine-controlled concatenation of stored-waveform speech elements is to synthesise speech from a set of parameters. This method requires much less machine memory than stored-waveform techniques and removes the need for recording a human voice. It makes available a virtually unlimited vocabulary and can consequently provide the attractive possibility of translating text directly into speech (see Chapter 12 section 12.3). These features impart enormous flexibility to machine speech which can be used to support a broad range of services, from quite limited announcements sets, in the case of Star Services, to full-blown interactive information services, with large and variable data-bases. Unfortunately, the algorithms currently available for generating speech sounds from coded input produce rather unnatural sounding results.

The use of synthetic speech exacerbates the problems inherent in presenting information by voice. Luce et al. (1983) demonstrated that synthetic speech places greater processing demands on 'working' memory than does natural speech and that this accounts in part for difficulties in perception and comprehension of the former. They speculate that this may be due to the relative lack of redundant information in synthesised speech. It is not yet entirely clear, however, that reduced performance levels with synthetic speech are not due to mere unfamiliarity.

Increasing the redundancy of the material can compensate for low intelligibility, to a certain extent (although this will obviously slow down the rate of information exchange), and realistic intonation can also provide cues to the listener. An example of a highly redundant message would be something like "It is necessary for you to identify your account by entering the account number. Please enter all the eight digits of your bank account number by pressing the appropriate keys on your telephone now." A similar message with little redundancy would be "Enter account number now." A recent experiment demonstrated that the choice of vocabulary used in messages can have a marked effect on intelligibility, but it is not possible to compensate for problem words by simply slowing down the delivery rate (see Chapter 7). In natural speech, rate varies with the redundancy of the material, so that highly redundant messages are typically spoken more rapidly than those with relatively little redundancy. This may be an attempt to optimise information exchange by holding the rate of processing constant for both speaker and listener. A sophisticated system could be capable of adjusting delivery rate in this way. This would certainly improve naturalness although it is not certain that the accuracy of information reception would be enhanced. Rate will not be a problem for relatively simple announcement sets, although it should be borne in mind that rate does affect such ascribed personality characteristics as competence and benevolence (e.g., Smith et al., 1975). Prosodic features are very significant in natural, unconstrained speech and can be used to convey intention, emotion, interpretation, elaboration, and even negation of the surface meaning. Pause durations, for example, have semantic significance and this suggests that the sorts of delay that can be experienced with VDT/teletype interactions cannot be tolerated with speech. If possible, pauses should be confined to natural breaks in the speech flow. It is possible that an inappropriate style of delivery would arouse ascriptions of personality or hidden meaning that might hinder the process of information exchange.

13.3 VOICE RECOGNITION

The use of speech recognition equipment (Automatic Speech Recognition or ASR) has several advantages over keyed input, principally because command words can be selected to match the functions they initiate, so that there is no need for the user to map functions onto arbitrary symbols. But the available technology does not, at present, lend itself to particularly comfortable interactions between man and machine, despite the claimed naturalness and convenience of the medium. Dialogue design must take account of the fact that the word 'recognised' will often be the wrong one, so

that the user will frequently need to confirm or correct the
input the machine has identified.

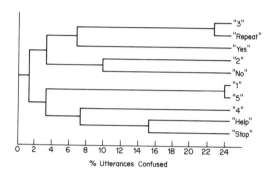

FIG. 13.1 Confusion tree for the digits 1 to 5 and five
command words. Items linked at the right hand side of the
tree are easily confused (e.g. "1" and "5"); items linked at
the left hand side are not easily confused (e.g. "No" and "1").

Measuring Recognition Accuracy

Choosing the most suitable recogniser for a particular task
can be fraught with difficulties. Manufacturers typically
quote figures of between 95 and 99% accuracy for their
products, of whatever type. But without considering other
information this is largely meaningless. Such figures are
presumably derived by very carefully selecting a small,
easily distinguishable vocabulary, and testing with
experienced users in ideal conditions. Accuracy of
recognition (in terms of the number of hits out of the
number of attempts) is important, but the circumstances
under which scores are obtained is crucial, and accuracy is
not the whole story; confusions, too, need to be taken into
account. We have found that confusion matrices and trees
are useful in selecting task vocabularies for particular
applications. A confusion tree of the digits 1 to 5 and
five command words, obtained from an inexpensive single-word

recogniser, is illustrated in Figure 13.1.   The results
shown are from 60 subjects, each repeating all ten words 20
times (i.e., 1200 utterances of each word).   Certain words
are very frequently confused (e.g., '1' and '5', and '3' and
'REPEAT'), whereas for others this is hardly ever the case
(e.g., '1' and 'REPEAT').

What the confusion tree does not show, although a
confusion matrix would, is that the pattern is often not
symmetrical.   In the same trials, 'REPEAT' was misrecognised
as '3' over three times more frequently than '3' was
misrecognised as 'REPEAT', for example.   Figure 13.2
presents a confusion tree for the digits 1 to 10 from 24
subjects, each repeating all ten words 32 times (i.e., 768
utterances of each word).   This clearly indicates that
certain digits, notably '5' and '9', should not be used
together with this device, if at all possible. If it proved
necessary to recognise all the digits, then users would have
to be encouraged to mispronounce the words to make them more
distinguishable (as with the "fife" and "niner" of Civil
Aviation English).   Consideration of the probable pattern of
vocabulary confusions is essential to successful command
word selection for a given application.

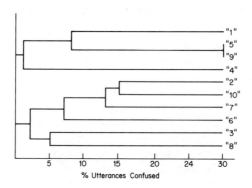

FIG. 13.2 Confusion tree for the digits 1 to 10.

Recognisers really need to be evaluated on the intended
vocabulary, perhaps using a procedure analogous to that

described for assessing speech synthesisers (see Chapter 7). Even better is testing the machine in the target application, but this cannot be done in advance of acquiring the device. An approach that is becoming popular is to provide standard vocabulary tapes for a range of different types of machine. Manufacturers will inevitably tailor their devices to perform well on the test tapes, however, so that the claimed performance may not be achieved in general use unless the material on the tapes is very carefully chosen.

The Limitations Imposed by Existing Systems

Currently available recognition systems impose a large number of constraints on the forms the man-machine interaction can be allowed to take. For example, they are usually only capable of recognising words spoken in isolation and often only by a speaker who has previously 'trained' the system on a particular and very limited vocabulary. With isolated word recognition, the system must interrogate the user in a way that encourages a 'legal' responding utterance. This means that careful consideration must be given to the design of the man-machine speech dialogue, to elicit appropriate responses from the user.

Many devices require the user to repeat the vocabulary of words to be recognised several times in order to 'train' the recogniser. The time and effort required to train a recogniser to a particular voice are likely greatly to inhibit the use of a system. It has been suggested that disguising the training session elicits utterances more similar to those produced during the actual task than when a formal training session is used, although the success of this approach was not tested. The method depends on the user's utterances being predictable, while the user gets the impression that he is actually deciding what to say. For the user, the distinction between training and use is supposed to disappear. While this may avoid some of the irritation generated by the training session, the extent to which the hidden training truly resembles the task situation, from the user's point of view, is more doubtful. It is very difficult to think of training tasks that realistically mimic the actual application, give the impression of subjective control, while being, in fact, totally determined. Such training tasks tend to be trivially easy for users, unlike actually using the system. So the claimed advantage of this technque, that similar utterances are produced in training and actual use, may be

more apparent than real. Voice prompting also has
implications in this area. We have observed that users who
are training a recogniser in response to synthetically
produced vocal prompts have a tendency to imitate the way in
which the prompts are pronounced. If this is also true
during actual use of the system, recognition might be
enhanced. But if the user does not also imitate the
prompting voice during use of the service recognition
performance will be degraded. The effects of visual versus
auditory prompting need to be tested. The use of a very
brief training session, to fine-tune preprogrammed templates
to a particular user, is likely to increase the
acceptability of 'user-dependent' devices in the future.

For a limited set of regular, motivated users, the need
to train the system, and occasionally update templates, is
not a major problem. Of course, the ultimate goal must be
to develop techniques whereby no training of the system by
the user is required, and this is particularly important for
telephone-accessible services used by the general public.
The user cannot be expected to train the system on his voice
every time he wants to know the time of a bus or a weather
report. Recognisers that are available now, and claim to be
speaker independent, have actually been trained by a large
set of users to produce several versions of each word
template, or merge many utterances into composite templates.
Unfortunately, neither approach is very satisfactory, and
the best way of producing general-user templates is not
known. British Telecom are currently investigating one
approach to this problem, that of using different voice
'type' exemplars as templates, from which a particular set
could be selected for each user on the basis of his first
utterances. However, it is unlikely that any one system
would be able to cope with the full range of British accents
and dialects, at least for the foreseeable future. And
there will always be a subset of the population for whom
automatic speech recognition is not possible, hence the need
for operator intervention in cases of serious difficulty.

Connected word recognition is now available, although
this usually still involves training on discrete single
words. The problems associated with using a recogniser can
actually increase with connected-word recognition, because
natural connected speech does not consist of a sequence of
complete, nonoverlapping whole words. Of course, the user
will only be successful if he uses words on which the system
has been trained, and he needs to speak in a very artificial
way. It is difficult to find a simple way of encouraging
the user to make acceptable responses. It is also much
harder to give the user a helpful model of how the system

operates than is the case with single-word machines. The concept of a speech recogniser that recognises all of some phrases, parts of others, and some not at all, is far from obvious. Another major disadvantage is that this approach is not practically extensible to continuous speech recognition from unconstrained discourse, because of lexical demands.

13.4 INTERACTIVE SYSTEMS

Introduction: The Design Process

Factors affecting speech generation and recognition should not be viewed in isolation from the two-way process of information exchange between user and system. For example, synthetic voices that appear unacceptable in highly constrained listening experiments can be more successfully received within the context of using an actual service. Voice recognition, on the other hand, is typically less successful in unconstrained situations than in controlled settings with a carefully enunciating speaker.

Our work in this area includes making specific recommendations for the design of particular interactive systems, using both keyed- and voice-input, and evaluating these systems in use by members of our subject panel. On the basis of an initial evaluation, systems are modified and then re-evaluated. With this approach, system development becomes an interactive cycle of design modification and evaluation, allowing us to develop a methodology for the evaluation of systems, as well as a 'feel' for the sorts of dialogue structures that are likely to be acceptable for particular applications.

Characterising a Human-Computer Dialogue

Although the actual application will have a profound influence on the fine structure of permissible exchanges, an attempt has been made to categorise the features that characterise man-machine vocal communication (Waterworth, 1982). This work was based on the distinction, drawn by Bunt et al. (1978), between two types of 'dialogue acts'; Goal-oriented acts and Dialogue control acts. The former involve the direct communication of goal-relevant information between system and user, the latter are implicated in the prevention and correction of mistakes, and

in the general flow of the dialogue itself, i.e., in the
control of the process of information exchange.

TABLE 13.1 Man-machine speech dialogue acts and subdialogues.

Dialogue Acts		
A Other	B Goal-Oriented	C Dialogue Control

Subdialogues		
(1) Prologue		
	(2) Main Body (Information In)	
		(3) Confirmation
		(4) Recovery/Repair
		(5) Help Safety Net
		(6) Extra Guidance
	(7) Information Out	
		(8) Stop Info./ Restart/Repeat
		(9) Start again/Exit
(10) Epilogue		

   Waterworth (1982) provided a breakdown of these dialogue
acts into specific 'subdialogues', on the basis of the
functions they fulfil in human-machine conversations, and
suggested the most appropriate modes of data entry for
particular subdialogues. Examples of these different types
of subdialogue are 'Prologue', where the system provides
initial greeting and identification of the system,
information on the scope of the information available, as
well as some preliminary guidance on its use, and
'Recovery/repair', resulting from repeated failure to

confirm an input, or difficulties in the successful
recognition of replies to prompts (see Table 13.1).

Waterworth suggested that voice data entry modes could be
ordered hierarchically on a dimension ranging from the most
sophisticated and least explicit (in terms of the extent to
which the user is informed of the system's requirements) at
the top, to the most explicit and basic at the bottom. And,
perhaps more contentiously, it was claimed that parallel
with this dimension is another, the size of the acceptable
user response class, with those modes with a large range of
possible inputs falling high in the hierarchy (Table 13.2).

TABLE 13.2 Voice data entry modes for interactive systems.

Level	Mode of Entry
1.	Command
	(no prompts)
2.	Direct
	("Input A,B,C,D.")
3.	Query
	("What is your price limit?")
4.	Menu
	("on a weekday, a Saturday, or a Sunday?")
5.	Yes/No
	("Travelling to London?") ("Yes or no?")
6.	Grunt
	("For trains to Cambridge make a noise now.")

Systems need to have the capability of dropping down, or
moving up, to an appropriate interaction level on the basis
of users' interactive behaviour. The 'Dialogue control'
approach suggests that one way to minimise user difficulty

with voice-based systems is to give control of the
interactive process, and in particular the presentation of
auditory information, to the user. If he can slow, speed
up, stop and repeat announcements, and 'page' backwards and
forwards through the dialogue, the memory problems arising
from the use of speech might seem to be obviated. But
problems remain. How, for example, are users to be informed
of these capabilities and the way to invoke them? This, in
itself, presents problems of information transfer unless
some other modality (e.g., textual guidance) is employed.
One approach is to make the system sensitive to the user, by
such strategies as reaction time measurement, looping
detection, etc. The user in difficulty (and the expert
user) can then be identified by the system itself and the
dialogue can be tailored accordingly. These two approaches
are actually complimentary. The first involves providing
control facilities, and giving the user a helpful model of
the system, so that he can take control of the dialogue; the
second is effectively an example of the system developing a
model of the user so that appropriate prompts and guidance
can be given automatically. In this way, the man-machine
interaction moves towards a closer approximation of the way
in which people converse together, and control the dialogue
process, on the basis of a model each holds of the other,
and of shared knowledge about conversational conventions.

Some Simple Rules

Synthetic speech should be implemented in such a way that
the user does not get an unrealistic view of the
capabilities of the system. Because of the temporary nature
of speech, and the limitations of human memory, information
must be presented in small enough 'packets' to be easily
assimilated and acted upon by the listener. Very unnatural
sounding speech will tend to decrease retention capacity
over and above any decrement due to poor intelligibility.
Redundancy in voice messages can help, and vocabulary should
be chosen to match users' expectations. Ideally, the output
of information should be user-controllable to avoid memory
overload. Other design strategies for speech output include
the use of an introductory 'blurb' with little informational
content. This allows the user to 'tune in' to the
particular synthesiser used without missing vital
information on the use of the system. Different voices can
also be used to highlight different levels or locations
within the dialogue structure. Such auditory cues are
analogous to the use of highlighting or colour in visual

displays, and can be used to help the user gain a clearer impression of the underlying structure of presented information.

Given the current state of the art, voice recognition should be treated with caution. Devices are very limited in their capabilities, and the structure of the dialogue, for example the choice of prompts to guide users to their goal, requires very careful consideration. Evaluation of a system in use by naive subjects, and subsequent modification, is highly desirable and probably necessary in most cases. Systems should be sensitive to users' behaviour and be capable of adapting the level of interaction (e.g., the specificity and complexity of prompts) accordingly. Future systems are likely to have a sophisticated model of user states and conversational behaviour.

13.5 SUMMARY

Interactive systems, using voice as the medium of information exchange in at least one direction, are already beginning to appear and will proliferate in the fairly near future. Their success depends to some extent on improved speech synthesis and recognition, but perhaps more particularly on the design of dialogues that take account of characteristics of speech and the unique relationships between people and the spoken word.

Good quality machine-generated speech is already available, using the principle of concatenation. But the extent to which it is equivalent to natural speech depends on the storage available, for good quality reproduction and for different versions of speech units appropriate to various contexts. Synthetic speech is potentially much more flexible and economical, but its use can increase the human problems of information assimilation. Characteristics of the voice used can influence users' view of the capabilities and 'personality' of the system.

Speech recognition technology will continue to develop along the path from trained, isolated-word, limited-vocabulary machines to very sophisticated, speaker-independent, extended-vocabulary systems capable of natural language understanding. This goal is still some way off, as the problems of speech recognition are proving more intractable than those of synthesis. To some extent, machines of intermediate sophistication can prove more problematic to the user than very simple systems. Dialogue design is critical and needs to take account of the limitations of recognition equipment and the characteristics

of human information processing capabilities and
conversational behaviour.

13.6 FURTHER READING

Good, general sources on computers and speech are Kuecken
(1983), Lea (1980), and Witten (1982a). Kuecken (1983), in
'Talking Computers and Telecommunications', gives fairly
technical coverage of the use of computer speech for
telecomms. applications, dealing particularly with speech
coding. Witten's (1982a) 'Principles of Computer Speech',
concentrates on speech output, and includes chapters on
man-machine dialogue design and commercially available
devices.
   The collection of chapters edited by Lea (1980), 'Trends
in Speech Recognition', provides a good summary of recent
approaches to speech recognition , including the
contributors to the American ARPA SUR project. More general
aspects of person-machine speech dialogues are covered by
Waterworth, J.A. (1982) and Bunt, H.C., Leopold, F.F.,
Muller, H.F., and van Katwijk, A.F.V. (1978).

CHAPTER 14

Human Factors Problems in the Design
and Use of Expert Systems

Alison Kidd

14.1 INTRODUCTION TO EXPERT SYSTEMS

Expert systems are a class of computer systems which have
evolved over the past ten years from the field of Artificial
Intelligence (AI) research. They embody the specialised
knowledge and experience of a human expert in a chosen
domain and a mechanism for applying this knowledge to solve
problems in that domain. Most expert systems act as
consultants in the sense that the user supplies information
about the problem and the system asks relevant questions and
then offers advice or makes a decision. Expert systems are
being used with considerable success to solve problems in a
number of scientific, medical and industrial applications.
   Obviously, computer systems that aid in decision-making
are not a new development. Conventional systems have proved
very effective for solving problems with a mathematical or
statistical basis or problems of a routine data processing
nature. However, in areas such as management, industry and
medicine, important problems exist which do not fit into
this category. Solving such problems is still critically
dependent on human expertise, skills such as identifying and
relating the key factors, weighing evidence, evaluating
alternatives, predicting outcomes and making complex
decisions. This can be summed up as the human's ability to
bring a wealth of diverse knowledge and years of experience
to bear on the problem in hand.

The problem of relying on human expertise alone in such areas is that expertise of this kind is often scarce; it may also be transient and is rarely economical. The use of expert systems means that expertise in a particular domain can be made more permanent and also more widely available to those who require it. A more important point is that the complexity of modern technology is giving rise to an increasing number of situations in industry and management where any one human expert is incapable of processing the sheer volume of information involved in making reliable and informed decisions. In principle, expert systems need not be constrained in this way by strict memory and processing limitations.

14.2 HOW EXPERT SYSTEMS WORK

How Knowledge is Represented

In an expert system, the knowledge is typically represented in the form of facts and rules. Facts are the type of domain knowledge found in specialist textbooks and journals whereas rules are the 'heuristics', or rules of thumb which experts build up over years of practical experience in the domain. These guide the use of the facts to solve problems.

There are many different ways of representing this kind of knowledge in program form; the most common way is to encode the knowledge in the form of 'production' or 'if-then' rules. For example, the following rules are typical of the things humans either know or learn in order to solve real world problems:

"IF a person has spots and a temperature THEN he may have measles."
"IF the car engine will not start and fuel is reaching the cylinders THEN the ignition system is faulty."

It seems that much real world and expert knowledge can be represented as collections of such rules. In an expert system, a whole set of 'production rules' are chained together to represent a complex decision process, e.g., fault diagnosis. Each condition (or left-hand) part of a rule refers to a fact which may or may not be recorded as true in the current data base. If the data base does not contain the fact, the system will ask the user whether it is true. For a rule to 'fire', all its conditions must be true and then the action (or right-hand) part of the rule is

executed. This action may specify which rule should be
considered next or, at the end of the chain, may state the
final conclusion (e.g., a diagnosis) to the user.

The main advantage of using production rules in expert
systems is that they capture in a manageable representation
scheme a certain type of problem-solving knowledge, i.e.,
knowledge about what to do in a specific situation. Although
this kind of knowledge is basically procedural, production
rules also possess many of the advantages of declarative
representation schemes, for example the modularity of the
rules. Individual rules in the knowledge base can be added,
deleted or modified independently. They behave basically
like independent pieces of knowledge. Another advantage is
that the rules have a certain psychological validity in that
they are structured in a similar way to the way people talk
about how they solve problems. This is why production rules
have been used as the basis for the development of most of
the major expert systems in existence today.

How Knowledge is Used to Solve Problems

There are two possible control strategies for using
production rules to solve problems. These can also be
identified as two common ways in which humans reason (see
Chapter 4).

(i) Forward chaining - here one starts from the
available information or assumptions (the 'IF' parts of a
production rule) and reasons forward to try to infer the
conclusions that are appropriate for the problem goal.
For example, in a medical diagnostic task, a doctor might
have no idea what is wrong with his patient so he may
work up through the set of reported symptoms until he has
narrowed down the set of possible diseases which can be
inferred.

(ii) Backward chaining - here one reasons in the
opposite direction; i.e., one starts with the desired
goal or conclusion (the 'THEN' part of a production rule)
and reasons backwards through the available data in order
to try to establish all the necessary evidence to support
that conclusion. For example, a doctor may expect from
the start that his patient has a particular disease and
he, therefore, works backwards from this hypothesis or
'goal' in order to discover which symptoms must be
present for this hypothesis to be supported.

Which of these two control strategies is implemented in a particular production system will depend on the characteristics of the problem space. In a diagnostic system, for example, forward chaining is a good technique to use if there are a large number of possible symptoms converging on only a small set of possible faults. On the other hand, backward chaining is a more efficient technique to use if the set of possible faults is large but the number of possible symptoms is relatively few. In the case of human reasoning, however, forward chaining seems to be flexibly mixed with backward chaining. This means, for example, that a doctor solving a diagnostic problem may use backward chaining because he has a hunch that the patient has a particular disease but he may switch automatically to forward chaining if an unexpected-but-relevant piece of information is suddenly volunteered by the patient. This is the sort of flexible control structure which the designers of expert systems are eventually seeking to emulate.

A problem with implementing knowledge in an expert system is that most real world problems involve decisions being made on the basis of uncertain information. Consequently, most expert systems incorporate some form of probablistic reasoning as part of their inference control mechanism, enabling the system to reason with uncertain information. This means that imprecise conclusions can be drawn from imprecise sets of premises.

Current Applications of Expert Systems

There are a growing number of expert systems in current practical use, principally in the United States, but more recently in the U.K. as well. The following list gives an idea of the range of current application areas:

    Medical diagnosis and prescription
    Equipment failure diagnosis
    Computer configuration
    Chemical data interpretation and structure elucidation
    Experiment planning
    Speech and image understanding
    Signal interpretation
    Mineral exploration
    Military threat assessment and targeting
    Crisis management
    Advising about computer systems
    Training and teaching
    VLSI design

```
Air traffic control
Database management
Intelligent interfaces
```

There are a number of important human factors issues
which can be identified in the design and use of expert
systems. The remainder of this chapter briefly discusses
three of these issues: acquiring knowledge from the human
expert, the representation and use of that knowledge to
solve problems and the user interface design.

14.3   ACQUIRING KNOWLEDGE FROM THE HUMAN EXPERT

The Nature of the Problem

The first step in building an expert system is to acquire
the necessary knowledge about the domain from the human
expert. This is an extremely difficult, messy and
time-consuming process and is recognised as the biggest
bottleneck in the production of these systems. Although
numerous expert systems have now —been constructed, an
effective standardised method for acquiring the expert's
knowledge has still not been developed. At present, the
process still constitutes more of an art than a science!
The problem is characterised on the one side by an
expert, unfamiliar with expert systems and unable to
articulate what knowledge he has and how he uses it to solve
problems; and on the other side by a knowledge engineer who
may well be totally ignorant about the domain of expertise.
Obviously, if expert systems are to be produced in multiple
applications then the process of knowledge acquisition
desperately needs streamlining for speed and efficiency.
Accuracy is a major problem as well. The use of
inappropriate techniques or badly interpreted data will
result in ineffective systems.

Techniques for Knowledge Acquisition

The first step of the knowledge acquisition process is to
define the problem and the basic concepts in the application
area. This initial structuring of the domain can be the
most difficult part. It seems that the most effective method
at this stage is to conduct in-depth interviews with the
expert. If possible, these should be tape-recorded so that
they can subsequently be transcribed and analysed in detail.

At the next stage, the interviewer (or 'knowledge engineer') must focus on the expert's experiential knowledge, including his assumptions, definitions, strategies, rules of thumb and guesses. To facilitate this task, the knowledge engineer usually presents the expert with a selection of hypothetical problems in which the relevant factors are systematically varied. The expert is encouraged to describe the rules he uses to arrive at his conclusions. He is then asked to try to analyse these rules at a more detailed level to uncover the data elements from which they are constructed. The choice of what level of detail is needed to describe these basic data elements may initially be just intuitive guesswork on the part of the knowledge engineer. Later, as the concepts and rules needed to answer the hypothetical questions are refined, the knowledge engineer and expert together may discover the level of representation best suited to the application in hand. Defining the basic concepts in the domain and representing them in an explicit and precise fashion is a difficult process and one not well understood at present. At the same time, decisions made at this stage are critical because they greatly influence the potential capabilities of the system, including its flexibility and power.

Alongside the interviews, other knowledge acquisition methods may be employed, for example:

(i) studying past and present problems and their solutions;

(ii) identifying prototypical or idealised problem types and associated solutions;

(iii) carrying out literature searches;

(iv) systematic observation of and collecting verbal protocols from experts at work in a real environment, solving actual, as opposed to hypothetical problems (this is vital in order to distinguish between the knowledge experts think they use and the knowledge they actually use in solving problems).

Once all this knowledge has been extracted and formalised, a prototype expert system is implemented. This system must then be rigorously tested to see if it is capable of predicting the expert's decisions on both old and new problems. Further interaction with the expert will be necessary at this stage in order to refine the system and make it model the expert more closely.

Tools

One attempt to alleviate the problem of knowledge acquisition has been the recent development of interactive programs that communicate with the expert to provide some of the kind of help a knowledge engineer provides. TEIRESIAS (Davis and Lenat, 1982) is probably the best developed example of this, but even it is currently limited to helping debug and fill out a knowledge base which has already been largely codified.

Another, very different approach to the problem, is the development of systems which can acquire their knowledge automatically. The process used for this is induction. Specific examples of a concept in the task domain (e.g., a 'serious fault') are input to the system as 'raw data' and the system uses inductive reasoning techniques to discover the simplest set of rules for correctly classifying examples according to the concept. All that is needed then in this case is a source of pre-classified examples. The claim is that however groping and confused experts may be at describing concepts, most of them are very good at categorising examples. However, it is not yet clear how useful this tool will be across a range of problems. There is also a major handicap that the rules output by such systems tend to be unstructured and extremely difficult to understand.

14.4   REPRESENTATION AND USE OF KNOWLEDGE BY THE SYSTEM

From a human factors point of view, there are two important requirements for the design of the knowledge representation and control strategy employed by an expert system: accuracy and intelligibility.

Accuracy

The knowledge representation and control strategy selected for an expert system should accurately reflect what the human expert knows and how he uses that knowledge to solve the problem. This does not mean that the system has to be a psychological model, exactly imitating a human's reasoning process, but it does mean that the representation chosen must be able to capture the fullest possible range and power of the human expert's knowledge in that particular domain. For example, in a fault-finding application, it may be very

important for the system to be able to represent explicitly
the cost of the different tests. This can often be a more
crucial factor determining the expert's problem solving
strategy, more so than the likelihood of different faults on
the system.

On these grounds, it is important for the knowledge
engineer to carry out at least an initial stage of knowledge
acquisition before he can intelligently commit himself to a
particular knowledge representation or control strategy.

Intelligibility

If an expert system is to be responsible for complex
decision making and giving advice, then it is vital that
there is compatibility, at the cognitive level, between the
user's model of the problem and the system's. In other
words, the knowledge representation and problem solving
processes employed by the system must be readily
intelligible to the user. Only if this is true will the
user both be able to interact competently and efficiently
with the system during its reasoning process and also be
confident in the system's reasoning and advice.

Because of the way that the knowledge is made explicit in
an expert system, there is the potential to provide some
form of limited explanation of the system's reasoning by
printing out, on request, a trace of the rules which have
fired on any program run. The ability of expert systems to
provide an explanation of their reasoning is obviously an
important aspect of their intelligibility to the user.
Unfortunately, the explanations provided by current expert
systems are often very poor. One reason for this is that
explanation is not treated as a task which requires
intelligence in itself. To provide useful explanations,
systems need to make use not only of knowledge about how to
solve problems in their respective domains but also
knowledge of how to communicate effectively an understanding
of this problem-solving process to the user. This involves
formalising the heuristics used to construct good
explanations. For example, in the case of human experts, an
appropriate explanation depends on the expert's assessment
of what the questioner has failed to understand and his
knowledge of how much the user knows about the domain.

14.5   USER INTERFACE DESIGN

There is no point in having a powerful knowledge-based
system if users cannot easily and efficiently communicate
with it under the constraints of a real-time task. This is
not necessarily a case of providing the system with a
natural language interface. More importantly, it is a
matter of ensuring that the dialogue facilities of an expert
system match the communication needs and constraints imposed
by the class of users for that system and the type of task
in question.

For example, most current expert systems act as
consultants and engage the user in a fairly rigid and often
laborious question/answer style dialogue in order to obtain
all the necessary information about his problem. In most
cases, the structure of this dialogue is directly controlled
by the system's inference strategy. In the case of backward
chaining, this often results in the user being asked a very
large number of questions, many of which may appear
frustratingly irrelevant to him. Controlled in this way,
the order of the questions may also be unnatural and
inefficient from the user's point of view.

Another important point is that the user should be able
to volunteer information concerning his problem easily and
rapidly to the system. This requires both a flexible
mixed-initiative style dialogue so that the user can easily
take over control from the system at any point and also the
development of appropriate interfaces (e.g., menus,
graphics, etc.) which will help the user to be able to enter
different types of information naturally and efficiently.

Intelligent Interfaces to Conventional Systems

The knowledge-based techniques discussed in this chapter
also have a valuable role to play in improving the usability
of interfaces to conventional computer systems. In the same
way as expert systems incorporate and make use of expert
knowledge to solve specific problems, so an intelligent
interface can be created in the form of a 'knowledgeable
assistant' whose task is to help (and possibly teach) the
user to interact more competently and efficiently with some
conventional system or package. Such an assistant would
need to incorporate the following types of knowledge:

(i)   knowledge about the application domain
(ii)   knowledge about the system or package being used

(iii)   knowledge about the different tasks the user might
want to carry out
(iv)   knowledge about the user:-
-   his level of competence with the system
-   his model of how the system works
-   his goals, needs, expectations, assumptions, etc.
-   his preferred method of interaction

Knowledge about the user can either be obtained by asking
the user questions at the beginning of a session or by the
system directly inferring it from the user's on-line
behaviour.

The knowledge listed above can be used to improve the
ease and efficiency of communication between the user and
the system. For example, at the simplest level, the
knowledge can be used to make run-time checking more
intelligent by checking whether the user's input makes sense
in the current context rather than just checking whether it
is a legal value. Knowledge can also be used to allow less
restricted input and output formatting, e.g., limited
natural language understanding and generation. The
assistant could also automatically carry out for the user
the more tedious or routine parts of his task or could
suggest to him more efficient ways of achieving certain
goals. Much research is currently in progress to develop
such intelligent interfaces.

14.6   SUMMARY

There is little doubt that if the development and
exploitation of expert system technology is successful then
it will have a substantial impact on computer and
communications industries all over the world. However, with
the advent of thinking, reasoning machines, the old problems
of man-machine compatibility have acquired a new
significance. The cognitive characteristics of the human
mind have become a critical design constraint in the design
of such systems. Three important human factors issues for
the design and use of expert systems are identified in this
chapter: acquiring knowledge from the human expert, the
representation and use of that knowledge within the system
and the user interface design. If the full potential of
expert system technology is to be realised then it is vital
that these human factors issues are taken into account in
the design and use of future systems.

14.7   FURTHER READING

A sound introduction to the field of artificial intelligence
is to be found in Barr and Feigenbaum (1981). The only
proper text book on the subject of expert systems is by
Hayes-Roth, Waterman and Lenat (1983), a very useful
reference book, containing a thorough introduction to the
relevant AI techniques and detailed descriptions of the
major expert systems in the USA. Other recommended books on
the subject are the useful selection of papers edited by
Michie (1982) and Welbank's useful review of the literature
in the area of knowledge acquisition techniques.

Clancey has published a number of very useful papers on
the subject of explanations; see for example Hasling,
Clancey and Rennels (1984). For further information on the
user interface and expert systems see Hayes and Reddy
(1983), Hayes and Szekely (1983) and Coombs and Alty (1984).

GLOSSARY

The items in this glossary have been chosen by a process of elimination, knowledge of which may help the reader find the information being sought. Terms which are explained in the text have not been included; this information can be accessed via the subject index. Computing terms have in general been excluded except where usage varies widely.

ACUITY. To measure a person's visual acuity is to measure the smallest "thing" (usually a gap or a line) that he can detect.

AI. Artificial intelligence (AI) is an academic discipline with some degree of overlap with the disciplines of Linguistics, Psychology and Computer Science. Research on AI is concerned with devising mechanisms (usually embodied in computer programs) to perform tasks we would normally view as intelligent: playing chess, image processing and natural language processing, for example. Much of the recent work in AI has been concerned with Expert Systems.

AMPLITUDE see FREQUENCY.

AMPLITUDE SPECTRUM. Any complex waveform can be considered to be composed of a number of sine waves (sinusoids) which have been added together. The amplitude (power) spectrum indicates the amplitude (power) of each component. To specify the waveform fully, its phase relationships must also be given. A sound spectrum (or spectral section) is usually the power spectrum of a sound (see also FILTER).

ANALYSIS OF VARIANCE. The stastistical analysis most commonly used for complex experimental designs is known as the analysis of variance. In an experiment with a factorial design two variables are manipulated; for example, one might be studying the effects of computing experience and age on the performance of some task. This could be done by having four groups of subjects: young computer naive users, young computer experienced users, old computer naive users and old computer experienced users. These four groups can be thought of as the 'factorial combination' of the two independent variables age and experience. If the analysis of variance is applied to the results of such an experiment it will tell

you the significance of each 'main effect' and the
'interaction'. The main effect of age is the difference
between the mean score of the two young groups and the
mean of the two old groups. Likewise, the main effect of
experience is the overall difference between naive and
experienced subjects. The interaction would be
significant if the effect of age depends on the degree of
experience or vice versa (e.g., if age has an effect when
comparing the two computer naive groups but not when
comparing the two computer experienced groups).

ARTIFICIAL INTELLIGENCE. See AI.

BANDWIDTH. See FILTER.

BUFFER. Computing machinery often contains information
buffers. This is a store or memory which temporarily
holds information from one part of the system while
another part deals with it. For example, a lineprinter,
which is a relatively slow device, may have a buffer to
hold a quantity of information from the relatively fast
CPU while it is printed. Biological information
processing systems may depend on memory mechanisms with a
similar function.

COGNITIVE. Cognitive Psychology is the study of higher
mental processes. It is common to distinguish between
perceptual or peripheral processes (processes dealing
with information from sensors such as the eye or ear) and
more central or cognitive processes which deal with more
abstract representations. Thus reasoning is thought to
be a cognitive task while colour discrimination is
perceptual.

COMPUTER NAIVE. It is common to distinguish between users
who are computer naive and those who are computer
sophisticated. Many computer systems have certain things
in common (e.g., pressing a 'return' or 'enter' key at
the end of a command) so that using one system can often
help (or hinder) learning about a new one. People with
little experience of computers are said to be computer
naive.

CONFOUNDED VARIABLE. See CONTROL GROUP.

CONTRAST SENSITIVITY. Visual stimuli can be presented at
varying contrasts. For example, two gratings of evenly
spaced stripes could be presented so that their mean
luminance is the same but the difference in luminance
between the dark and light stripes is different. If
contrast is reduced, then at some point the stripes will
not be discernable. The minimum contrast at which the
stripes can be detected is the contrast threshold. The
contrast sensitivity is the inverse of the contrast
threshold.

CONTRAST THRESHOLD. See CONTRAST SENSITIVITY.

CONTROL GROUP.   A control group is often employed in
behavioural experiments. The treatment of the control
group should be similar in every way to the experimental
group, apart from the variable being studied. For
example, to study the effect of environmental noise on
performance there should be two groups of subjects. One
would work in quiet conditions, the other in noisy
conditions. The task performed, the equipment used and
every other detail must be the same for the two groups if
we are to attribute any difference between them to the
presence of noise. This degree of experimental control
is often difficult to achieve in applied work. If some
variable cannot be controlled and it varies with the one
you are manipulating, it is said to be a confounded
variable and the two variables are said to be confounded
with one another. An example would be age and experience
which are often confounded.

CRT DISPLAY.   A CRT display is strictly speaking a display
using a Cathode Ray Tube ('Video'). It is also commonly
used to mean a terminal with a video display and a key
board. (See also VDT and VDU).

DISPLAY RESOLUTION. A CRT display can be thought of as an n
x m array of points. At any moment some of these points
will be 'brighted up' and some will not. The elements in
the array, the points, are known as pixels and the number
of them in the array determines its resolution. With a
large array (high resolution) it is possible to include
much more detail than with a small array. This makes it
possible to display smooth curves and straight lines at
arbitrary angles. Low resolution displays can do this
less effectively as it is less likely there will be a
pixel at the precise position required. As a rule of
thumb, displays with an array of at least 1024 x 768
points are considered high resolution displays, those
with 256 x 256 or less points are considered low
resolution and medium resolution displays have around 512
x 512 points.

EMULATION. In the process of developing a computer-based
system it is common practice to emulate or simulate the
system using hardware more powerful than the hardware
which will eventually be used. Emulation can be
distinguished from simulation on the basis of
verisimilitude. A prototype which includes only a part
of the specification or which differs from the final
system in important details is a simulation. On the
other hand, from the point of view of the user, an
emulation is indistinguishable from the final product.

(One could simulate the exploding of an atomic bomb, but it would be foolish to emulate it!)

FACTORIAL DESIGN. See ANALYSIS OF VARIANCE.

FILTER. Any complex waveform can be considered to be composed of a number of sine waves (sinusoids) which have been added together. A filter selectively modifies the 'power' of these components. A high-pass filter reduces the intensity of low frequency components but has relatively little effect on high frequency components. Similarly, a low-pass filter lets through low frequency components and attenuates high frequency components. Other filters have a 'pass-band' of frequencies which are unaffected and everything either side of the pass-band is attenuated. In fact all electronic and biological systems act as filters of a kind. That is to say there are frequencies below and above which the system will not respond. Consider, for example, a HiFi amplifier. The range of frequencies over which the system functions normally is called the 'bandwidth' of the system. (See also AMPLITUDE SPECTRUM.)

FREQUENCY. A sinusoidal waveform has an amplitude and a frequency. The frequency is the number of times it repeats itself in some unit of time, commonly cycles per second or 'Hz'. The amplitude is the magnitude of the wave, for example, the peak-to-peak amplitude.

HIGH-PASS FILTER. See FILTER.

HIGH-RESOLUTION DISPLAY. See DISPLAY RESOLUTION

Hz. See FREQUENCY.

INTERACTION. See ANALYSIS OF VARIANCE.

j.n.d. The Just Noticeable Difference is the smallest change in some physical characteristic of a stimulus (e.g., intensity) that can be identified. (See THRESHOLD)

LOW-PASS FILTER. See FILTER.

LOW-RESOLUTION DISPLAY. See DISPLAY RESOLUTION.

MAIN EFFECT. See ANALYSIS OF VARIANCE.

MEAN. The (arithmetic) mean of a set of numbers is computed by adding them all up and dividing by the number of numbers.

MEASURE OF CENTRAL TENDENCY. The mean or average is a measure of central tendency as are the median and the mode. Measures of central tendency can be distinguished from measures of dispersion, which are also used to characterise a set of numbers or scores. Measures of dispersion characterise the spread of scores. The range and standard deviation are examples of measures of dispersion.

MEASURES OF DISPERSION. See MEASURES OF CENTRAL TENDENCY.

MEDIUM-RESOLUTION DISPLAY. See DISPLAY RESOLUTION
NEURON. See SYNAPSE.
NONSENSE WORD. In an effort to minimise the effects of
    previous experience with linguistic materials,
    psychologists often use nonsense words or nonsense
    syllables (e.g., GAX, FLUNT).
OCTAVE. If a wave has a frequency twice that of another the
    former is said to be an octave higher.
PERIPHERAL PROCESSING. See COGNITIVE.
PERIPHERAL VISION. See POINT OF FIXATION.
PIXEL. See DISPLAY RESOLUTION
POINT OF FIXATION. The point of fixation is the point in a
    visual display on which the eyes are focussing. It
    corresponds to the part of the display in foveal or
    central vision, everything else is in peripheral vision.
    Also known as the 'Point of Regard'.
POINT OF REGARD. See POINT OF FIXATION.
POWER SPECTRUM. See AMPLITUDE SPECTRUM.
PRESTEL. Prestel is a data bank publicly available in Great
    Britain via the telephone. It uses a domestic television
    as its visual display and has a rudimentary keypad for
    input. This type of facility is sometimes known as
    Viewdata. (See TELETEXT)
SEMANTIC. A semantic analysis has to do with the meaning of
    the thing being analysed. Semantics are often contrasted
    with Syntax which refers to grammar. (See also SYNTAX)
SOUND SPECTRUM. See AMPLITUDE SPECTRUM.
STIMULUS. The classical view of behaviour is one of
    responses being elicited from an organism by stimuli,
    i.e., situations which stimulate its sense organs. The
    materials presented in an experiment, or elsewhere, are
    still commonly referred to as stimuli.
SUBJECT. An experimental subject is a person who takes part
    in an experiment, what the general public might call a
    'guinea pig'.
SYNAPSE. The nervous system contains cells known as
    neurons. These neurons communicate with one another by
    means of electro-chemical impulses. The structure
    through which one neuron communicates with another is
    known as the synapse.
SYNTAX. A syntactic analysis has to do with the grammar of
    the thing being analysed. For example, in English an
    article ('the' or 'a') is always followed by a noun,
    adverb or adjective. In PASCAL a ":=" is always followed
    by an 'expression'. (See also SEMANTIC)
TELETEXT. Teletext is the generic term for publicly
    available data bases which use the domestic television as
    a display device. This would include Prestel and Viewdata

as well as less interactive versions where the information is broadcast with the television signal.

TEMPLATE. At some point in any mechanical recognition system some representation of the object to be recognised, or some part of it, must be compared with a set of stored representations with known names. These stored representations are the 'templates'. The template which matches the object to be recognised most closely is identified and its name is given to the object. For example, if the template for the letter 'A' is most similar then the object is recognised as an 'A'. Template matching is sometimes contrasted with the feature analysis approach to recognition. There components of the stimulus (features) are recognised and then rules are applied to determine what object is specified by that combination of features. However, this really only postpones the problem as templates of some kind are still needed to recognise the features.

THRESHOLD. The 'intensity threshold' or absolute threshold is the intensity below which a stimulus cannot be detected. The 'difference threshold' is the smallest change in some characteristic of a stimulus that can be identified, i.e., the 'just noticeable difference' (see j.n.d.).

VDT. A Visual Display Terminal is a terminal with a video screen and a key-board. VDTs are also known as VDUs and 'CRT displays' depending upon which part of the world you are in.

VDU. See VDT.

VIEWDATA. See PRESTEL.

WORKING MEMORY. One obvious potential function for short term memory is as a 'working memory', that is as a temporary store to be used as a part of some cognitive process; for example, holding a string of words in memory while its grammar and meaning is extracted or holding part answers while doing mental arithmetic.

REFERENCES

ACM Computing Surveys. (March 1981). Special issue on "The Psychology of Human-Computer Interaction". 13(1), 71-99.

Allen, R.B. & Scerbo, M.W. (1983). Details of command-language keystrokes. ACM Transactions on Office Information Systems, 1, 159-178.

Akin, O. (1981). Efficient computer-user interface in electronic mail systems. Working Papers in User-Computer Interface. Carnegie-Mellon University.

Alvi, M.A., Daskalakis, C., & Powner, E.T. (1982). The design of man-machine software interfaces. IEE International Conference on Man/Machine Systems, Manchester (pp 6-10).

Anastasi, A. (1982) Psychological Testing. 5th edition. Macmillan, New York.

Anderson, J.R. (1976). Language, Memory and Thought. Erlbaum, Hillsdale, N.J.

Anderson, J.R. (1980). Cognitive Psychology and its Implications. W.H. Freeman & Co., San Francisco.

Anderson, J.R. & Bower, G.H. (1973). Human Associative Memory. V.H. Winston & Sons, Washington, D.C.

Archer (Jr.), J. & Conway, R. (1981). COPE: A cooperative programming environment. TR 81-459, Cornell University.

Baddeley, A.D. (1976). The Psychology of Memory. Harper & Row, New York.

Baddeley, A.D., Eldridge, M. & Lewis, V. (1981). The role of subvocalisation in reading. Quarterly Journal of Experimental Psychology, 33A, 439-454.

Baddeley, A.D. (1983) Your Memory: A User's Guide. Penguin, Harmondsworth, Middx.

Bailey, R.W. (1982) Human performance engineering: a guide for system designers. Prentice Hall: Englewood Cliffs, N.J.

Baker, C.L. (1967). JOSS: Rubrics, P-3560, RAND Corp. Available from Ministry of Defence Library, Old War Office Building, London S.W.1.

Bamford, R.J., Weller, D.L. & Williams, R. (1979). Source code generation method utilizing a programmable graphics display system. IBM Technical Disclosure Bulletin, 22, 2493-2495.

Barnard, P.J. (1983). Applying the products of research on interactive dialogues. In: M.J. Elphick (ed.) Man-Machine Interaction: Proceedings of the Joint

IBM/University of Newcastle Seminar.

Barnard, P.J. & Hammond, N.V. (1982). Usability and its multiple determination for the occasional user of interactive systems. In: M.B. Williams (ed.) Pathways to the Information Society: Sixth International Conference on Computer Communication. North-Holland: Amsterdam.

Barnard, P.J., Hammond, N.V., MacLean, A. & Morton, J. (1982). Learning and remembering interactive commands in a text-editing task. Behaviour and Information Technology, 1, 347-358.

Barnard, P.J., Hammond, N.V., Morton, J., Long, J.B. & Clark, I.A. (1981). Consistency and compatibility in human-computer dialogue. International Journal of Man-machine Studies, 15, 87-134.

Barr, A. & Feigenbaum, E.A. (1981). The Handbook of Artificial Intelligence, Volumes 1-3. Pitman Books Ltd., London.

Bauer, D. & Cavonius, C.R. (1980). Improving the legibility of visual display units through contrast reversal. In: Grandjean, E. & Vigliani, E. (eds.), Egonomic Aspects of Visual Display Terminals. Taylor & Francis, London.

Bennett, J.L. (1979). Incorporating usability into system design. Design '79 Symposium. Monterey, California.

Boarder, J.C. (1980). Graphical programming for parallel processing systems. Internal Report, Oxford Polytechnic, Oxford.

Boarder, J.C. (1981). The graphical parallel programming language LZ. Sixth Annual Microprocessor Workshop on Microprocessor Applications, Liverpool.

Braddick, O.J. & Sleigh, A.C. (eds.) (1983). Physical and Biological Processing of Images, Springer-Verlag, Berlin.

Bradshaw, J. (1975). Three interrelated problems in reading: A review. Memory and Cognition, 3, 123-134.

Broadbent, D.E., Cooper, P.F., FitzGerald, P. & Parkes, K.R. (1982). The cognitive failures questionaire (CFQ) and its correlates. Brit. J. of Psychology, 50, 253-290.

Broadbent, D.E. (1958). Perception and Communication. Pergamon Press, London.

Brooks, F.P. (1977). The Computer 'Scientist' as Toolsmith - Studies in Interactive Computer Graphics, in Gilchrist, E.B. (ed) IFIP Conference Information Processing '77, 625-634.

Brown, J.W. (1982). Controlling the complexity of menu networks. Communications of the ACM, 25(7), 412-418.

Bruder, G.A. (1978). Role of visual familiarity in the word

superiority effects obtained with the simultaneous-matching task. Journal of Experimental Psychology: Human Perception and Performance, $\underline{4}$, 88-100.

Buchanan, B.G. (1979). Issues of representation in conveying the scope and limitations of intelligent assistant programs. In Hayes, J.E., Michie, D. & Mikulich, L.I. (eds.) Machine Intelligence $\underline{9}$. Ellis Horwood Ltd., Chichester.

Bunt, H.C., Leopold, F.F., Muller, H.F., & van Katwijk, A.F.V. (1978). In search of pragmatic principles in man-machine dialogues. IPO Annual Progress Report, $\underline{13}$, 94-98.

Cakir, A., Hart, D.J. & Stewart, T.F.M. (1979). The VDT Manual. Inca-Fief Research Associates, Darmstadt.

Campbell, F.W. & Maffei, L. (1974). Contrast and spatial frequency. Scientific American, $\underline{231}$, 106-114.

Card, S.K., English, W.K., & Burr, B.J. (1978). Evaluation of mouse, rate-controlled isometric joystick, step keys and text keys for text selection on a CRT. Ergonomics, $\underline{21}$, 601-613.

Card, S.K., Moran, T.P. & Newell, A. (1980). Computer text-editing: An information-processing analysis of a routine cognitive skill. Cognitive Psychology, $\underline{12}$, 32-74.

Card, S.K., Moran, T. & Newell, A. (1983). The Psychology of Human-Computer Interaction. Erlbaum, Hillsdale, N.J.

Carlson, E.D., Giddings, G.M. & Williams, R. (1977). Multiple colors and image mixing in graphics terminals. IFIP Congress 77, $\underline{7}$, 179-182.

Carroll, J.M. (1982). The Adventure of Getting to Know a Computer, IEEE Computer, $\underline{15}$, 49-58.

Carroll, J.M. & Rosson, M.B. (In Press) Usability specifications as a tool in interactive development. In Hartson, H.R. (ed.) Advances in Human-Computer Interaction. Ablex Publishing, Norwood, New Jersey.

Carroll, J.M. & Thomas, J.C. (1982). Metaphor and the Cognitive Representation of Computing Systems, IEEE Transactions on Systems, Man, and Cybernetics, $\underline{SMC-12}$, 107-116.

Chapanis, A. (1981). Interactive Human Communication: Some Lessons Learned from Laboratory Experiments, in Shackel, B. (ed) Man-Computer Interaction: Human Factors Aspects of Computers & People, NATO Advanced Study Institutes Series E: No. 44 Sijthoff & Noordhoff, The Netherlands (pp65-114).

CHI '83: Human Factors in Computing Systems, Boston, December 1983. ACM, New York. (Special issue of SIGCHI Bulletin).

Christ, R.E. (1975). Review and analysis of color coding research for visual displays. Human Factors, 17(6), 542-570.

Clark, H.H. & Carlson, T.B. (1981). Context for comprehension. In: Long, J.B. & Baddeley, A.D. (eds.) Attention and Performance 9. Erlbaum, Hillsdale, N.J.

Cole, R.A. (ed.) (1980). Perception and Production of Fluent Speech. Erlbaum, Hillsdale, N.J.

Coltheart, M. (1978). Lexical access in simple reading tasks. In: Underwood, G. (ed.), Strategies of Information Processing. Academic Press, London.

Coombs, M.J. & Alty, J.L. (eds.) (1981). Computing Skills and the User Interface. Academic Press, London.

Coombs, M.J. & Alty, J.L. (1984). Expert systems: an alternative paradigm. International Journal Man-Machine Studies, 20(1), 21-43.

Cox, A.C. & Cooper, M.B. (1981). Selecting a voice for a specified task: the example of telephone announcements. Language and Speech, 24, 233-243.

Craik, F. & Lockhart, R. (1972). Levels of processing: A framework for memory research. Journal of Verbal Learning and Verbal Behaviour, 11, 671-684.

Crowder, R.G. (1982). The Psychology of Reading. Oxford University Press.

Cuff, R.N. (1980). On casual users. International Journal of Man-Machine Studies, 12, 163-187.

Dallimonti, R. (1980). Principles of design for man-machine interfaces in process control. In: Man-Machine Interfaces for Industrial Control. Control Engineering (April) (pp 13-34).

Danchak, M.M. (1976). CRT displays for power plants. Instrumentation Technology, 23, 29-36.

Danchak, M.M. (1977). Alphanumeric displays for the man-process interface. Advances in Instrumentation, 32 (ISA Conference - Niagara Falls part 1 pp 197-213).

Davies, D.W. & Yates, D.M. (1978). Human factors in display terminal procedures. In: Inose, H. (ed.) Evolutions in Computer Communications. North Holland, Amsterdam (pp 777-783).

Davis, R. & King, J. (1979). An overview of production systems. In Elcock, E. & Michie, D. (eds.) Machine Intelligence 8. Ellis Horwood Ltd., Chichester.

Davis, R. & Lenat, D.B. (1982). Knowledge-Based Systems in Artificial Intelligence. McGraw-Hill, New York.

Deatherage, B.H. (1972). Auditory and other sensory forms of information presentation. In Van Cott, H.P. & Kinkade, R.G. (eds.) Human Engineering Guide to Equipment Design. US Department of Defense.

DeMars, S.A. (1975). Human factors considerations for the use of color in display systems. NTIS (NASA-TM-X-72196), NASA, J.F. Kennedy Space Centre.

Dodd, D.H. & White, R.M. (1980). Cognition: Mental Structures and Processes. Allyn & Bacon, Mass.

Donelson, W.C. (1978). Spatial management of information. SIGGRAPH '78 Proceedings, 12(3), 203-209.

Du Boulay, B., O'Shea, T. & Monk, J. (1981). The black box inside the glass box: Presenting computer concepts to novices. International Journal of Man-Machine Studies, 14, 237-249.

Embley, D.W. & Nagy, G. (1981). Behavioral aspects of text editors. ACM Computing Surveys (Special Issue: The Psychology of Human-Computer Interaction), 13(1), 33-70.

Engel, S.E. & Granda, R.E. (1975). Guidelines for Man/Display Interfaces. (TR 00.2720). IBM, Poughkeepsie, N.Y.

ETH. (1982). Source code debugger for Modula-2 programs. Edgenossische Technische Hochschule, Zurich.

Evans, J.StB.T. (1982). The Psychology of Deductive Reasoning. Routledge & Kegan Paul, London.

Feigenbaum, E. & Feldman, J. (1963). Computers and Thought. McGraw-Hill, New York.

Ferguson, G.A. (1981). Statistical Analysis in Psychology and Education. 5th edition. McGraw-Hill, London.

Fitter, M.J. (1979). Towards more "natural" interactive systems. International Journal of Man-Machine Studies, 11, 339-350.

Fitts, P.M. & Posner, M.I. (1967) Human Performance. Brooks/Cole, Belmont, California.

Flanagan, J.L. (1972). The synthesis of speech. Scientific American, 226, 48-62.

Foley, J.D. & Wallace, V.L. (1974). The art of natural graphic man-machine conversation. Proceedings of the IEEE, 62(4), 462-471.

Foley, J.D., Wallace, V.L. & Chan, P. (1981). The human factors of graphic interaction - tasks and techniques. George Washington University, Washington DC.

Frei, H.P., Weller, D.L. & Williams, R. (1978). A graphics-based programming-support system. SIGGRAPH-ACM, 12(3), 43-49.

Frisby, J.P. (1979). Seeing: Illusion, Brain and Mind. Oxford University Press.

Fry, D.B. (1977). Homo Loquens. Cambridge University Press.

Fry, D.B. (1979). The Physics of Speech. Cambridge University Press.

Gaines, B.R. (1976). On the Complexity of Causal Models,

IEEE Transactions on Systems, Man & Cybernetics, SMC-6, 56-59.

Gaines, B.R. (1978). Man-computer communication - what next? International Journal of Man-Machine Studies, 10, 225-232.

Gaines, B.R. (1981). The technology of interaction - dialogue programming rules. International Journal of Man-Machine Studies, 14, 133-150.

Gall, J. (1975). Systemantics, Pocket Books, New York.

Gibson, E. & Levin, H. (1975). The Psychology of Reading. MIT Press, Mass.

Gilhooly, K.J. (1982). Thinking: Directed, Undirected and Creative. Academic Press, London.

Gilliland, J. (1972). Readability. Unibooks, London.

Gould, J.D., Conti, J. & Hovanycez, T. (1983). Composing letters with a simulated listening typewriter. Communications of the ACM, 26, 295-308.

Gould, J.D. & Lewis, C. (1983). Designing for usability - key principles and what designers think. In: Proceedings of CHI '83: Human Factors in Computing Systems, Boston, December. ACM, New York.

Grandjean, E. & Vigliani, E. (1982). Ergonomic Aspects of Visual Display Terminals. Taylor & Francis, London.

Green, T.R.G. & Payne, S.J. (1983). Higher-Order Rules in the Perception of Grammars, Memo 544, MRC Social and Applied Psychology Unit, Sheffield University.

Green, T.R.G., Payne, S.J. and van de Veer, G. The Psychology of Computer Use. Academic Press, London.

Green, T.R.G., Sime, M.E. & Cornah, A.J. (1979). 'GUIDO': A software tool to help the average programmer. MRC Social and Applied Psychology Unit Report. (MRC Social and Applied Psychology Unit, Department of Psychology, University of Sheffield, England.)

Gregory, R. (1977) (3rd edition) Eye and Brain: The Psychology of Seeing. Weidenfeld & Nicolson, London.

Grether, W.F. & Baker, C.A. (1972) Visual presentation of information. In van Cott, H.P. & Kinkade, R.G. (Eds.) Human egineering guide to equipment design, Rev. Ed., U.S. Govt. Printing Ofdfice, Washington, D.C.

Grusec, T. (1976). Learnin' a machine to talk proper. Telesis, 4, 227-233.

Gunnarsson, E. & Soderberg, I. (1983). Eye strain resulting from VDT work at the Swedish Telecommunications Administration. Applied Ergonomics, 14, 61-69.

Guttag, J. & Horning J.J. (1980). Formal Specification as a Design Tool, in 7th ACM Symposium on POPL, Las Vegas.

Halasz, F. & Moran, T.P. (1982). Analogy considered harmful. In: Proceedings of Conference on Human Factors in Computer Systems, Gaithersburg, March. ACM, New York.

Hammond, N.V., Barnard, P.J., Clark, I.A., Morton, J. & Long, J.B. (1980). Structure and content in interactive dialogue. Human Factors Report HF034, IBM UK Laboratories, Hursley Park.

Hammond, N.V., Hinton, G., Barnard, P.J., MacLean, A., Long, J.B. & Whitefield, A. (1984). Evaluating the interface of a document processor: A comparison of expert judgement and user observation. In: Shackel, B. (ed.) Interact '84: First IFIP Conference on Human-Computer Interaction. IFIP, North Holland, Amsterdam.

Hammond, N.V., Jorgensen, A.H., MacLean, A., Barnard, P.J. & Long, J.B. (1983). Design practice and interface usability: Evidence from interviews with designers. In: Proceedings of CHI '83: Human Factors in Computing Systems, Boston, December. ACM, New York.

Hammond, N.V., Long, J.B., Clark, I.A., Barnard, P.J. & Morton, J. (1980). Documenting human-computer mismatch in interactive systems. Proceedings of the Ninth International Symposium on Human Factors in Telecommunication, Red Bank, N.J.

Hammond, N.V., Long, J.B., Clark, I.A., Morton, J. & Barnard, P.J. (1980). Documenting human-computer mismatch in interactive systems: Annotated protocols. Human Factors Report HF024, IBM UK Laboratories, Hursley park.

Hammond, N.V., MacLean, A., Hinton, G., Long, J.B., Barnard, P.J. & Clark, I.A. (1983). Novice use of an interactive graph-plotting system. Human Factors Report HF083, IBM UK Laboratories, Hursley Park.

Hammond, N.V., Morton, J., Barnard, P.J., Long, J.B. & Clark, I.A. (in preparation). Characterising user performance in command-driven dialogue.

Hansel, C.E.M. & Stafford, E.M. (1982). Optimum colour specifications for use in VDU based systems. IEE International Conference on Man/Machine Systems, Manchester (pp 157-159).

Hansen, W.J., Doring, R. & Whitlock, L.R. (1978). Why an examination was slower on-line than on paper. International Journal of Man-Machine Studies, 15, 507-519.

Harrison, M.D. & Thimbleby, H.W. (in preparation). Formalising User Requirements for a Display Editor, University of York.

Hartley, J.T., Harker, K.O. & Walsh, D.O. (1980). Contemporary issues and new directions in adult development of learning and memory. In Poon, L.W. (ed.)

Aging in the 1980s. American Psychological Society.

Hartson, H.R. (ed.) (In Press) Advances in Human-Computer Interaction. Ablex Publishing, Norwood, New Jersey.

Hasling, D.W., Clancey, W.J. & Rennels, G. (1984). Strategic explanations for a diagnostic explanation system. International Journal of Man-Machine Studies, 20(1), 3-19.

Hawley, M.E. (ed.) (1977). Speech Intelligibility and Speaker Recognition: Benchmark Papers in Acoustics 11. Dowden, Hutchinson & Ross, Stroudsburg, Pa.

Hayes, P.J. (1982). Cooperative command interaction through the COUSIN system. IEE International Conference on Man/Machine Systems. Manchester (pp 59-63).

Hayes, P.J. & Reddy, D.R. (1983). Steps toward graceful interaction in spoken and written man-machine communication. International Journal of Man-Machine Studies, 19(3), 231-284.

Hayes, P.J. & Szekely, P.A. (1983). Graceful interaction through the COUSIN interface. International Journal of Man-Machine Studies, 19(3), 285-306.

Hayes-Roth, F., Waterman, D.A. & Lenat, D.B. (1983). Building Expert Systems. Addison-Wesley, New York.

Hebalkar, P.G. & Zilles, S.N. (1978). TELL: A system for graphically representing software designs. IBM Research Report RJ2351(31523)9/22/78 (IBM Research Laboratory, San Jose, California).

Herot, C.F. (1980). A spatial graphic man-machine interface. In: Lavington, S. (ed.) Information Processing 80. North Holland, Amsterdam (pp 1039-1044).

Herot, C.F., Brown, G.P., Carling, R.T., Friedell, M., Kramlich, D. & Baecker, R.M. (1982). An integrated environment for program visualization. In: Schneider, H.J. & Wasserman, A.I. (eds.) Automated Tools for Information Systems Design. North Holland, Amsterdam (pp 237-259).

Herot, C.F., Carling, R.T., Friedell, M. & Kramlich, D. (1980). A prototype spatial data management system. SIGGRAPH '80 Proceedings, 14, 63-70.

Hinton, G.E. & Anderson, J.A. (1981). Parallel Models of Associative Memory. Erlbaum, Hillsdale, N.J.

Hodge, D.C. (1962). Legibility of uniform-strokewidth alphabet: I. Relative legibility of upper and lower case letters. Journal of Engineering Psychology, 1, 34-46.

Huckle, B.A. (1980). Designing a command language for inexperienced computer users. In Beech, G. (ed.) Command Language Directions. North Holland, Amsterdam.

Human Factors in Computer Systems. Conference held at

Gaithsburg, MD, March 1982. ACM, New York.
Hurvich, L.M. (1981). Color Vision. Sinauer Associates Inc. Sunderland, Mass.
Infotech State of the Art Report on Man/Computer Communication (2 volumes). Infotech International Ltd., Maidenhead, Berks.
Interact '84: First IFIP Conference on Human-Computer Interaction. Shackel, B. (ed.) IFIP, North Holland, Amsterdam.
International Journal of Man-Machine Studies. (1981). Special issue on "The Semantics and Syntax of Human-Computer Interaction". 15(1).
Irby, C.H. (1974). Display techniques for interactive text manipulation. National Computer Conference 1974 (pp 247-255).
Isensee, S.H. & Bennett, C.A. (1983). The perception of Flicker and glare on computer CRT displays. Human Factors, 25, 177-184.
Jacob, R.J.K. (1983). Executable specifications for a human-computer interface. In: Proceedings of CHI '83: Human Factors in Computing Systems, Boston, December. ACM, New York.
Johnson-Laird, P.N. & Wason, P.C. (1977). Thinking. Cambridge University Press.
Johnson-Laird, P.N. (1982). Ninth Bartlett Memorial Lecture: Thinking as a skill. Quarterly Journal of Experimental Psychology, 34A, 1-29.
Johnson-Laird, P.N. (1983). Mental Models. Cambridge University Press.
Jones, P.F. (1978). Four principles of man-computer dialogue. CAD Computer Aided Design, 10(3), 197-202.
Kay, A.C. (1977). Microelectronics and the Personal Computer. In: Morrison, P. (ed.), Microelectronics: A Scientific American Book. Freeman, San Francisco (pp 124-135).
Kay, A. (1980). SMALLTALK. In: Guedj, R.A., ten Hagen, P.J.W., Hopgood, F.R.A., Tucker, H.A. & Duce, D.A. (eds.) Methodology of Interaction. North Holland, Amsterdam (pp 7-11).
Kirk, R.E. (1968). Experimental Design: Procedures for the Behavioural Sciences. Brooks/Cole, Belmont, California.
Klatt, D.H. (1977). Review of the ARPA Speech Understanding Project. Journal of the Acoustical Society of America, 62, 1345-1366.
Klatt, D.H. (1980). Speech perception: a model of acoustic-phonetic analysis and lexical access. In: Cole, R. (ed.) Perception and Production of Fluent

Speech. Erlbaum Assoc., Hillsdale, N.J.

Kleiman, G.M. (1975). Speech recoding in reading. Journal of Verbal Learning and Verbal Behaviour, 14, 323-339.

Kofer, R. (1983). Ease of use in office communication. Proceedings International Computing Symposium (ICS 83). Teubner Verlag, Nuremberg.

Kolers, P.A., Dachnicky, R.L. & Ferguson, D.C. (1981). Eye movement measurement of readability of CRT displays. Human Factors, 23, 517-527.

Kolers, P.A., Wrolstead, M.E. & Bouma, H. (1977). Processing of Visible Language, 1. Plenum, New York.

Kolers, P.A., Wrolstead, M.E. & Bouma, H. (1980). Processing of Visible Language, 2. Plenum, New York.

Kramlich, D., Brown, G.P., Carling, R.T. & Herot, C.F. (Pers. Com.). Program visualization: graphics support for software development.

Ladefoged, P. (1962). Elements of acoustic phonetics. University of Chicago Press.

Lampson, B.W. (1983). Hints for computer system design, ACM Symposium on Operating System Principles. Bretton Woods (pp 33-48).

Lass, N.J. (ed.) (1976). Contemporary Issues in Experimental Phonetics. Academic Press, London.

Lea, W.A. (ed.) (1980). Trends in Speech Recognition. Prentice-Hall, Englewood Cliffs, New Jersey.

Lehiste, I. (1967). Readings in Acoustic Phonetics. MIT Press, Mass.

Leler, W.J. (1980). Human vision, anti-aliasing, and the cheap 4000 line display. SIGGRAPH '80 Proceedings, 14, 308-313.

Lesk, M.E. (1975). Lex - A Lexical Analyser Generator, Computer Science Technical Report No. 32, Bell Laboratories, Murray Hill, New Jersey.

Levinson, S.E. & Liberman, M.Y. (1981). Speech recognition by computer. Scientific American, 244, 56-78.

Liberman, A.M., Cooper, F.S., Shankweiler, D.S. & Studdert-Kennedy, M. (1967). Perception of the speech code. Psychological Review, 74, 431-461.

Lindsay, P.H. & Norman, D.A. (1977). Human Information Processing: An Introduction to Psychology. Academic Press, London.

Lodding, K.N. (1983). Iconic interfacing. IEEE Computer Grahics and Applications, 3, 11-20.

Long, J.B., Hammond, N.V., Barnard, P.J., Morton, J. & Clark, I.A. (1983). Introducing the interactive computer at work: The users' views. Behaviour and Information Technology, 2, 39-106.

Lowerre, B.T. & Reddy, D.R. (1980). The Harpy speech

understanding system. In: Lea, W.A. (ed.) Trends in
Speech Recognition.   Prentice Hall, Englewood Cliffs,
N.J.

Luce, P.A., Feustel, T.C. & Pisoni, D.B. (1983). Capacity
demands in short-term memory for synthetic and natural
speech. Human Factors, 25, 17-32.

McCann, C. (1978). Graphic display interaction. Part II.
Information structure and basic functions. AD-A055403/0,
Defence and Civil Inst. of Environmental Medicine,
Canada.

Mack, R.L., Lewis, C.H. & Carroll, J.M. (1983). Learning
to use word processors: problems and prospects. ACM
Transactions on Office Information Processing, 1,
254-271.

Malhotra, A., Thomas, J.C., Carroll, J.M. & Miller, L.A.
(1980). Cognitive processes in design. International
Journal of Man-Machine Studies, 12, 119-140.

Marr, D. (1982). Vision. Freeman, San Francisco.

Marshall, C.J. (1982). The intelligibility of synthetic
speech for machine to man communication. Final year
project report, Loughborough University of Technology.

Mayer, R.E. (1977). Thinking and Problem Solving. Scott,
Foresman, Glenview.

Medina-Mora, R. (1982). Syntax-directed editing: towards
integrated programming environments. Ph.D Thesis,
Department of Computer Science, Carnegie-Mellon
University, Pittsburgh.

Michie. D. (Ed.) (1982) Introductory readings in expert
systems, Gordon and Breach, New York.

Miller, G.A. (1956). The magical number seven, plus or
minus two: Some limits on our capacity for processing
information. Psychological Review, 63(2), 81-97.

Miller, G.A. (ed.) (1973). Communication, Language and
Meaning: Psychological Perspectives. Basic Books, New
York.

Miller, L.A. & Thomas, J.C. (1977). Behavioural issues in
the use of interactive systems. International Journal of
Man-Machine Studies, 9, 509-536.

Mitchell, D. (1982). The Process of Reading. Wiley,
London.

Moore, B.C.J. (1982). An Introduction to the Psychology of
Learning. Academic Press, London.

Moran, T.P. (1981a). An applied psychology of the user.
Computer Surveys, 13, 1-11.

Moran, T.P. (1981b). The command language grammar: A
representation for the user interface of interactive
computer systems. International Journal of Man-Machine
Studies, 15, 3-50.

Morse, A. (1979). Some principles for the effective display of data. SIGGRAPH '79 Proceedings, 13, 94-101.

Morton, J., Barnard, P.J., Hammond, N.V. & Long, J. (1979). Interacting with the computer: A framework. In Boutmy E.J. and Danthine A. (eds.), Teleinformatics '79. North-Holland, Amsterdam (pp 201-208).

Morvis, J.G. (1979). Using color in industrial control graphics. Control Engineering, (July).

Murrell, K.F.H. (1965). Ergonomics. Chapman & Hall, London.

Muter, P., Latremouille, S.A., Treurniet, W.C., & Beam, P. (1982). Extended reading of continuous text on television screens. Human Factors, 24, 501-508.

Myers, B.A. (1980). Displaying data structures for interactive debugging. Xerox Parc Report CSL-80-7, Xerox Palo Alto Research Centre.

Naisbitt, J. (1984). Megatrends. (2nd edition). Macdonald & Co., London & Sydney.

Naur, P. (1983). Program development studies based on diaries. In Green, T.R.G., Payne, S.J. and van de Veer, G.C. The Psychology of Computer Use. Academic Press, London.

Nesslage, R.L. (1976). The design of a user interface for a color, raster scan graphics device. AD-A028442/2, Naval Postgraduate School.

Newell, A. (1977). Notes for a model of human performance in ZOG. Department of Computer Science, Carnegie-Mellon University, Pittsburgh.

Newell, A., Barnett, J., Forgie, J.W., Green, C., Klatt, D.H., Licklider, J.C.R., Munson, J., Reddy, D.R. & Woods, W.A. (1973). Speech Understanding Systems: Final Report of a Study Group. North Holland/American Elsevier, New York.

Newell, A., McCracken, D.L., Robertson, G.G. & Akscyn, R.M. (1982). ZOG and the USS CARL VINSON. Computer Science Research Review, Carnegie-Mellon University 1980-81. CMU, Pittsburgh (pp 95-118).

Newell, A. & Simon, H.A. (1972). Human Problem Solving. Prentice-Hall, Englewood Cliffs, New Jersey.

Newman, W.M. & Sproull, R.F. (1979). Principles of Interactive Computer Graphics. (2nd edition.) McGraw-Hill, New York.

Ng, N. (1978). A graphical editor for programming using structure charts. IBM Research Report RJ2344(31476)9/19/78. IBM Research Laboratory, San Jose, California.

Nickerson, R.S. (1981). Why interactive computer systems are sometimes not used by the people who might benefit from them. International Journal of Man-Machine Studies, 15, 469-483.

Nievergelt, J. (1982). Errors in dialogue design and how to avoid them. Proceedings 1982 International Zurich Seminar on Digital Communications, Zurich, March, 1982 (pp 199-205). (Eidgenossische Technische Hochschule (ETH), Institut fur Informatik, Zurich, Switzerland).

Norman, D.A. (1976). Memory and Attention: An Introduction to Human Information Processing. (2nd edition.) Wiley, New York.

Norman, D.A. (1981). The trouble with UNIX. Datamation, 27, 139-150.

Norman, D.A. (1982). Learning and Memory. W.H. Freeman & Co., San Francisco.

Otway, H.J. & Peltu, M. (1983). New Office Technology, Human and Organizatorial Aspects. Pinter, London.

Palme, J. (1981). Interactive software for humans. In Shackel, B. (ed.) Man-Computer Interaction: Human Factors Aspects of Computers & People. NATO Advanced Study Institutes Series E: No. 44. Sijthoff & Noordhoff, The Netherlands (pp 167 213).

Pearson, D.E. (1975). Transmission and Display of Pictorial Information. Pentech Press, London.

Pike, K.L. (1945). General characteristics of intonation. In: Bolinger, D. (1972). Intonation - Selected Readings. Penguin, Harmondsworth, Middx.

Rabiner, L.R. & Schafer, R.W. (1978). Digital Processing of Speech Signals. Prentice-Hall, Englewood Cliffs, New Jersey.

Radl, G.W. (1980). Experimental investigations for optimal presentation-mode and colours of symbols on the CRT-screen. In: Grandjean, E. & Vigliani, E. (eds.), Ergonomic Aspects of Visual Display Terminals. Taylor & Francis, London.

Rasmussen, J. (1983). Skills, rules and knowledge; signals, signs and symbols, and other distinctions in human performance models. IEEE Transactions on Systems, Man and Cybernetics, SMC-13, 257-266.

Rayner, K. (1975). The perceptual span and peripheral cues in reading. Cognitive Psychology, 7, 65-81.

Rayner, K. (1978). Eye movements in reading and information processing. Psychological Bulletin, 85, 618-660.

Reisner, P. (1982). Further developments toward using formal grammar as a design tool. In: Proceedings of Conference on Human Factors in Computer Systems, Gaithersburg, March. ACM, New York.

Roach, J.W. & Nickson, M. (1983). Formal specifications for modelling and developing human/computer interfaces. In:

Proceedings of CHI '83:   Human Factors in Computing
Systems, Boston, December. ACM, New York.
Roberts, T.R. & Moran, T.P. (1983). The evaluation of text
editors: Methodology   and   empirical   results.
communications of the ACM, 26, 265-283.
Robinson, W.P.   (1972).   Language and Social Behaviour.
Penguin, Harmondsworth, Middx.
Robson, C. (1973). Experimental Design and Statistics in
Psychology. Penguin, Harmondsworth, Middx.
Rovamo, J. & Virsu, V.   (1979).   An estimation and
application of the human cortical magnification factor.
Experimental Brain Research, 37, 495-510.
Rowson, J.R. & Salama, B.   (1978).   Virtual displays.
Electronic Displays, London.
Savage, R.E., Habinek, J.K. & Barnhart, T.W. (1982). The
design, simulation and evaluation of a menu driver user
interface. In: Proceedings of Conference on Human
Factors in Computer Systems, Gaithersburg, March. ACM,
New York (pp 36-40).
Sauter, S.L. Gottlieb, M.S., Jones, K.C., Dodson, V.H. &
Rohrer .   (1983).   Job and health implications of VDT
use: Initial results of the Wisconsin-NIOSH study.
Communications of the ACM, 26(4), 284-294.
Schegloff, E.A., & Sacks, H. (1973). Opening up closings.
Semiotica, 8, 289-327.
Schiff, W. (1980).   Perception, An Applied Approach.
Houghton Mifflin Company, Boston.
Shackel, B. (ed.) Interact '84: First IFIP Conference on
Human-Computer Interaction.   IFIP, North Holland,
Amsterdam.
Shaw, M.   (1980).   On Becoming a Personal Scientist.
Academic Press, New York.
Shneiderman, B.   (1980).   Software Psychology. Winthrop
Publishers Inc., Cambridge, Mass.
Shneiderman, B. (1983). Direct Manipulation: A Step Beyond
Programming Languages, IEEE Computer, 16, 57-69.
Singleton, W.T. (1976). Ergonomics: Where have we been
and where are we going: IV. Ergonomics, 19, 208-313.
Smith, B.L., Brown, B.L., Strong, W.J. & Rencher, A.C.
(1975).   Effects of speech rate on personality
perception. Language and Speech, 18, 145-152.
Smith, D.C. (1975). PYGMALION: A creative programming
environment. AD-A016811/2, Stanford University.
Smith, H.T. & Green, T.R.G. (eds.) (1980).   Human
Interaction with Computers. Academic Press, London.
Smith, S.L.   (1982).   User-System Interface Design for
Computer-Based Information Systems. ESD-TR-82-132, MITRE
Corp. Bedford, Mass.

Smith, S.L. & Goodwin, N.C. (1971). Blinking code for information display. Human Factors, 13(3), 283-290.

Smith, S.L. & Goodwin, N.C. (1972). Another look at blinking displays. Human Factors, 14(4), 345-347.

Spence, R. & Apperley, M. (1982). Hierarchical dialogue structures in interactive computer systems. IEE International Conference on Man/Machine Systems, Manchester (pp 11-15).

Sproull, R.F. (1979). Raster graphics for interactive programming environments. SIGGRAPH-ACM, 13(2), 83-93.

Stevens, K.N. (1980). Acoustic correlates of some phonetic categories. Journal of the Acoustical Society of America, 68, 836-842.

Stockenberg, J.E. & van Dam, A. (1975). STRUCT programming analysis system. IEEE Transactions on Software Engineering, SE-1, 384-389.

Sturt, J. (1982). Raster-scanned colour meets CAD. Systems International (GB), 10(11), 39-42.

Sufrin, B. (1981). Formal Specification of a Display Editor, PRG-21. Oxford University Computing Laboratory.

Teitelman, W. (1977). A display oriented programmer's assistant. 5th International Joint Conference on Artificial Intelligence, Cambridge, Mass. (pp 905-915).

Terrana, T., Merluzzi, F. & Gindici, E. (1980). Electromagnetic radiations emitted by visual display units. In: Grandjean, E. & Vigliani, E. (eds.), Ergonomic Aspects of Visual Display Terminals. Taylor & Francis, London.

Thimbleby, H. (1978). A note on menu selection. Computer Bulletin, 2(18), 20-21, 23.

Thimbleby, H.W. (1979). Interactive technology: the role of passivity. In: Bensel, C.K. (ed.) Proceedings Human Factors Society, 23, 80-84.

Thimbleby, H.W. (1980). Dialogue determination. International Journal of Man-Machine Studies, 13, 295-304.

Thimbleby, H.W. (1982a). Character level ambiguity: consequences for user interface design. International Journal of Man-Machine Studies, 16, 211-225.

Thimbleby, H.W. (1982b). Basic user engineering principles for display editors. Proceedings 6th International Conference on Computer Communications, London 1982. North Holland, Amsterdam (pp 537-542).

Thimbleby, H.W. (1983a). Guidelines for 'manipulative' text editing. Behaviour and Information Technology, 2, 127-161.

Thimbleby, H.W. (1983b). "What you see is what you have got" - a user engineering principle for manipulative display? Proceedings of ACM Conference on Software Ergonomics, Nuremberg, April 1983 (pp 70-84).

Thomas, J.C. & Gould, J.D. (1975). A psychological study of Query-by-Example. In: Proceedings of 1975 National Computer Conference.

Thomas. J.C. & Schneider, M. (1983) Human factors in computing systems. Ablex Corp., Norwood, N.J.

Tinker, M.A. (1955). Prolonged reading tasks in visual search. Journal of Applied Psychology, 39, 444-446.

Tinker, M.A. (1965). Bases For Effective Reading. University of Minnesota Press.

Tourangeau, R. & Sternberg, R.S. (1982). Understading and appreciating metaphors. Cognition, 11, 203-244.

Truckenbrod, J.R. (1981). Effective use of color in computer graphics. SIGGRAPH '81 Proceedings, 15(3) 83-90, Dallas, Texas.

Tulving, E. & Donaldson, W. (eds.) (1972). Organization of Memory. Academic Press, London.

Usher, D.M. (1982). A touch-sensitive VDU compared with a computer-aided keypad for controlling power generating plant. IEE International Conference on Man/Machine Systems, Manchester (pp 250-252).

Wason, P.C. (1960). On the failure to eliminate hypotheses in a conceptual task. Quarterly Journal of Experimental Psychology, 12, 129-140.

Wason, P.C. (1966). Reasoning. In Foss, B.M. (ed.) New Horizons in Psychology. Penguin, Harmondsworth, Middx.

Waterman, D.A. (1979). User-oriented systems for capturing expertise: a rule-based approach. In Michie, D. (ed.) Expert Systems in the Microelectronic Age. Edinburgh University Press, Edinburgh.

Waterman, D.A. & Hayes-Roth, F. (1978). Pattern-Directed Inference Systems. Academic Press, New York.

Waterworth, J.A. (1982). Man-machine speech "dialogue acts". Applied Ergonomics, 13, 203-207.

Waterworth, J.A. (1983). Effect of intonation form and pause durations of automatic telephone number announcements on subjective preference and memory performance. Applied Ergonomics, 14, 39-42.

Watson, A.B. & Ahumada, A.J. (1983). A Look at Motion in the Frequency Domain. NASA Technical Memorandum 84352. (Point of contact: Dr A.B. Watson, Ames Research Center, M/S 239-2, Moffett Field, Calif. 94035, U.S.A.)

Weizenbaum, J. (1976). Computer Power and Human Reason. W.H. Freeman, San Francisco.

Weizenbaum, J. (1980). Human choice in the interstices of the megamachine. In: Mowshowitz, A. (ed.) IFIP Conference Human Choice and Computers, 2, 271-278. North-Holland.

Welbank, M. (1983). A Review of Knowledge Acquisition Techniques for Expert Systems. Martlesham Consultancy Services, British Telecom Research Laboratories, Ipswich.

Witten, I.H. (1980). Communicating with Microcomputers. Academic Press, London.

Witten, I.H. (1982a). Principles of Computer Speech. Academic Press, London.

Witten, I.H. (1982b). An interactive computer terminal interface which predicts user entries. IEE International Conference on Man/Machine Systems, Manchester (pp 1-5).

Yarwood, E. (1977). Toward program illustration. Technical Report CSRG-84 Computer Systems Research Group, University of Toronto.

Young, R.M. (1981). The machine inside the machine: Users' models of pocket calculators. International Journal of Man-Machine Studies, 15, 51-85.

Young, R.M. & Hull, A. (1982). Cognitive aspects of the selection of Viewdata options by casual users. In: Williams, M.B. (ed.) Pathways to the Information Society: Sixth International Conference on Computer Communication. North Holland, Amsterdam.

Zimmerman, L.L. (1967). On-line program debugging - a graphic approach. Computers and Automation, 16(1), 30-34.

Author Index

Subject Index

A

Accent, regional, 99, 208
Accessibility of user knowledge, 141
Accuracy of speech recognisers, 218, 227-231
Acoustic boundaries in speech, 204
Acoustics
theory of, 200-203
relation to linguistics, 196, 204-209
Acquisition of knowledge
by users, 127, 135-139
for expert systems, 241-243
Acuity, 11, 16-25, 249
in peripheral vision, 23-25, 38
luminance and, 11
measurement of, 16-18
Adaptive differential PCM (ADPCM), 213
Adaptation, dark, 10
After image, 117
Age and intelligibility of synthetic speech, 97, 100
Age-related hearing loss, 97, 100
AI, see Artificial Intelligence
Alarms, 114
Aliasing
anti- (displays), 111, 120
error (speech), 213
All capital printing, 42, 114
Allophones, 208
Alphanumeric keys, 108, 110, 120, 167
Amplitude, 249

Amplitude spectrum, 201-203, 249
Analogy, 140
Analysis of variance, 94, 100, 249
Angle of inclination, 117, 121
Anomalous colour vision, 14
Announcements, public, 89
Anti-aliasing, 111, 120
Applications of expert systems, 240-241
Apple Lisa, 118
Arabic, phonology of, 197
Argument order, 146-152
ARPA SUR, 236
Articulation
in speech, 200-203
place of, 198
Articulators, 195
Articulatory dynamics, 200-203
Articulatory loop, 51, 224
Artificial intelligence, 237, 247, 250
Ascribed personality, 223
ASR, see Automatic speech recognition
Attitude
measurement of 74, 79
to synthetic speech, 94, 99, 223
Audition, 203-204
Auditory menus, 224
Automatic knowledge acquisition, 243
Automatic speech recognition, 216-218
accuracy of, 227-229
advantages of, 226
connected speech and, 217, 230